David Noland

TRAVELS ALONG THE EDGE

David Noland is a freelance writer specializing in adventure travel, sports, and science. He is a regular contributor to *Outside* magazine and his articles have appeared in *Sports Illustrated, Discover, Smithsonian Air & Space,* and *The New York Times* travel section. An avid outdoorsman and adventurer, he lives in Mountainville, New York.

TRAVELS ALONG THE EDGE

TRAVELS ALONG THE EDGE

40 Ultimate Adventures
for the Modern Nomad —
From Crossing the Sahara to
Bicycling through Vietnam

DAVID NOLAND

vintage departures
vintage books
a division of random house, inc.• new york

A Vintage Departures Original, August 1997
First Edition

Five of the chapters in this work, "Sikkim," "New Zealand," "Belize," "Wyoming," and "Mexico," were originally published in greatly altered form in *The New York Times* travel section.

Grateful acknowledgment is made to the following for permission to reprint previously published material:
Penguin Books Ltd.: Excerpt from *Wainwright's Coast-to-Coast Walk* by Alfred Wainwright (Michael Joseph Ltd., 1987), copyright © 1987 by The Estate of the late A. Wainwright. Reprinted by permission of Penguin Books Ltd., London.

Nick Shipton: Excerpt from *Land of Tempest* by Eric Shipton (E. P. Dutton, 1963), copyright © 1963 by Nick Shipton. Reprinted by permission of Nick Shipton.

University Press of Florida: Excerpt from *Totch: A Life in the Everglades* by Totch Brown. Reprinted by permission of the University Press of Florida.

Library of Congress Cataloging-in-Publication Data
Noland, David.
Travels along the edge: 40 ultimate adventures for the modern nomad—
from crossing the Sahara to bicycling through Vietnam / by David
Noland.—1st ed.
p.   cm.—(Vintage departures)
"A Vintage departures original"—T.p. verso.
ISBN 0-679-76344-9
1. Outdoor recreation.   2. Adventure and adventurers.   I. Title.
GV191.6.N65   1997
796.5—dc21   97-11594
CIP

Random House Web address: http://www.randomhouse.com/

Book design by Debbie Glasserman

Printed in the United States of America
10 9 8 7 6 5 4 3 2

To Lisa Lou, who keeps the home fires ever burning.

Magellan Travel Books suggested a number of books for the Recommended Reading section, as did my book-mad friend Jay Frogel.

Virtually every outfitter listed in the book helped in my research, but Jim Sano (Geographic Expeditions), Jim Traverso (Overseas Adventure Travel), Irma Turtle (Turtle Tours), Linda Svendsen (Boojum Expeditions), Gary Ziegler (Adventure Specialists), Olaf Malver (Mountain Travel-Sobek), and Lou Wilkinson (Sierra Club Outings) suffered the most from my insatiable thirst for information. No one contributed more to my research than Janet Baldwin, the librarian at the Explorers Club in New York, who put that vast and enchanting resource at my disposal. My main regret in finishing the book is that I no longer have a pretext to hang out in that armchair adventurer's paradise.

ACKNOWLEDGMENTS

In the adventure that was the writing of this book, help came from many quarters. Lisa Chase at *Outside* magazine planted the seed in 1991 when she assigned me to write the first of three "Trip-Finders," the magazine's annual listing of the fifty best adventure trips. Her successors, Kathy Martin and Leslie Weeden, kept it growing. Kris Dahl of International Creative Management made the book project happen: I'll never forget her we've-got-a-deal phone call, which I received over a static-filled radiotelephone in a climber's hut at 15,000 feet in the Italian Alps. At Vintage Books, Dawn Davis broke in a rookie book writer with careful and enthusiastic editing.

Wilson Hubbell, Bob Hempstead, and Leslye Abbey made the always risky decision to open up their lives to a writer and allow themselves to be profiled in some detail. Jim Anderson, Jackie Steakley, Steve Colf, Susan Olsen, John and Kathy Attig, Gary Richter, and Debbie Lovci also told me some great stories about their trips. My friends Howard Davis and Ted Buhl let me poke fun at their outdoor exploits. Don Heyneman and George Fuller served as my tropical disease gurus. Beth Krusi at

CONTENTS

INTRODUCTION

ad·ven·ture - *n*. 1. an undertaking involving risk, unforeseeable danger, or unexpected excitement. 2. an exciting or remarkable experience.

Adventure is a personal matter. Everyone has his own definition of it, his own threshold of risk, danger, or excitement. Take, for example, Manhattan writer Fran Lebowitz, who defines the outdoors as "a place you must pass through in order to get from your apartment into a taxicab." To Fran, a twenty-minute walk through the New Jersey suburbs would qualify as an adventurous undertaking, fraught with the risk of falling branches, the unforeseeable danger of Lyme disease, and the unexpected excitement of an encounter with a squirrel. To mountaineer Reinhold Messner, on the other hand, an expedition to the summit of Mount Everest, using supplemental oxygen, probably would not qualify as a particularly exciting or remarkable experience, since he's already climbed Everest a couple of times without oxygen, once by himself.

Whether you're a Lebowitz or a Messner, an adventure is an experience that pushes your personal envelope, that forces you out of your day-to-day comfort zone. A true adventure, in addition to being exhilarating and inspiring, should also make you tired, nervous, disoriented, a little scared. My own personal definition goes like this: It's not really an adventure unless, at some point during the trip, I say to myself, "What the fuck am I doing here?"

I have uttered those precise words on any number of occasions: Lost in the jungles of Trinidad as daylight fades. Trapped in a stalled bus about to topple over a cliff on the road to Darjeeling. Dangling exhausted from a rope 200 feet down into a 700-foot-deep rock crevasse in Utah. Puking my guts out on the upper slopes of Kilimanjaro. These were all genuinely scary or miserable moments that, fortunately, passed without serious mishap. And I now have extraordinarily fond memories of each.

An estimated 15 million Americans spent roughly $8 billion on adventure travel in 1996, making it the fastest-growing segment of the travel industry. I imagine that not all of these 15 million people qualified as adventurers by my definition. But it's safe to assume that each was looking for something more than the usual Caribbean beach vacation, European museum tour, or Disney World pilgrimage with the kids. They wanted to get off the beaten path and actually do something: trek in the Himalayas, paddle a sea kayak in Belize, ride a raft down a raging river in Chile, climb a mountain in Africa, ride a bicycle through the wine country of Portugal, stay in an Indian village in the Venezuelan rain forest. They wanted physical and mental challenge, excitement, uncertainty—maybe even a hint of danger.

What they didn't want, however, was the hassle of arranging the trips themselves: choosing precise routes, hiring guides and porters, assembling equipment and food, getting permits, and all the other myriad nitpicking detail required to organize an off-the-beaten-path journey in a remote, possibly primitive part of the world.

To tap into this growing market of people whose lust is for adventure rather than logistics, a number of outfitters have sprung up in the last couple of decades to offer all-inclusive adventure trips to virtually every part of the world. Mountain Travel (now merged with Sobek Expeditions and known as Mountain Travel-Sobek) essentially invented the business in the late sixties when it began to run guided treks in a little-known Himalayan country called Nepal. A number of other large, well-established companies also offer full menus of adventure trips all over the world. Among the best known are Wilderness Travel, Geographic Expeditions, Backroads, and Overseas Adventure Travel. There are dozens of others. A whole different tier of companies focus on specific activities—sea kayaking, for example, or mountaineering, or dogsledding, or whitewater rafting—in particular areas. There are literally hundreds of these smaller, more specialized outfitters.

Big or small, they have hit upon a formula that seems to appeal to a lot of people. A small group of travelers—typically five to fifteen—strikes out on foot, bicycle, ski, or horseback; in dugout canoes, rafts, or jeeps. Their focus is a beautiful, rugged landscape, unusual wildlife, or a "primitive" culture—often all three. Extreme physical fitness isn't required for most trips (mountaineering ascents are often the exception), and the hardships along the way are usually rather modest for an active, flexible, good-humored person. On a typical Himalayan trek, for example, porters carry all the camp supplies and luggage, and the trekking staff puts up the tents, cooks, does the dishes, and even hands you a cup of steaming hot tea through your tent flap each morning. Essentially, all the trekker has to do is walk, eat, and sleep.

There are those who will insist that such all-inclusive trips are not really adventures, that they're too safe, too well managed. How can it be an adventure if your sole logistical responsibility is to get off the plane in Kathmandu and find the guy with the sign that says "Above the Clouds Trekking"?

They've got a point. Unplanned itineraries and do-it-yourself logistics often bring the delight of the unexpected. In the process of blundering your way through, getting lost, asking around, standing in line, taking detours, and struggling to make yourself understood in the local language, you'll meet people and see places you never imagined. Hitchhiking through Belize a few years ago, I got picked up by a guy who owned a jungle lodge that wasn't in any guidebook, and ended up spending three marvelous days there. That would have never happened on an outfitted trip. And even lacking such serendipity, there is a certain satisfaction and reward in taking responsibility for yourself.

But do-it-yourself planning can be time-consuming and expensive. On a recent on-my-own climbing and hiking trip in Italy, for example, I had to get from the alpine village of Alagna to Selva, another village 200 miles away in the Dolomites. The exhausting all-day journey required a bus, three trains, and a $75 taxi ride that got me to my hotel in Selva too late for dinner. An outfitter's mini-bus could have gotten me there by noon, at half the cost, leaving the rest of the day free for a hike to Sassolungo. Given a choice between a hike and a train ride, well, I'll take the hike every time.

Apparently a lot of people agree with me, particularly people with ample funds and less-than-ample vacation time. Mountain Travel-Sobek reports that its typical customer is a forty-six-year-old professional who has a graduate degree, makes about $75,000 a year, and lives in a major metropolitan area. With the glaring exception of a rather more modest income, I happen to match that profile almost exactly. They've got me pegged. They know that when I get off a 747 in a remote third-world city, brutally jet-lagged, there's no sweeter sight than the guy holding the sign.

Demographics aside, this book is designed for adventurers

with limited time and a low threshold for logistical hassle. The vast majority of the adventure trips described here take from two to four weeks, well within most people's vacation quotas. In each, the logistics are taken care of and included in the price of the trip: hotels, meals, transportation, guides, porters, permits. Basically, your sole logistical responsibility is to call the 800 number, give them your credit-card number, buy the stuff on the equipment list, and get to the airport on time.

Relieved of the niggling details, you'll be free to focus on the real adventure. With a little bit of luck, you'll soon be asking yourself what the fuck you're doing there.

TRAVELS ALONG THE EDGE

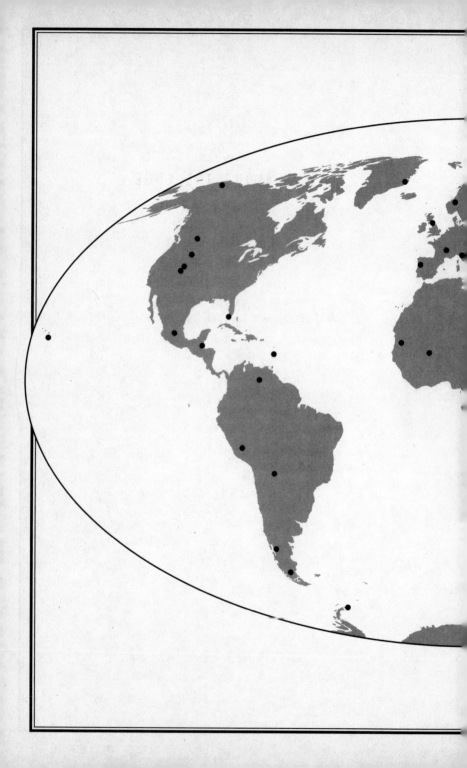

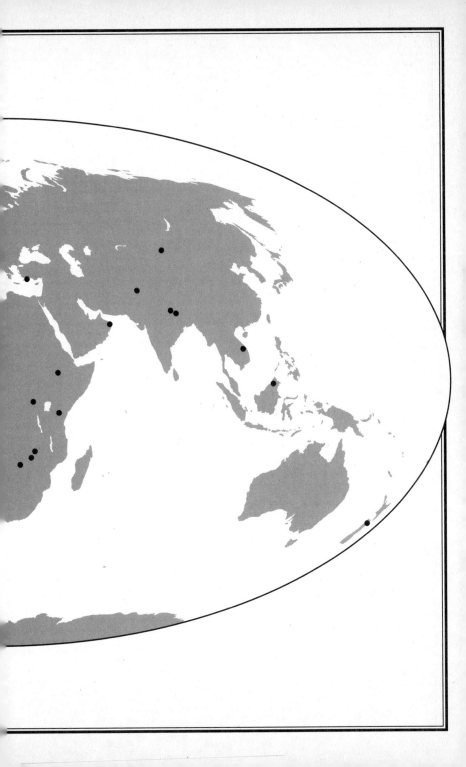

CHOOSING A TRIP

That well-known rain forest eco-traveler Pogo Possum once lamented that he was "confronted with insurmountable opportunities." He might well have been talking about the daunting task of choosing among the thousands of adventure trips available today. This book winnows your choices down to a more manageable forty, but that's still a mind-boggling selection, a lifetime of travel. Where to begin?

Begin with the reference section at the end of each trip narrative. A number of trips will probably eliminate themselves right off the bat because they're too expensive or run at the wrong time of year.

The reference section also contains ratings of the physical challenge, mental challenge, and skills required for each trip. These ratings will help you get through the second round of elimination: those trips that are either too difficult or not challenging enough.

The demands of each trip are rated 1 through 5, with 1 the easiest and 5 the most difficult. Such ratings are notoriously subjective, of course, but it's assumed you are a healthy, well-adjusted, self-sufficient, modestly active, and reasonably well-coordinated person—someone who can, say, briskly walk up two flights of stairs without pain, wheezing, or risk of cardiac arrest. Someone who, if absolutely necessary, could change a tire—or at least be willing to learn how.

PHYSICAL CHALLENGE

Virtually every trip in this book requires some sort of physical effort beyond the normal daily routine of the average American—that's part of the attraction, part of the adventure. Physical demands range from a leisurely half-hour stroll along a riverbank to several weeks of hauling 60-pound loads uphill through hip-deep snow at elevations above 24,000 feet.

Here's what the ratings mean:

1. Couch potatoes welcome; no physical challenge at all. Any healthy person can manage with little effort. Hikes, if any, are optional and short. No pretrip physical conditioning necessary.
2. Modest effort required, enough to get the heart pumping now and then. You might be called upon to hike for four or five hours over generally level terrain at low altitude, or ride a bike 20 or 30 miles in a day. While the habitually slothful would require pretrip conditioning, a reasonably fit person could manage without. European inn-to-inn walking trips typically carry a 2 rating.
3. Be prepared for some serious huffing and puffing. Avid runners or cyclists should take 3-rated trips in stride, but if regular aerobic exercise isn't a part of your life, you'll need a pretrip workout program. A typical 3-rated trip might include daily bicycle rides of 40 to 70 miles, or daily hikes of six to eight hours over sometimes steep ter-

rain at altitudes above 10,000 feet. Many Himalayan and Andean treks fall into this category.

4. Even if you're in very good shape, expect to be seriously challenged. There may be days when you are as physically exhausted as you've ever been. Some sort of vigorous pretrip aerobic workout program is mandatory. Most 4-rated trips are ascents of "beginner" mountains such as Kilimanjaro or Popocatepetl, involving steep terrain, altitudes up to 20,000 feet, and possibly a grueling twelve-to eighteen-hour summit day.

5. If you have to ask, you probably can't do it. The one 5-rated trip in this book—a climb of Mount Everest—demands extended periods of high-altitude climbing through deep snow with heavy packs. In addition to extraordinary cardiovascular fitness and stamina, you'll need robust overall health to cope with altitude sickness, dehydration, and hypothermia.

Rating a trip is easy, but how does one rate oneself? You must be mercilessly objective in evaluating your own physical fitness. Not how fit you were back in college. Not how fit you could be in a few months if you joined the health club. How fit you are right now. An accurate self-assessment can spell the difference between the adventure of a lifetime and a fiasco.

A sad example: A few years ago, I took an African trek that included ascents of Mount Kenya and Kilimanjaro. The trip had been labeled "strenuous walking, high elevation" in the catalog, and pretrip paperwork clearly laid out what to expect, including one eighteen-hour day that began at one A.M. with a steep 4,000-foot ascent to more than 19,000 feet. Yet two of the group members—a fiftyish sedentary mobile-home salesman and a retired newscaster in his late sixties—were physically overmatched from the first day. They struggled on the easier Mount Kenya trek, arriving exhausted and miserable at camp each day, several hours behind the rest of us. Both were too wiped out to try the two-hour walk to the 16,300-foot trekking summit. The group leader wisely didn't permit them to even begin the much tougher, longer climb of Kilimanjaro. They both had a wretched time, fled for home early, and essentially flushed $6,000 down the toilet—all because they wildly overestimated their own physical fitness.

Such expensive self-delusion is not the sole province of the aging. On another climbing trip, this one in Mexico, a muscular young army officer in our group found himself gasping and floundering like a blowfish barely halfway up the first mountain we attempted. He retreated to base camp, and the next day packed up his biceps and went home, missing the final eight days of the twelve-day trip. Three thousand more dollars down the toilet. On a three-day instructional climb on Mount Rainier, I once watched a slightly overweight young fellow in his mid-twenties give up, exhausted, fifteen minutes from the base lodge.

If you have any doubts about your fitness, call the outfitter. But keep in mind that some companies, loath to turn away paying customers, take an unrealistically upbeat you-can-do-it attitude. (After all, they get to keep your money if you can't hack it.) And even if you waltz through the trip with ease, a company's reluctance to properly screen its clients may mean that other overmatched trekkers slow you and the rest of the group down.

In almost all cases, a pretrip workout program is a very good idea. Your specific program depends on the trip, of course. But at the least, it should include some sort of vigorous physical exercise for twenty minutes, three times a week. With that as a base, tailor your exercise program to your specific activity.

For a hike or trek, the best preparation is simply to walk a lot, preferably with a light pack. Prepare for hilly country by hitting the Stairmaster or, better yet, simply hiking up and down a lot of steep hills. If there aren't any nearby, improvise. A small-town midwesterner I know gets in shape for his treks by shouldering a heavy pack and repeatedly walking up and down the stairs of the tallest building in town—a six-story office "tower."

MENTAL CHALLENGE

It takes more than muscle tone and aerobic capacity to enjoy an adventure trip. You gotta have an attitude.

An adventure trip challenges the mind as well as the body. Along with the stunning vistas, intriguing people, and exotic wildlife go sudden rainstorms, bad roads, recalcitrant bureaucrats, blisters, smelly toilet pits, and a myriad of other minor unpleasantries that are part and parcel of being off the beaten path. Many trips have the potential of more serious hazards as well: nasty diseases, altitude sickness, dangerous roads, and isolation from help in case of injury or illness.

The mental-challenge ratings quantify these discomforts and potential hazards. Here are the criteria:

1. Virtually all the comforts of home. No camping—you'll stay in reasonably nice hotels or lodges, eat good food in restaurants, and encounter little in the way of bad weather or other discomfort. You won't be tested or challenged in any way. Essentially, your level of comfort will be pretty much like it is at home.
2. A few of the comforts of home, such as rustic cabins or large stand-up tents with cots, maybe even indoor plumbing some of the time. You may get a little dusty or sweaty, but the potential for serious discomfort due to weather, fatigue, or other factors is small.

3. None of the comforts of home. You'll be camping out in small two-person tents or huts and away from hot water for long periods of time. You'll be peeing in a hole or behind a bush. You may get wet or cold on occasion. You'll be tired at the end of the day, and probably won't smell very good after a while. But for an experienced outdoorsperson, a 3-rated trip should be a piece of cake. Call it full-service backpacking—you won't have to carry a heavy pack, cook, or wash dishes. Your tent may even be set up for you when you arrive at camp.

4. Difficult conditions even for an experienced outdoorsperson. You may be challenged by severe weather, exhaustion, gastrointestinal distress, or altitude sickness. The food may be lousy at times, and you will have to pitch in with camp chores. Periodically, you will long to be at home in your own bed.

5. You could die out there. Crevasses, avalanches, bitter cold, altitude sickness, and relentless, exhausting physical effort may all be part of the game. And don't count on being treated like a guest; you'll be expected to pitch in for your share of the scut work and pull your weight in an emergency.

"The Attitude"—the proper spirit of adventure to deal with the vagaries of off-the-beaten-path travel—has a number of facets. It is a cheerful, flexible, easygoing nature and a sense of humor. It's the ability to shrug off—or even relish—minor hardships. A stoicism in the face of difficulty. A willingness to suck it up and keep going when you'd really rather quit. The ability to adjust quickly when things go wrong—because things will almost certainly go wrong on any adventure trip. (If they don't, your outfitter is either very lucky or playing it very safe, in which case you're not getting much of an adventure at all.)

The Attitude is personified by the British explorer Wilfrid Thesiger, who spent years roaming the sands of Arabia in the company of Bedu nomads. Thesiger despised the comfort and security of civilized life. "I long for the chaos, the smells, the untidiness, and the haphazard life," he wrote. "I want color and savagery and hardship. . . . " Now, it's not necessary to actually *long for* bad smells and hardship as Thesiger did, but you must be able to at least tolerate them with some measure of good cheer.

Once again, a scrupulously objective self-assessment is critical. Unfortunately, judging one's own mental toughness is even harder than judging one's physical fitness. Most of us, if prodded, might be willing to concede that, well, okay, maybe I'm not really in that great a shape physically. But how many among us could bring ourselves to admit, "Yeah, I guess when you get right down to it, I'm a spoiled, self-pitying whiner who freaks out at the first hint of a problem."

Ask yourself some questions: Am I the type of person who makes a big stink in a restaurant if a spoon is dirty? Am I the type who checks the spoons in the first place? Does being wet and cold ruin my whole day? Does a dirty bathroom gross me out? Are most of the people I meet real jerks? Would I bring along twenty-two pairs of clean underwear for a twenty-two-day Himalayan trek? (Don't laugh, a trekmate of mine once did just that.) Does waiting around drive me nuts?

A "yes" answer to any of these questions is not a good sign. You are not a Trekker With Attitude. Perhaps you should stick to the Hiltons and put this book back on the shelf.

I recall a trek during which one middle-aged woman, traveling alone, whined incessantly about the food, the weather, the cold, her boots, everything. We could hear her every night, literally whimpering and moaning in her tent. The grand finale came when she claimed she was too tired to walk up a particularly long, steep hill, and demanded that a porter carry her up piggyback. The poor fellow actually did so. Needless to say, she didn't win many friends on the trip, or have much fun.

Group dynamics play a big role on any adventure trip. You'll be spending a lot of time in close quarters with five, ten, or fifteen strangers. For some, this is the fatal drawback of outfitted adventure travel: They simply don't want to take the risk of being stuck with a real asshole for three weeks.

But one man's "real asshole" is another man's "idiosyncratic personality that can easily be ignored." The ability to get along with—or at least tolerate—all sorts of people is a basic part of The Attitude.

In my experience, the asshole-quotient on adventure trips is surprisingly low, and more than compensated by the high likelihood of meeting some absolutely splendid people. Group adventure travel seems to self-select out most of the spoiled whiners. In the dozen or so adventure trips I've taken, I can recall only one true psycho (the piggyback woman), maybe three moderately annoying jerks, a smattering of bores, an overwhelming majority of fine folks, and a couple of dozen true soul mates. After one trip, five of the seven group members—including one guy from Australia—showed up for a one-year reunion party at my house. Eight years later, I'm still in touch with all of them. Friends like that are worth the occasional jerk.

Your ability to get along with people applies to the local population as well as your trekmates. Many Americans are surprised at the intelligence, sensitivity, and sophistication of people who at first glance might be considered "primitive" or "backward." Thesiger, writing of the Arabian nomads with whom he traveled, admitted, "I went there with a belief in my own racial superiority, but in their tents, I felt like an uncouth, inarticulate barbarian, an intruder from a shoddy and materialistic world." Once again, you may not go to Thesiger's extremes, but smug preconceptions about the inferiority of "primitive" people are definitely not part of The Attitude.

SKILLS

A number of the trips in this book require certain specific skills: paddling a sea kayak, riding a horse, self-arresting with an ice ax, or negotiating technical terrain on a mountain bike. Sometimes the outfitter can teach you what you need to know during the trip; in other cases you'll need to bring well-honed skills with you.

Here's what the ratings mean:

1. No special skills required at all. Even if you can't walk and chew gum at the same time, spit out the gum and just walk. Hiking and trekking trips fall into this category.
2. A few basic skills required, but they can be learned during the trip. No previous experience is necessary, nor will run-of-the-mill klutziness ruin your trip or threaten your safety. Smooth-water canoeing or sea kayaking trips typically fall into this category, as does nontechnical mountain biking.
3. Some skills definitely required. Previous experience is highly recommended, but an apt, determined beginner can probably pick up enough pointers on the trip to get through it without a mishap. Insufficiently skilled people, however, will miss some of the fun. They'll have to walk their mountain bikes around particularly rough, steep sections of trail, for example, or portage kayaks around some rapids.
4. Accomplished veterans only. No way even the most talented beginner can learn enough along the way. The

insufficiently skilled will not only ruin his own trip but will also be a big pain in the butt—and possibly a hazard—for the entire group.

5. Experts only. If you can't hack it, you could die.

Once again, assessing your own skill level can be tricky. A few skills like rock climbing, hang gliding, and whitewater kayaking have objective rating criteria. But how do you assess your ability to climb a mountain, ride a horse, handle a sea kayak in rough water, or do technical mountain biking?

If in doubt, call an outfitter for advice. Try to avoid vague terms like "intermediate"; ask specific questions: Do I need to know how to Eskimo roll? Make surf landings? Do linked telemark turns in crust? Once again, beware the upbeat outfitter who says, "Hey, no problem, you can do it. What's your credit-card number?"

Okay, you've eliminated the trips that don't meet your schedule or budget, as well as those that are beyond your physical, mental, or skill limits. Now what?

Maybe the choice will be easy. Maybe you've always been just dying to see Mount Everest, or watch the sun rise at Machu Picchu, or come face-to-face with a hippopotamus. Most likely, though, it won't be that simple. You'll still have to pick from dozens of really cool-sounding trips.

If you're less fixated on a place, pick an activity first. Heretical as it may seem, I'm a firm believer that the destination counts less than what you do once you get there. Trekking is equally wonderful in the Himalayas, the Andes, or the Karako ram. Sea kayaking in Belize isn't much different from sea kayaking in the Solomon Islands. But any trekking trip is vastly different from any sea kayaking trip.

Choose an activity you know, or at least one for which you have some affinity. Hiking and trekking trips make good first adventures because virtually everybody has hiked at some point in his life. Bike trips also have near-universal appeal.

Finally, pick your destination. If no country leaps to mind, choose a place that might have some special significance in your life, however small. Maybe your merchant seaman uncle told you tall tales about Borneo when you were a kid. Maybe you were entranced by Beryl Markham's descriptions of colonial life in Kenya from *West with the Night*. Perhaps you're intrigued by Buddhist monasteries. Whatever your choice of place, don't be afraid to make it on the most ethereal of whims. Following your dream is what adventure travel is all about.

CHOOSING
AN OUTFITTER

Okay, you've finished the fun part: figuring out where to go and what to do when you get there. Now comes the not-quite-so-fun part: picking an outfitter.

If only one outfitter runs your trip, great—send off your deposit and skip the rest of this chapter. But for most of the trips in this book, several outfitters are given.

The outfitters are listed in alphabetical order. There are no ratings, no stars next to any outfitter's name. To accurately rate each outfitter against its competition is virtually impossible. To be thorough and fair, a self-appointed arbiter would have to personally make all of the one hundred-plus outfitters' trips listed here. An enviable task, perhaps, but one that would require ten years of nonstop travel and a budget of, oh, half a million dollars. (The publisher, sadly, rejected my plea to fund just such a research program.)

In the absence of a star-rating system, I can state with reasonable assurance that all the outfitters listed here are good, solid companies. Each has its own strengths, weaknesses, and personalities that may or may not be a good fit for you. It's up to you to sort them out for yourself.

- Step one is to call and ask for a catalog. Outfitter promotional material runs the gamut from a single typewritten sheet to a huge glossy volume that would sit nicely on a Park Avenue coffee table. (The catalogs of Geographic Expeditions and Wilderness Travel are particularly seductive; anyone who can page through either and not give serious thought to quitting his job, leaving his family, and spending the rest of his life adventure traveling is a hard case indeed.)

You can't judge a company solely by its catalog, of course, but it does give a perspective. Check the number and types of trips offered. Does the company specialize in one particular area or activity? (Concordia Expeditions, for example, specializes in Pakistan. International Expeditions runs mostly nature-oriented trips.) Or does it offer a smorgasbord of trekking, rafting, climbing, and paddling all over the world?

The big guys have broad experience in adventure travel, but the small specialists sometimes—and I emphasize the sometimes—have more expertise in their specialties. Indeed, the big adventure-supermarket companies sometimes use the specialists to operate the trips they sell.

The catalog will also give you a feel for the style of the company: macho or soothing, corporate or mom-and-pop, slick or hokey.

- Step two is to ask for the detailed day-to-day itinerary and predeparture information package. Compare the itineraries from several outfitters carefully. There are likely to be major differences in routing, accommodations, rest days, and so forth.

Note the thoroughness and frankness of the pretrip info package. There should be detailed lists of recommended clothing and equipment, medical and physical fitness advice, and warnings of potential discomforts or hazards. If one outfitter mentions voracious black flies while another doesn't, beware the Pollyanna.

- Once you've made the first cut of outfitters based on their printed material, get on the phone and start asking some tough questions: How long has the outfitter been in business? How long have they been running this trip? Do they run the trip themselves or subcontract it to a local operator? How long have they been working with that local operator? What is their cancellation/refund policy?

- Ask about the trip leader, who may be the most important single factor on any adventure trip. He or she serves as your guide, interpreter, teacher, mother hen, drill sergeant, and group psychologist. (Among my most memorable trip leaders have been the first Latin American to climb Everest, a renowned marine biologist, and the wife of famed Sherpa mountaineer Tenzing Norgay.) Blitz each outfitter with questions about the trip leader: How long has he worked for you? What is her experience and background in this country? How long has he been leading this particular itinerary? Does she have any special knowledge about the local geology, culture, or natural environment?

American trip leader or local? Both have their pros and cons. An American (or British) leader clearly has the upper hand in communication and cultural understanding of trip members' needs. A native of the country, on the other hand, can provide an insider's perspective that is unmatched. Your choice.

Ask the outfitter for the trip leader's phone number. Even if you have to call overseas, the cost of the call will be a small price to pay for a chat with the person who, more than anyone else, will determine how much you'll enjoy your trip.

· Then ask the outfitter for the phone numbers of several people who've taken that same trip. Call them all. (Don't be shy; people love to talk about their adventure trips.) A savvy outfitter won't give you the name of an unhappy client, so you may have to read between the lines. Does the former client rave about the trip or merely endorse it? Does she seem to share your priorities about what makes a good trip?

This second round of inquiry should winnow the outfitters to a short list that match your needs and karma pretty closely. Now it's crunch time: How much are you willing to pay?

Adventure trips can be surprisingly expensive. I recall the astonishment in my friends' eyes a few years back when I told them about my mountaineering trip to Africa. Alas, it was not my rhapsodic account of sunrise from the summit of Kilimanjaro that so amazed them. It was the cost of the trip: $3,890 for nineteen days. "Are you serious?" one incredulous friend asked. "You paid $200 a day to sleep in a tent and eat beans and rice?"

Not exactly. But you can't blame people for puzzling over the high cost of roughing it in the far corners of the globe. The trips featured in this book have per-diem costs ranging from about $80 (a no-frills mountaineering trip to Mexico) to $1,275 (a dogsled trip to the North Pole). The average is about $200 a day—right up there with big-city, four-star hotels. (Keep in mind that the prices listed for each trip were current as of early 1997. Listed prices assume a full travel group; some outfitters use "tier-pricing," adding a surcharge if the group size turns out to be small. Prices also assume double occupancy. Most trips have a "single supplement" of a few hundred dollars.)

So where do the adventure traveler's hard-earned dollars go? Probably not into the outfitters' pockets. "Nobody's making huge sums of money in this business," says Ben Wallace of Himalayan Travel. Indeed, industry stalwarts like Mountain Travel and Overseas Adventure Travel suffered financial turbulence in the early nineties.

A surprisingly large percentage of the money you pay for an adventure trip goes toward the peripherals and extras: hotels in the staging city, transportation, trip-leader salaries, office overhead, and so on.

Why do two outfitters charge significantly different prices for what appears to be the same trip? Rarely is there a ripoff. In most cases, different prices simply reflect different levels of service and amenities. You almost always get what you pay for. The trick is to pay for only what you want, to find an outfitter that shares your priorities about what makes a great adventure.

Do you want a fancy hotel to come back to after the trek, or is one star sufficient? When traveling within the country, do you want to fly or take a bus? Do you want a Western trip leader or a local? How good do you want your pretrip customer service to be? The true bargain is the trip that has the frills you like but lacks the ones you don't.

In the end, your choice of an outfitter should come down to a gut feel based on the maximum amount of information—about both yourself and the outfitter.

Made up your mind? Good. Take a deep breath, call the toll-free number, and have your credit card handy. Now it's time to start getting ready.

GETTING READY

This chapter won't tell you how to apply for a passport or get a visa. It won't remind you to buy traveler's checks or have a neighbor collect your mail while you're away. You know that stuff already. That's Traveling 101.

Adventure travel, even the full-service outfitted variety, demands more than undergraduate-level trip-planning skills. Arcane matters like helicopter evacuation insurance, State Department warnings of guerrilla activity, malaria pills, and moisture-wicking underwear can loom large and confusing to the uninitiated.

A sure path to discomfort and embarrassment on an adventure trip is to get caught unprepared when everyone else in the group is prepared. I still remember the guy who, ignoring the outfitter's stern guidelines, showed up for a Caribbean sea-kayaking trip with no tent and a wardrobe that consisted primarily of cotton shorts and T-shirts. "Tent, schment," he said. "This is the tropics. It's warm. I'll just sleep in my hammock." (I'm not making this up; the guy literally said, "Tent, schment.") Of course, there was a downpour the first night, and he ended up wet and shivering in somebody else's tent (not mine, I can assure you), an imposition that was not particularly well received by the rest of the group. He was certainly uncomfortable, and should have been embarrassed, although this clown may have been beyond embarrassment.

It sounds pathetically obvious, but here it is: The single best way to prepare for any adventure trip is to carefully read the outfitter's pretrip recommended equipment list, and then make sure you have everything on it.

Astonishingly and inexplicably, vast legions of adventure travelers fail to do so. Jim Traverso of Overseas Adventure Travel recalls a Nepal trekker who showed up in Kathmandu without hiking boots, claiming that the pretrip equipment list hadn't emphasized them. In fact, as Traverso patiently pointed out to her, the equipment list for that particular trek began with the words, "The most important item you'll bring along on your trek is your hiking boots. . . . "

The better companies put immense effort into their pretrip packets. (Remember, you picked your outfitter partly on the basis of it.) Your outfitter has probably taken several hundred clients on your particular trip, and its recommendations are a distillation of that collected wisdom. They know what works. Listen to them. Says Traverso wearily, "Every day I get calls from clients asking, 'Do I really need . . . ?' My answer is always, 'Yes, you really need . . . '"

That said, there are still a number of decisions you'll have to make yourself. Here are some words of advice on various aspects of pretrip planning.

INSURANCE

Although the whole concept of insurance flies directly in the face of the risk-taking philosophy of adventure travel, most outfitters will be happy to sell you all sorts of coverage. (An exception is Geographic Expeditions, which includes medical and evacuation insurance in the price of its trips.) Mountain Travel-Sobek offers a full package of medical, evacuation, trip cancellation, and life insurance for $189 and up, depending on the trip. Wilderness Travel, which requires medical/evacuation insurance for treks in the Alps and Himalayas, has a deal with Travelers Insurance. Most other outfitters either have connections with, or at least can refer you to, travel insurance firms such as Travel Guard International (800-826-1300) and Tele-Trip (800-228-9792). Since general insurance agents don't typically sell specialized travel policies, your first move should be to call your outfitter and see what they have.

You'll be offered a variety of insurance. Trip cancellation/ interruption insurance, which reimburses you if some unforeseen emergency prevents you from starting or finishing your trip, typically costs around $5.50 per $100 of coverage. For a $4,000 trip, that amounts to $220, not a trivial amount. (Heck, you could buy a nice windproof Patagonia fleece jacket for $220.) Personally, I've never bought trip cancellation insurance, and have thereby saved myself several thousands of dollars over the last decade. (Fortunately, that time I broke my collarbone skating at the local pond, I had no trip scheduled for the next few months.) You'll have to make your own decision, based on your personal risk/cash/peace-of-mind dynamic.

Health insurance is something to think about because your exposure to disease and injury is higher on an adventure trip. Most standard health insurance policies cover accident or illness abroad, but check to make sure yours does. If not, consider extra coverage. One thing to remember, though: Virtually every country in the world has medical costs far lower than the fantastic charges that are the rule in the United States. Mending a broken ankle in Gangtok will cost closer to $50 than $5,000. Jim Sano of Geographic Expeditions tells the story of a client who suffered a stroke in Tibet. He was evacuated to a topnotch state-of-the-art hospital in Singapore, where he spent a week in the intensive care unit. His total hospital bill: $2,200.

Evacuation insurance covers the cost of a helicopter rescue from a remote area and a flight to a nearby hospital. Without insurance, such a rescue in Nepal, for example, would cost $8,000. (In some cases, the insurance also covers the cost of a medevac flight by jet back to the States.) Helicopter evacuations are extremely rare, however; Overseas Adventure Travel has taken nearly three thousand people trekking in Nepal in the last ten years, with a grand total of three chopper rescues. Healthy, stoic sorts may choose to go without coverage on the grounds that if there is a truly life-threatening emergency, they'll be perfectly happy to pay the $8,000.

HEALTH

In matters of health, Americans have a tendency to rely on benevolent all-knowing authorities like the family doctor and the federal Centers for Disease Control and Prevention. But neither of these august institutions is likely to be of much direct help for the adventure traveler. Marcus Welby is too busy patting runny-nosed moppets on the head to keep up to date on the South American cholera epidemic. And the CDCP, although a font of knowledge, is too big and bureaucratic to offer more than ultraconservative cover-their-ass shotgun advice. If you call the CDCP's International Travelers' Hotline (404-332-4559) seeking information about recommended inoculations for, say, Zambia, you'll get a labyrinthine six-minute journey through push-button hell, with stern recorded lectures on tetanus, diphtheria, polio, measles, mumps, and rubella— but nary a word about malaria. Don't even bother.

As always, first check your outfitter's pretrip info package. Ideally, you should find specific, up-to-date medical advice for your particular destination, not just the boilerplate "check with your physician." For a trip I took to Borneo, Overseas Adventure Travel sent three pages of advice on various inoculations and exotic diseases, plus several more pages on altitude sickness and general hygiene.

If your outfitter doesn't come up to that standard, consult a travel clinic or physician who specializes in travel medicine. Check the Yellow Pages, or the *Travelers' Medical Resource* from ICS Books.

The number-one medical concern of international travelers, of course, is shots. Which ones you'll need depends entirely on where you're going, so no specific advice can be offered here. (Again, ask your outfitter or travel clinic.) But keep in mind that, because of the American legal climate, your advisers are likely to take an ultraconservative approach to inoculations and prophylactic medicine—after all, it's you, not they, who pays for all those shots and pills, and you, not they, who gets your arms punctured and suffers all the side effects.

You may want to think twice about certain "recommended" inoculations. Yellow fever shots, for example, are necessary mostly to satisfy bureaucrats in a few African countries; no American has contacted the disease since the mid-1980s. Cholera vaccine usually doesn't work and can make you sick as a dog. And some old African hands prefer the antimalarial drug Paludrine, not available in the United States, to the usual Lariam regimen, which in rare cases can have serious side effects. These are things you should discuss with your doctor.

Beyond inoculations, the second big health concern of adventure travelers is gastrointestinal distress. Third-world sanitation is simply not up to Western standards, nor are our GI tracts accustomed to some of the exotic bugs to be found in far-off places. If you have chosen a competent outfitter and follow

basic precautions when you're on your own—drink only bottled water, eat only food that has been cooked or that you have
peeled yourself—you'll probably be fine. But diarrhea medicine is cheap, so you might as well take some along.

For mild bouts of the runs, good old Pepto-Bismol and
Kaopectate are reasonably effective, and some people take it as
a precaution before meals and bedtime. (Those with horrible
childhood memories of a slimy pink liquid will be glad to
know that Pepto-Bismol is also available in pill form these
days.) For more serious or long-term cases of diarrhea, many
travel specialists prescribe the antibiotic Ciprofloxacin. For
short-term relief of the exploding-bowel variety, try over-the-
counter Imodium, but not if you have a fever or bloody stool.
In any case (hedge, hedge) be sure to consult with a physician,
preferably a travel specialist, for possible side effects and con-
traindications.

There's one adventure-travel health hazard you won't learn
much about even from travel clinics: altitude sickness. A mysterious malady triggered by the lower levels of oxygen found at
high altitudes—above 10,000 feet or so—it has an array of
symptoms ranging from headache, nausea, and lethargy to potentially fatal cerebral and pulmonary edema. Different people
are affected in different ways, and susceptibility seems unre-
lated to age, general health, or physical fitness.

The best way to prevent altitude sickness is to ascend gradually, ideally no more than 1,000 feet per day once above 10,000
feet. This gives the body time to acclimate to the lower oxygen
levels. You should also drink copious amounts of water. The
prescription drug Diamox helps reduce symptoms in many
people by making the blood more acidic, thereby increasing
one's rate of breathing during sleep. Your outfitter or travel
clinic may not tell you this flat out, but I will: If you're going
above 12,000 feet, take Diamox. It has saved my ass on a number of occasions.

CLOTHING

Once again, what you need depends entirely on your destination and the time of year. Your outfitter should provide a detailed clothing list, but here are some general guidelines:

- Avoid cotton in cool or cold weather. Although it feels good against the skin, cotton has little insulating value when dry and none at all when wet. A sweat-soaked T-shirt can chill you to the bone; a cold, wet pair of jeans can be life-threatening under some conditions. Instead, take clothes of wool or quick-drying polyester fabrics like Polartec or Capilene. This may require a great philosophical shift for followers of indoor fashion, where cotton has traditionally meant classy and polyester is considered cheap and tacky. But in the outdoors, the only fashion is function.

- In cool or cold weather, dress in layers. This allows you to quickly remove or add items as the temperature and your activity level vary. The standard layering strategy has three prongs: a thin inner layer of synthetic material, such as Capilene, that will wick away excess perspiration; a heavier middle insulating layer of wool or quick-drying warm-when-wet polyester fleece (Polartec, for example); and a thin breathable waterproof outer shell, such as Gore-Tex. Mix and match the layers as necessary.

- Avoid cotton in hot, humid climates as well. It gets quickly soaked with sweat and stays clammy for days. For tropical climes, take clothes of quick-drying no-iron synthetic fabrics like Coolmax or Supplex. Long pants and long-sleeve shirts, which are necessary for sun and bug protection in the tropics, can be hard to find in lightweight 100 percent synthetic fabric, so you may have to settle for a cotton/synthetic blend. Try to keep the cotton to no more than 50 percent. One hundred percent cotton is acceptable—although still inferior to synthetics, in my opinion—only in hot, dry climates like East and North Africa.

The prestige brands in outdoor clothing are Patagonia (800-638-6464), North Face (800-362-4963), and Marmot (707-544-4590). Although their stuff is very good, it is breathtakingly expensive and lends itself to snobbery and pretension. (God forbid one of your trekmates is a wealthy outdoor novice all decked out for his first hike in $1,000 worth of Patagonia gear.) There are a number of excellent, reasonably priced retail and mail-order outlets; my favorites are L.L. Bean (800-341-4341), REI (800-426-4840), Travelsmith (800-950-1600), and Campmor (800-226-7667). I'd also recommend Sierra Trading Post (800-713-4534), a discounter that offers astonishing bargains in discontinued and irregular name-brand clothing and equipment.

- Make sure your chosen footgear is very comfortable and well broken in. When it comes to outdoor footgear, I happen to be a bit of an iconoclast who dares to challenge the hiking-boot dogma of stiff soles and full ankle support. (It seems to me that an ultrastiff sole actually promotes ankle-twisting by torquing abruptly around off-center obstacles instead of squishing around them like a soft-soled sneaker. But I digress.) For all but the most extreme hiking conditions, I prefer the comfort, cushioning, and light weight of low-cut running or cross-training shoes. I've happily worn Nike runners while climbing to 15,000 feet on Kilimanjaro, trekking for twenty-four days in Nepal, and humping a 40-pound pack for a week in New Zealand.

My views are so heretical that I would not urge them on others. I will point out, however, that Nepalese porters often go barefoot while carrying their 60-pound loads through the Himalayas. And can you guess the preferred trekking footwear of the most experienced American trip leader I know, a man who has led literally hundreds of Himalayan treks? Flip-flops.

- You must address the hat question. At the bare minimum, most of the trips in this book require some sort of baseball hat for sun protection. Many veteran travelers prefer all-around brims, but aesthetic discretion is advised. A brown, rakishly floppy Indiana Jones hat may look great on Harrison Ford or a cover model in *Outside* magazine, but on the head of a mere mortal it can border on caricature.

- In third-world countries, women should seriously consider making their primary travel garment a long, loose skirt. It has a number of practical advantages—light weight, cool in hot weather, ideal for discreet pit stops in open treeless areas—but the primary plus is cultural. By conforming to the more conservative dress codes of the local people, you'll bring out the friendly feelings that most local women already have for foreign visitors, and avoid leers from the males, who may be shocked and titillated to see a bare, or even trousered, female leg.

OTHER STUFF

- Sun protection gear is critically important on virtually every trip in this book. High altitude, tropical latitude, snow, and water can dramatically intensify sunlight and the attendant ultraviolet radiation. At the summit of Kilimanjaro—near the equator, 19,000 feet above sea level, surrounded by snow—an unprotected person can be badly sunburned in a matter of minutes. In addition to a good hat, you'll need sunglasses that block 100 percent of ultraviolet radiation. In snowy areas, "glacier glasses" with sun-blocking side panels are necessary. And of course you'll be slathering on the sun block, minimum SPF 20 and preferably SPF 40.

Your outfitter will almost certainly pound home the need for adequate sun protection, but here are some suggestions for handy items you may not find on your outfitter's equipment list:

- Ziploc bags. Clear plastic bags are invaluable for storing items that must stay dry, isolating wet and/or dirty clothes, and generally organizing your stuff. For the compulsive sorter, the possibilities are endless. Emergency pills in one bag, daily vitamins in another. Socks in one bag, underwear in another. A bag just for batteries (camera, flashlight, Walkman). A bag for paper, postcards, and pen. The see-through bags allow you to find things instantly, without rummaging. And if it rains, or the luggage raft capsizes, everything stays dry.

- Mini tape recorder. Audio memories—children giggling, the porters singing around the campfire, the roar of a lion—can be more fun than photographs. And local kids are invariably astonished and delighted when you play back their own voices to them.

- Compact binoculars. Beyond the obvious advantages for observing wildlife, it's fun to watch the snow blow off a 25,000-foot peak, check out the porter's progress behind you, or just people-watch from afar. A 9 x 25 model is a good compromise among magnification, light-gathering power, weight, and size.

- Pee bottle for men. Assuming you have an understanding tentmate, a wide-mouth plastic bottle by your sleeping bag will save a bone-chilling midnight trip to the toilet tent. Be sure to mark the bottle clearly with a skull and crossbones so you (or someone else) won't mistakingly fill it with drinking water.

- Inflatable sleeping pad, such as a Therm-a-Rest. After one night on an inflatable, a return to an old-fashioned foam pad becomes unthinkable.

- Small toys to entertain local kids. Frisbees, whiffle balls, magic tricks, finger puppets, and wind-up toys are all wonderful ice-breakers. (A guy on a Nepal trek I took a few years ago became an instant hero in every village when he took out a Hacky Sack and started kicking it around with the local kids.) An inflatable globe is eye-catching and lets you point to where you live. Avoid electronic doodads like Gameboys, whose high-tech allure tends to mesmerize kids. The idea, after all, is to open up communication, not shut it off.

- Duffel bags instead of suitcases. Your bags may be in for some rough treatment—strapped to a yak, lashed to the roof of a jeep, pelted with spray in the bottom of a jungle river longboat. Veteran travelers like Jim Traverso of Overseas Adventure Travel use duffels within duffels—three or four medium-size bags nested within one big one. He sorts the smaller ones according to function: one for on-the-trail clothes, one for city clothes, one for personal gear, and so on.

- Medium-size day pack of about 1,500 to 2,000 cubic inches. Use it on the airplane as your carry-on bag for indispensable items (documents, valuables, spare clothes in

case of lost luggage) and during the trip for all the little
things you'll need during the day when your luggage is un-
available (camera, snacks, water bottle, spare sweater).

· Snapshots of your family and hometown. More great ice-
  breakers. Imagine the reaction of a Mongolian yak herder
  upon seeing a picture of a Kansas field full of cows. Along
  the same line, a Polaroid camera lets you present local people with instant snapshots of themselves, an unfailing trigger for delighted guffaws. If you have an artistic bent, take
  along a small sketchbook or watercolor set.

· Lead-lined film bag. Third-world airports may not have
  the latest low-dose X-ray machines.

· Personal journal. Snapshots are okay, but you'll find that a
  written record of your thoughts and feelings will bring a
  knowing smile years from now. Write down those what-
  the-fuck-am-I-doing-here moments. Adventure travel, because it so removes you from everyday life, invariably
  stimulates unaccustomed self-reflection and musing. Should
  I quit my boring job when I get back home? Does it really
  matter who wins the Super Bowl? Am I really ready to settle down and get married? And does this guy Buddha
  really hold the secret to life and death? Write these
  thoughts down. Years from now you'll be amazed at what
  went through your head.

I could keep going here, but I fear I've already flouted the
first rule of getting ready for adventure travel: Keep it to a minimum. As our old friend Wilfred Thesiger puts it, "Anything
that is not a necessity becomes an encumbrance."

NORTH
AMERICA

ALASKA

paddle-rafting the
kongakut

Hanging out in camp after a day on the river, John Attig glanced out over the tundra and noticed that the western horizon—a broad, gentle ridge several miles away—appeared oddly blurred in the evening light. "Kinda fuzzy," he recalls. Curious, Attig reached for his binoculars. What he saw made him gasp in astonishment: a horizon of antlers, a wall of caribou marching shoulder-to-shoulder over the ridge, directly toward the campsite.

It was not by accident that Attig and his river-rafting mates were camped in Caribou Alley, a narrow strip of tundra between the icebergs of the Beaufort Sea and the foothills of the Brooks Range. This coastal plain on the far northern edge of Alaska, part of the Arctic National Wildlife Refuge, has been called America's Serengeti. During the wink-of-an-eye Arctic summer, nonstop sunlight and warmish temperatures lure a deluge of wildlife: moose, wolves, arctic foxes, wolverines, musk oxen, Dall sheep, and unfathomable numbers of birds, along with the two fiercest predators in North America, the grizzly bear and polar bear.

But the dominant summer species of this wildlife-rich tundra—the boss of the moss, so to speak—is the caribou. Every June, some 160,000 caribou of the Porcupine herd migrate here from their wintering grounds in the mountains to the south. Like the wildebeest of East Africa's Serengeti Plain, the caribou are instinctive nomads, following the relentless rhythm of the seasons. They spend a dark, bitter winter in the stunted forests surrounding the Porcupine River, which cuts the Alaska-Yukon border just above the Arctic Circle. In April, after months of pawing holes in the snow in search of lichen, the cows—skinny, hungry, and pregnant—begin moving north in small bands. (The bulls, juveniles, and unpregnant females follow a month or so later.) Plodding single file, each group of caribou is a tributary to a living stream that grows ever larger as it flows north toward the sea.

The caribou are canny travelers. They follow frozen streambeds for better footing, and in deep snow trace each other's tracks to save energy. Harassed by wolves, smothered by spring blizzards, hunted by Inuits, they press relentlessly northward for 300, 400, even 500 miles, like waves of attacking soldiers in the face of withering fire. Fearless swimmers, they ford rushing ice-choked rivers with heads high and legs churning. Nothing deters the tide of hooves.

In mid-May, the pregnant cows flood out of the mountains into the flat, open tundra region sliced by the Kongakut, Aichilik, Jago, and Hulahula Rivers. There they settle down to fill their stomachs on the burgeoning plant life, give birth to the next generation of caribou, and gather strength for the return trip.

Virtually all the calves are born during the first week of June, a marvelous synchronism that cuts losses to wolves, bears, and eagles. The newborns are up and walking within minutes; at ten days old, a caribou calf can outrun a grizzly. Coalescing into larger and larger groups, the cows and calves forage for cotton grass, willow shrub leaves, and lousewort. Later in the month they are joined by the late-starting bulls and juveniles. By the first of July, aggregations as large as 90,000 animals are wandering the tundra.

Kind-hearted humans, if it were in our power, would no doubt grant the Porcupine herd a pleasant, relaxed summer as a respite from their long winter's suffering. Nature, on the other hand, arranges for unimaginable swarms of mosquitoes to arise from the tundra bogs around the first of July. Legendarily large, numerous, and aggressive, arctic mosquitoes are reputed to kill moose by sucking them dry of blood, drive men to suicide, carry off babies, and herd caribou into the sea. The first three phenomena are as yet unconfirmed by scientific authorities, but a report by the International Porcupine Caribou Board declares flatly that during the first two weeks in July, caribou herds travel "primarily in response to insect harassment." Crowding together to reduce exposed skin area—or perhaps simply because misery loves company—the caribou will gallop en masse for 20 miles seeking out high, windy areas, where the weak-flying mosquitoes are grounded. Or, lacking wind, they may wade haunch-deep into shallow lagoons or estuaries along the coast. In desperation, the caribou sometimes shake their heads and kick and buck, spooking each other into huge stampedes.

As if mosquitoes from Hell were not enough, the caribou must also suffer July attacks from botflies and warble flies. Botflies, too fast to be outrun, dart into the caribou's nostrils and deposit larva, which grow and infest the nasal passages. (To fend off botflies, caribou have been observed standing for hours on end with their heads buried in bushes.) Warble flies bombard the caribou's legs, laying eggs that eventually hatch into larva. The worms bore through the skin and migrate underneath to the back, rump, and shoulders. There the grubs, by now thumb-sized, bore airholes to the surface, through which they breathe as they swell into festering abscesses. A typical caribou hide will have several hundred warble fly holes; one poor half-dead calf was found to be infested with nearly two thousand larvae.

Along with wolves, bears, eagles, and bugs, there is another killer of migrating caribou: rivers. Blindly plunging into deep, fast-moving torrents, caribou often drown or break their legs against rocks as they are pulled into rapids. Calves are routinely swept away from their mothers—a death sentence, for no cow will accept another's calf. In 1984, Quebec's George River caribou herd, driven more by instinct than good sense, tried to cross the Carniapiscau River, swollen by an ill-advised release of water from a HydroQuebec dam upstream. For five suicidal days, caribou marched into the raging water, only to be swept over a waterfall just below the ford. By the time the carnage ended, ten thousand carcasses littered the banks of the river for 50 miles downstream.

On the day that John Attig and his rafting pals on the Kongakut watched the wall of caribou approach their camp, the river was at its normal summer level—one to 8 feet deep, running 5 or 6 knots of current. The leading edge of the herd halted at the water's edge, milling nervously on a gravel bar. Behind them, bleating and snorting, followers began to pile up. The opposite bank of the river quickly became a seething, snorting, hairy, horny mass of confusion. A few animals would start to splash across, then panic and bolt back to shore. "It was chaos," recalls Susan Olsen, another trip member. "There seemed to be no rhyme nor reason to their behavior."

At last a cow and her calf plunged in and began to swim strongly out into the roiling water. The cow stayed just upstream of her little one, shielding it from the current as best she could. After several minutes of struggle, they clambered ashore perhaps 50 yards downstream from the camp. Then others began to plunge in. "They would charge at the water, almost in a panic," reports Attig. The sound of hundreds of hooves ripping the water was that of distant thunder. A few addled animals swam across, scrambled out of the water, then inexplicably turned around and swam back. Some cows stayed near their calves, others swam across alone and waited. "I have a very vivid memory of a young calf, only a week or two old, swimming its heart out in the middle of the river, bleating and bleating and going nowhere against the current, while its mother waited on the shore," says Attig's wife, Katherine. "It was heart-wrenching to watch." In the confusion, she never saw whether the youngster made it safely across.

The tide of caribou poured across the river all that night. The rafters, crouched in a ravine above the campsite to avoid spooking the animals, stayed up most of the "night" to watch the spectacle. (It was broad daylight, of course. Land of the midnight sun.) Finally, at about three A.M. the rafters, exhilarated and exhausted, crawled into their sleeping bags and fell asleep to a cacophonous lullaby of snorting, bleating, stomping, and splashing, all against the backbeat of incessant clicking that a caribou's ankle bone makes with every step. Figure 1,000 caribou an hour passing by your tent, four ankle bones each, say 50 steps each within earshot. Would 200,000 clicks an hour lull you to sleep or drive you mad?

When the rafters awoke the next morning, the caribou tide was still at full flood, and it continued unabated all day. "At any point you could walk up a little rise behind camp and see thousands of caribou," recalls John Attig. The animals steered clear of the actual campsight, but the rafters, by walking away from the camp a few hundred yards and hiding behind rocks, could immerse themselves in the flow, watching the animals from 10

feet away or less. Sagas of caribou joy and heartbreak, of desperation and fear, unfolded before their eyes. Mama cows
hopefully sniffed lost calves and bellowed in delight when they
found them. Others sniffed and turned away to continue the
search for their own, leaving the orphan calf bleating in terror.
Forlorn calves in their desperation even approached rafters,
only to spook away when they smelled Gore-Tex and DEET
instead of Mom. (Not to worry. According to Ken Whitten, a
caribou maven with the Alaska Fish and Game Department,
"Caribou calves and cows are very adept at finding one another,
even in very large crowds.")

After three days the caribou flood finally abated, and once
again there was only the sound of the wind. Thick clumps
of caribou hair lined the riverbank like a soap ring in a bathtub,
turning every rock and stick furry. Turds littered the tundra.
And everywhere the ground was laced with a dense network of
newly gouged trails, fresh scars on the fragile earth. In its after-
math, America's grandest wildlife spectacle bore a remarkable
resemblance to a convention of drunken dirt bikers.

OUTFITTERS

ABEC, Alaska Discovery, Arctic Treks, and *Wilderness: Alaska/
Mexico* offer pretty much the same itinerary on the Kongakut: a
three-hour Cessna 185 or Helio Courier flight from Fairbanks to
a suitable landing place ("suitable" by the liberal definition of
Alaskan bush pilots, that is) on a gravel bar at Drain Creek, followed by eight leisurely days of paddling and floating on the river,
covering a total of about 60 miles. The Kongakut is generally
shallow and fast-moving, often flowing in multiple braided chan-
nels, with lots of small rapids. A 3-mile stretch through a small
canyon has Class III rapids. The usual takeout and bush-plane
pickup is a gravel bar near Caribou Pass, about 35 river miles upstream from the Beaufort Sea, overlooking the coastal plain.

There's typically a one- or two-day layover for extended hiking, as well as short hikes from camp. Trips are usually scheduled to coincide with peak caribou migration, but there's no guarantee you'll see vast herds. Caribou movement is notoriously unpredictable from year to year. ("Nobody knows the wind or the caribou," the Inuit say.)

With the exception of Alaska Discovery, each outfitter offers optional backpacking expeditions in the Kongakut headwaters area before the raft trip. Only the sturdy need apply; trekkers carry a 50–60-pound pack anywhere from eight to twelve days over rough or nonexistent trails.

WHAT TO EXPECT

Although trip participants paddle the rafts themselves, the pace is leisurely and the rapids in general not very demanding. Hiking on layover days is moderate and at low altitude.

The optional pretrip backpack expedition is much tougher; you'll start off with a 60-pound pack and eat your way down to perhaps a 45-pounder by the last day. The highest passes crossed are at 4,000 to 4,500 feet, with daily elevation gains up to 1,800 feet.

The camping is not quite full service. Meals are prepared by the camp staff, but you'll be asked to put up and take down your own tent and help load and unload the rafts.

Weather is very changeable, with temperatures from the 30s to the 90s possible on each trip. Periods of rain are probable, snow possible. Cool weather, frigid river water (35 to 50 degrees), wind, and the low-activity level on the raft can combine to make you very cold and uncomfortable. Although there is little danger on the trip, the great isolation from help in case of an injury adds to the mental challenge.

And then there are the mosquitoes. Most trips are scheduled for mid- to late June to avoid the peak swarms in mid-July.

Even so, most outfitters recommend bringing along jumbo-size bottles of bug repellent, head nets, and even repellent-soaked fine-mesh mosquito suits.

Paddling a raft demands certain basic techniques, but they are quickly learned. Even if you're a total klutz, other paddlers can take up the slack.

All trips run in mid- to late June.

RECOMMENDED READING

Coming into the Country by John McPhee. The classic account of the author's wanderings through Alaska and his encounters with its fiercely independent inhabitants.

IN BRIEF

ABEC, 907-457-8907: 11 days, $2,300; with backpacking option: 18 days, $2,800, or 22 days, $3,000

Alaska Discovery, 800-586-1911: 10 days, $2,990

Arctic Treks, 907-455-6502: 10 days, $2,575; with backpacking option, 19 days, $3,475

Wilderness: Alaska/Mexico, 907-479-8203: 11 days, $2,400; with backpacking option, 22 days, $3,100

Physical challenge, 2; Mental challenge, 3; Skills 2.

THE ARCTIC
skiing to the
north pole

Of all the myriad dangers inherent in a journey by ski and dogsled across a frozen ocean, perhaps the most worrisome is the possibility of falling through the ice. During the spring—the only period when such a journey is feasible—the frozen surface of the sea is constantly shifting, cracking, opening up, and refreezing. An unlucky step onto thin or soft ice may, with no warning, plunge an expeditioner into 29-degree water, where the normal human life expectancy is between three and five minutes. This can be problematic when the nearest heated enclosure is 500 miles away.

Paul Schurke and Rick Sweitzer, leaders of a two-week ski/dogsled trip to the North Pole, sincerely want to help their clients conquer this fear of falling through the ice. So, each January, three months before the trip departs, they bring clients to Schurke's northern Minnesota lodge. A hole is chainsawed into a frozen lake and clients, fully clothed, are invited to jump into the icy water. Not invited, actually. Ordered. No dunk, no trip.

"You'd actually feel a lot warmer if you went in naked," says Sweitzer. "The wet clothes keep sucking the heat right out of you even after you've climbed out of the water."

The icy plunge is the grand finale of a mandatory six-day training camp for trip participants. Sweitzer and Schurke—a veteran polar explorer who, with Will Steger, led an epic two-month dogsled trip to the North Pole in 1986—instruct the troops in the basics of Nordic skiing, mushing, dog handling, winter survival, and expedition psychology. Clients learn first-hand, for example, that a fully clothed plunge into 29-degree water is in fact quite survivable—invigorating, really—as long as a tent and a complete set of dry clothing are immediately at hand.

The idea for the North Pole trip is simple enough: use modern technology to give adventurous clients a taste of old-fashioned polar exploration in the manner of pioneering Arctic explorers Robert Peary and Robert Falcon Scott. Using chartered planes, the group flies to within about 100 miles of the North Pole, lands on the ice, and then slogs the rest of the way solely on muscle power (both the clients' and the dogs'). The plane returns two weeks later to pick up the group at the nearest suitable landing spot to the Pole.

Fifteen people signed up for the 1993 inaugural trip—among them were a social worker, an insurance salesman, a pastry chef, a homemaker, and a jingle writer. They ranged in age from thirty-two to sixty-three, in physical strength from superfit to barely fit, and in outdoor experience from veteran mountaineer to "didn't know one end of a sleeping bag from another." Four bowed out during training camp, leaving a motley crew of eleven whose only common denominator was an uncommon mental toughness. "After you've jumped into a hole in the ice when the windchill is 30 below, not many things bother you," shrugged one training-camp survivor.

After a lengthy series of northbound flights in planes of ever diminishing size, thirteen people, two sleds, sixteen dogs, and 2,200 pounds of gear disembarked from two ski-equipped

Twin Otters into the middle of an unbroken white wasteland at latitude 88.25. The frozen surface was laced with long fissures of open water called leads. All around them lay pressure ridges—mounds of broken ice up to 20 feet high created by the enormous pressures of shifting ice. The Pole was 109 miles away. As the Twin Otters disappeared into the distance, the vast silence was broken only by the excited yipping of the dogs.

Although it was one A.M., there was no time for sleep. The humans were just as pumped up as the dogs, and a hazy sun was shining. (This time of year, the polar sun circles low in the sky in a perpetual late afternoon.) Moreover, weather had delayed the last flight, and the expedition was already three days behind schedule. With barely a pause to ponder the eerie beauty of their surroundings, the expeditioners hooked up the dogs—eight huskies and two people to a team—and clicked into their cross-country skis. The party moved off into the vast frigid whiteness chattering and huffing with excitement.

Less than two hours later, Jim Anderson and Tim Goodsell fell through the ice. Schurke, leading the way on skis, had threaded his way through several pressure ridges and across a 20-foot lead that had recently refrozen. The fresh ice was thick enough to support him, several following skiers, and the first team of dogs. But under the 800-pound weight of the second sled, with Anderson and Goodsell pushing alongside, a section of ice began to sink. After a heart-stopping second, the sled broke through, and the two men tumbled into the slushy water.

Anderson doesn't remember his head going under, but he does recall thinking that the water didn't feel as cold as his practice dunk back in Minnesota. As the frigid water penetrated his clothing, he kept saying to himself, "I wonder how deep this is?" (About 3 miles, it turned out.) Buoyed yet encumbered by his bulky winter clothing, he struggled to swim the 6 feet to the edge of the ice. Kicking madly, Anderson flopped his upper body up onto the ice like a seal, then clawed and rolled the rest of the way out, just as he'd been taught back in Minnesota. The ice held, and he stood up with a massive sense of relief, fear draining away. Then suddenly he broke through the crust again, plunging in up to his neck. Anderson struggled up onto the ice once more, but this time crawled and rolled until he reached solid pack ice.

The postdunk drill called for rolling around in the snow, which acts like a sponge to absorb water from wet clothes. Still soaked to the skin and rapidly chilling, Anderson and Good-sell, who had also hauled himself out, could see Schurke on the other side of the frozen lead, waving them over. The two men walked 50 yards along the lead to a narrow spot in the slush. Hopping from one frozen chunk to the next, they reached the other side, where Schurke began putting up a warming tent. (Fortunately, the dogs had managed to pull the sled out of the water before it sank completely.) The two changed into their backup sets of dry clothes, huddled around the small cooking stove, and were soon warmed and out of danger. Since it was now three A.M., Schurke called it a night.

Sweitzer now admits that, after such a near disaster so early in the trip, he had serious forebodings. But in the name of group morale, he kept quiet. Nor did Anderson waste a lot of time thinking what might happen if he fell through the ice again, this time with no dry clothes to change into. (His wet clothes would remain frozen stiff and useless for the remainder of the trip.)

They covered 8 miles the second day, a rate not nearly suffi-cient to make the Pole in the nine days remaining. But the group was gaining strength and expertise, and each day the sleds got lighter by 60 pounds as dog food, people food, and stove fuel were consumed. Day three was better, almost 12 miles. And no dunks.

The ice kept fighting them. Each morning Schurke would awake, check the Global Positioning System (GPS) satellite navigator, and discover that they had drifted back southward in the ocean currents anywhere from one to three miles during the night. As they neared the Pole, the pressure ridges and leads became more numerous. On day eight, another musher fell through the ice, setting them back a few more hours. Time was growing short.

By radio, Schurke learned that a group of Canadian scientists had just set up a temporary camp only 5 miles from the Pole, at a suitable landing site for Twin Otters. Although it would be a detour, Schurke decided to head for the camp, since it was a known landing site and could serve as a base from which to make a final dash to the Pole if time permitted.

On day ten, they came to a zone of especially jumbled, fractured ice. From the top of a pressure ridge, Schurke could see the loose ice ahead drifting in all directions. Although passable on skis, the terrain would be exceedingly difficult to pull the heavy sleds across. Schurke went ahead to scout the route, and radioed back that he'd found a way through. But many in the group, exhausted and intimidated by the rugged terrain ahead, had doubts about proceeding. They had made a valiant effort, but the Canadian camp was still 15 miles away—if they could find it on the shifting ice—and the Pole 5 miles farther still. They had less than thirty-six hours to reach the Pole and get back to the camp in time for the Twin Otter pickup. The prudent course would be to retreat to the last suitable landing spot they'd seen, about 3 miles back.

Sweitzer, convinced that the group was up to the task, persuaded them to press on. The ice was so soft in spots that it billowed and jiggled under their weight like a waterbed. They built bridges across narrow leads by lining up small icebergs. After a difficult struggle, they caught up with Schurke.

The feeling of renewed determination and confidence, however, was short-lived. A few hours later they came up against a
seemingly impassable 25-foot-wide fissure of open water that
slashed across their path, stretching left and right as far as they
could see. Schurke, borrowing a technique used by Scott nearly
seventy years before, walked onto a small peninsula of ice and
cut it loose with a saw brought along for just such an eventual-
ity. The raft of ice, although unstable, was just large enough to
support one sled. Using ropes to pull the ice ferry back and
forth across the lead, the team bridged the gap in a few minutes. "We began to feel invincible," recalls Sweitzer.

Shortly thereafter, Schurke, standing atop an ice ridge, spotted a tent and a radio antenna ahead—the Canadian camp. Exhausted both mentally and physically after their harrowing day,
the group greeted the surprised scientists and set up their tents.
It was now about 10 P.M.; the pickup planes would arrive in
twenty hours—just enough time for dinner, a good night's
sleep, and the final 10-mile round-trip dash to the Pole.
Schurke unpacked the radio and GPS.

The news was disheartening. The Twin Otter pilots reported
from their base that a five-day storm was forecast to commence
the next afternoon, and the planes would now arrive for the
pickup at two P.M., four hours earlier than planned. That dead-
line was absolute; if the group was not back by then, the planes
would leave without them. Worse yet, the GPS revealed that
the camp had drifted 6 miles south in the last two days. Counting tomorrow's anticipated drift, they would be facing a 26-
mile round-trip to the Pole, and now had only sixteen hours in
which to accomplish it. Up to that point, they'd never managed
to cover more than 15 miles in one day. It looked hopeless.

But if they left the dogs and sleds behind, and traveled light,
maybe it could be done. Still feeling invincible, they decided to
sleep a few hours and leave at two A.M. That would give them
twelve hours to cover those 26 miles.

The insurance salesman and the housewife and the jingle writer skied with all the energy they could muster. By the second rest stop, they'd covered 10 miles in five hours, a good clip that left them just 3 miles from the Pole. But 16 miles still remained, and only seven hours in which to cover them. Even at their current all-out pace, it would take them eight hours. The pitiless mathematics of distance and time left no choice: After eleven days and 106 miles of struggle, they would have to turn back literally within sight of the North Pole.

It was then, sitting in despair and exhaustion, that they heard a whining whup-whup-whup sound up ahead. On the horizon, a bright orange helicopter was coming in to land, apparently right over the Pole. Schurke, a veteran of a Siberian dogsled trip a few years previously, recognized the chopper as a Russian Mil. Hoping the group might be able to catch a lift back to the base camp on the helicopter, he madly sprinted ahead, while the others straggled behind in breathless pursuit. Sweitzer, staying back with the slowest skiers, realized they had now passed the "point of no return" back to the base camp. They could not possibly get back by two o'clock. In their last gasp to flag down the helicopter, they had burned their bridges behind them. Their fate lay entirely in the hands of a crew of Russians who didn't even know they existed.

To Sweitzer's horror, the chopper took off again. Apparently, Schurke had not reached it in time, and it was returning home, wherever that might be. But then the Mil banked toward the skiers and circled overhead. Sweitzer could see faces at the window and hands waving. The helicopter returned to its landing spot.

As Sweitzer and the stragglers rounded a last pressure ridge, they saw a sight they could hardly believe. Swarms of people milled about on a big red X painted on the ice. Flags fluttered in the breeze while TV camera crews scurried about. People danced arm-in-arm, Cossack style, to the music of a wheezing concertina.

The German tourists who'd chartered the Russian helicopter for their North Pole junket were astonished and delighted to see the unexpected party crashers. They cheered and clapped for the skiers as they arrived one by one. They were toasted with champagne, vodka, and caviar. They wolfed down fried chicken and beer. There were hugs and tears and high-fives at the very top of the world.

One detail yet remained. Schurke recognized one of the helicopter crewmen as an old pal from his Siberian trip. The two quickly got down to business, and terms were proposed: the $1,200 GPS navigator in exchange for a five-minute, 13-mile hop back to the base camp. The deal was done. And so was the adventure.

OUTFITTER

Not surprisingly, the key word in *Northwest Passage*'s itinerary is "north." The trip begins at Resolute Bay in Canada's Northwest Territories, the northernmost outpost in the world reachable by scheduled air service. From there, the party flies about 400 miles north by chartered Twin Otter to Eureka, a weather station on Ellsmere Island. Then it's a five-hour northerly flight (in two legs, with a stop along the way at a cache of fuel drums) to the drop-off point at about 88 degrees North latitude. Precise location will vary according to ice conditions, but the target distance from the Pole is 100 to 150 miles.

From there, it's about a two-week ski/mush to the Pole. The expedition will be picked up by Twin Otters somewhere in the vicinity of the Pole—again depending on where there happens to be 1,500 feet of smooth ice on which to land—and ferried back to Resolute.

The trip package also includes a mandatory six-day training camp at Paul Schurke's lodge in Ely, Minnesota, three months before the trip. You'll learn the basics of dogsledding, skiing, and winter survival, and find out if you've got the stuff for the trip. (If you or Northwest Passage decides you're not up to it, you may cancel with no penalty.)

WHAT TO EXPECT

Long, arduous days of skiing and mushing while carrying a 30-pound pack will challenge even the fittest. Do not harbor the illusion that driving a dogsled is physically easy; you'll be required to help push the 1,000-pound sleds, not ride along shouting commands while your hair blows dramatically in the wind. Hauling sleds over ice ridges is a particularly exhausting task.

Thankfully, the route is mostly dead level, and altitude, of course, is not a problem. But overall, this trip is as physically demanding as most mountain climbs.

How cold does it get? Typical temperatures range from 10 below to 10 above, but it's possible you'll see 40 below. Obviously, camping out under these conditions is difficult. But cold is just the beginning. There's also the danger of falling through the ice, the isolation from rescue, the likelihood of being turned back by weather, open water, or impassable ice ridges, and the sheer drudgery of hauling heavy loads across an endlessly monotonous landscape. There's also the chance that weather may prevent a pickup or rescue, leaving you stranded for days in an Arctic blizzard. And don't forget the polar bears, among the most aggressive animals toward humans. Y'all be careful now, hear?

On the other hand, the dogs are great fun to work with. And the expedition has a couple of modern gizmos to enhance safety: a high-frequency radio to keep in touch with Resolute and a GPS position-finder that makes it virtually impossible to get lost.

About the only skill necessary to make this trip is a moderate level of competence on cross-country skis. More advanced skiing techniques, dogsled driving, and winter survival skills are taught in the mandatory training camp, so by the time you're ready to go, you'll have well-honed skills.

The trip departs in late April from Edmonton, Alberta.

RECOMMENDED READING

North to the Pole by Will Steger and Paul Schurke. A firsthand account of the authors' epic fifty-five-day, 1,000-mile ski-dogsled run to the North Pole in 1986.

IN BRIEF

The Northwest Passage, 800-732-7328: 20 days, $25,500

Physical challenge, 4; Mental challenge, 5; Skills, 2.

ARIZONA

horseback riding in
monument valley

First came the gay caballeros of Andy Warhol's *Lonesome Cowboys,* who wore tights with their Stetsons and used the hitchin' post in front of the saloon as a ballet barre to practice their demi-pliés. Then came Mitzi, Felicia, and Bernadette, the dazzling transvestites of *Priscilla, Queen of the Desert,* who strutted in satin gowns and plumed hats amid the cliffs and mesas of the Australian Outback.

And now here am I, a novice cowboy loping across the rolling sand and sagebrush amid a surreal landscape of red-rock buttes and spires, with my lower body sheathed in skintight see-through stretch nylon. The outfitter's pretrip "Helpful Hints" had suggested that unpracticed riders might want to wear panty hose under their jeans to prevent chafing and saddle sores. Sound advice, perhaps, but hardly in keeping with the cowboy aesthetic, it seemed to me. John Wayne, who made a half dozen movies here in Monument Valley, probably didn't wear panty hose to prevent chafing and saddle sores. Chafing and saddle sores were part of the cowboy game. Like all cowboys, he stoically endured the hardships of a tough world.

Don't complain, don't explain. Suck it up. Take responsibility for yourself.

But I soon came to learn there is another little-known canon in the modern-day cowboy code: play tricks on the hapless dudes at every opportunity. One grizzled wrangler advised a woman guest on a Monument Valley ride, "Hon, I'll tell you once an' only once how you know if a cowboy's lyin'—it's when his lips is movin'." It occurred to me as I rode across the sage-brush that this whole panty-hose thing might just be a huge practical joke dreamed up by the wranglers around a campfire.

"Lemme tell you, Milt. These eastern city dudes are dumber than storm drains. They'll believe any kind of ridiculous horse-shit you tell 'em. Today I had a bunch of 'em shoutin' into a damn hole in the rock. Told 'em to listen for the echo. Sure enough, one after the other, they'd yell into the hole, and then nod and smile and say how that was one hell of an echo. Damnedest thing I ever seen."

"Sheeit, Cliff, that ain't nothin'. I had a guy ask me yesterday what made them holes in the rock in the first place. So I told him it was the rockpecker birds, makin' a place for a nest. So he nods and smiles and says to his wife, ain't this wildlife unusual out here in Arizona."

"Hell, we could get these dudes to do anything. I'll bet you a pitcher of beer back in Gallup that if we told the men to wear panty hose, some dumb sumbitch would show up walkin' funny."

"Aw, c'mon, Cliff. Not even a goddam New Jersey lawyer is that dumb. You got yourself a bet."

Our initiation into the cowboy code began with the subsec-tion about taking responsibility for yourself. At breakfast on the first day back in Gallup, before we ever got near a horse, we had been presented with liability waivers to sign. "I acknowl-edge that a horse may . . . regardless of training and past performance . . . without warning or apparent cause, buck, stumble, fall, rear, bite, kick, spook, jump obstacles, step on a person's feet, push or shove a person. . . . I voluntarily assume the risk and danger of injury or death inherent in the use of the horse. . . . "

Say what? The brochure had made no mention of bucking, stumbling, falling, rearing, kicking, biting, or spooking. This curious document in front of me seemed to imply that as a cowboy—even a novice cowboy—I would be required to actually assume the risk myself for these multifarious hazards. Moreover, I would forfeit the right to blame or sue anyone else. It seemed downright un-American.

Nevertheless, I signed the waiver. There's more to being a cowboy, after all, than sitting on a horse wearing a ten-gallon hat. I was going to take responsibility for myself, by God, just like the Duke.

Down at the bottom of the waiver a second paragraph required another signature. "It is recommended that all riders wear a protective helmet. It is my understanding that a protective helmet is available and has been offered for my own safety. . . . " I hesitated. Panty hose, maybe. But panty hose and a helmet? With reckless abandon, I signed the line that said "I hereby refuse to use it." Man, if my friends back East could see me now, casually refusing recommended safety equipment!

Of course, everyone else refused the offer of helmets as well. Don Donnelly, our trip leader and the owner of the horseback tour company, said he couldn't recall anyone ever wearing a helmet in all his years of leading rides in Monument Valley. But if somebody insisted, he could probably dig one out of the bottom of a horse trailer somewhere. "But I tell you what," he added, "if somebody refuses to sign the helmet waiver, we'd make damn sure they never took off the helmet. They'd be sleepin' in it."

If you squint a little bit, Donnelly, who is 6-foot-4 (not counting boots and hat) and 250-plus pounds, looks like John Wayne with a friendly twinkle in his eye and some extra padding around the middle. He has spent most of his life on horses, and most of the last thirty-four years taking folks for rides in beautiful places. He walks the walk and talks the talk. A representative sample of Donnellyisms:

"I think I'll go lay down for a while till this dark spell passes." (Said just before bedtime.)

"We're exactly partway there." (Answer to inevitable dumb dude question. How much farther?)

"Clear clouds followed by dry drizzle." (Answer to inevitable dumb dude question, What will the weather be tomorrow?)

"Round about lunchtime." (Answer to inevitable dumb dude question, When's lunch?)

"They was runnin' around here kissin' on each other somethin' awful. It sounded like cows pullin' their feet outta the mud." (Description of a romance between a wrangler and a female guest on a previous trip.)

Romance is part of the cowboy ethic, of course—mostly romance gone bad. One of our wranglers was reputed to have been married fourteen times. A camp cook, getting over her second divorce in Pennsylvania, ran off to Arizona with a man she'd known for two weeks. A wrangler named Bud ("like the beer," he told me as he introduced himself), a fine guitar player, sang us a song around the campfire about his third ex-wife. (As I recall, it included the words *bitch* and *slut*.) Bud's heartbreaks go beyond the romantic; a few years ago he recorded a country/western song by an unknown songwriter named Lyle Lovett. The record went nowhere. Six months later, Lovett, using the same producer and the same band, recorded the same song. It went platinum. Hell, that's a country song right there.

But for pain and heartbreak, not even cowboys can match the Navajo, who lived in Monument Valley for centuries until the white man moved in and burned their homes and farms and began herding them into concentration camps in the 1860s. Perhaps feeling a bit guilty, the U.S. government eventually gave the Navajos some of their land back, and Monument Valley, with its famous mittenlike buttes and needle spires, is now a tribal park that lies entirely within the Navajo reservation. Outsiders are not allowed to venture off the scenic-loop road without a Navajo guide.

Our guide was Lonnie Yazzi, an easygoing forty-eight-year-old with a braided ponytail and a face darkened by a lifetime of desert sun. He was born in a mud hogan just round the other side of Thunderbird Mesa from our base camp. At age two he was assigned by his mother the task of assistant herder of the family sheep flock, under the command of his older brother. By age six, he had moved up to head family sheepherder, but admits he was too curious and restless for the job. "I'd get to exploring around the mesas, looking for caves and petroglyphs, and all of a sudden I'd realize the sun was going down, and, oh man, where were my sheep?"

His sheepherding career ended when he was sent off to the first grade at a Navajo boarding school. He eventually graduated from Navajo Community College, and is now a part-time teacher. But he still spends much of the year living at Thunderbird Mesa and guiding Donnelly's groups around his vast backyard.

The Navajo songs Lonnie sang for us around the campfire that first night, like Bud's country/western tunes, were heavy with loneliness and despair.

> *I lost my gal and I lost my home*
> *Because I drink that wine, oh wine.*
> *Cold in the country, cold in the town*
> *Cold to sleep on the ground. Wine, oh wine.*
>
> *Call me a drifter, call me a bum.*
> *Where, oh where can a wino hide from the wine*
> *From the pretty red wine.*

He also told us the story of his great-great-great-grandmother. Herding sheep one day around 1866, just a butte or two away from our present campsite, she was captured by legendary Indian fighter Kit Carson. Along with other victims of the Navajo roundup, she was blindfolded and forced to walk 400 miles to a concentration camp at Fort Sumner, New Mexico. Along the way, when her blindfold was briefly removed for food and water breaks, she memorized landmarks.

After a year in captivity at Fort Sumner, during which hundreds of her fellow Navajos died of disease and starvation, Great-great-great-grandma Yazzi escaped across the desert, fleeing barefoot through dense cactus to a nearby mountain. She spent the night in a tree, and awoke to find her feet so swollen and infected from cactus thorns that she was unable to walk. She hid out in the tree, smearing her feet with sap and crawling out at night on her hands and knees in search of water and berries. After two months she peeled the dried sap from her feet. They had healed. It was time to go home.

For a year she walked through the desert, following the landmarks locked in her memory. Usually traveling at night, she stayed off roads and trails to avoid U.S. Cavalry patrols and unfriendly Comanche. She spoke not a single word during the journey, and when she finally arrived home in Monument Valley, she was mute, unable to speak even to her family. But a medicine man cast a spell on her and brought back her voice.

A few months later, herding sheep in virtually the same place, she was captured again by Carson's men. But just after she arrived at Fort Sumner for the second time, the peace treaty of 1868 was signed. She walked home again, this time proudly, right out in the open.

Sitting there in the glow of the campfire, listening to Lonnie's soft singsongy voice, the threat of chafing and saddle sores suddenly seemed rather trivial. And so, after we'd all filed back to our tents for the night, I quietly returned to the still-flickering campfire, panty hose in hand, and tossed them into the flames. The foul-smelling smoke rose into the starry Monument Valley sky.

OUTFITTER

Don Donnelly Stables' weeklong trip begins with a van ride five hours north from Gallup, New Mexico, to Monument Valley. After saddling up at a corral near the visitors' center, you'll ride a half day into the heart of the park, past several of the best-known picture-postcard buttes and spires, to an isolated base camp at Thunderbird Mesa. From there, you'll make day rides to various remote parts of Monument Valley, returning to camp each night. On the last full day, you'll ride up a steep, winding trail to the top of Mitchell Mesa, accessible only by foot or horseback with a Navajo guide, where there is a commanding view of the entire Four Corners area. There are four full days of riding, plus half days going in and out from the base camp.

WHAT TO EXPECT

For the experienced rider, this trip is about as aerobically challenging as watching TV from a Barcalounger. The horse does
all the work, after all. The novice or occasional rider, however,
will find a myriad of new muscles coming into play. And then
there is the pain. If you have never ridden a horse before, or
have not ridden in a long time, you will most definitely experience what a woman in our group came to call "that special feeling" in your crotch, butt, and inner thighs. After the opening
half-day ride to base camp, one novice rider in our group dis-
mounted and literally fell to the ground moaning.

To minimize the pain, beginners and lapsed riders should
take at least two—and preferably three or four—riding lessons
the week prior to the trip. This will get your riding muscles in
reasonable shape and get the break-in pain out of the way early.
But in any case, bring the ibuprofen.

Donnelly allows rank beginners to take the Monument Valley trip, and most do okay. But some riding experience makes
this trip far more rewarding, allowing you to actually enjoy the
astounding scenery instead of just clinging desperately to your
horse and trying to ignore the pain in your tailbone.

During a typical day's ride, your horse will do a lot of walking and trotting over moderately rough, rolling terrain. There
are plenty of opportunities to canter (or "lope" in Western par-
lance). Expert riders may essentially do anything they wish,
fanning out across the open range at whatever pace they prefer.

Although Donnelly's horses are unusually calm and well be-
haved, there is a very real danger of being thrown from a horse
that bucks, stumbles, falls, rears, and so on. (On my trip, two
guests fell off, fortunately without injury, when their horses
spooked.) For the beginner, dealing with a 1,200-pound animal can be a bit scary at times.

Out of the saddle, the amenities border on the luxurious. "This is no skim-milk deal," says Donnelly. There are even hot showers and open-air sinks with mirrors. The tents, which sleep two people each on cots, are large stand-up models. "So you don't have to get down on your belly and crawl in like a snake," as Donnelly puts it. Food is hearty cowboy cuisine; health-conscious types will probably eat more red meat this week than in a typical month. Breakfast, for example, typically includes eggs, pancakes, oatmeal, sausage, ham, bacon, grits, and hash browns. For the abstemious, there is cereal, fruit, and 1 percent milk—but, like Don says, no skim.

The desert weather can be unpredictable. Thunderstorms and high winds are common; several riders in our group were caught in a violent hail and lightning storm.

Trips run in the spring and fall: May, June, September, and October. Guests meet in Gallup, New Mexico, which is accessible by commuter plane from Phoenix, and by Amtrak or rental car from Albuquerque.

RECOMMENDED READING/VIEWING

Tall Sheep by Samuel Moon. A biography, mostly in the form of interviews, of the legendary Harry Goulding, who ran a trading post in Monument Valley from 1925 to 1965.

Fort Apache, Cheyenne Autumn, My Darling Clementine, and *The Searchers,* all directed by John Ford and filmed in Monument Valley. You'll ride through many of the places where these movies were shot. For instance, there is a narrow gap in the rock that John Wayne and his men ride through just before the Duke says, "I don't like the looks of this." That gap, called The Hole, is just a few hundred yards from your base camp, and you'll ride through it several times.

IN BRIEF

Don Donnelly Stables, 800-346-4403: 7 days, $1,400. The
   trip may also be booked through American Wilderness Experience, 800-444-0099, and Equitour FITS, 800-545-
   0019.

Physical challenge, 1; Mental challenge, 2; Skills, 2.

THE CANADIAN ROCKIES
bicycling the icefields parkway

When I told my local bike-shop manager, a short bald guy named George, that I was planning a five-day ride through the wilds of the Canadian Rockies, he offered this wise and generous counsel: "Your legs will turn to rubber after three days. You'll get the worst case of crotch rot you can possibly imagine. And some lonesome lumberjack is gonna see you ride by in those tight black shorts and those purple shoes, and he's gonna chase you down, lay you over a log, and make you squeal like a pig. Man, didn't you ever see *Deliverance*?"

Sorry, George. Rubbery legs, maybe. Crotch rot, maybe. But no lumberjacks. The millions of acres of spruce and hardwood forest that flank the road from Banff to Jasper are part of two national parks, immune to the chainsaw. The only thing that could conceivably chase me down is a grizzly bear. (Actually happened to a cyclist a few years back, they tell me. Killed the poor chap. Never knew what hit him.)

The Canadian Rockies are a well-kept secret south of the border, perhaps because they are an affront to America's national fixation for being the biggest/best. But we must face facts: In terms of scenic grandeur, Canada's Rocky Mountains blow ours away. By comparison, Colorado is a bland collection of hills, the Tetons diminutive wanna-bes sadly deficient in glaciers. I first began to get the hint during a conversation with a trip leader for Backroads, a big bike-tour outfitter that runs trips in places like Bali and the Loire Valley. "If you could lead any trip your company runs," I asked her, "which would you choose?"

"Canadian Rockies," she answered without hesitation. "Every leader in the company would kill for that assignment."

So here we are, pedaling north out of Banff on the wide, smooth, nearly traffic-free Bow Valley Parkway, headed for Jasper. Carpets of dark green pine trees sweep up to jagged peaks festooned with glaciers. Emerald lakes sparkle. But these scenic delights fail to erase my dark forebodings of rubber legs and crotch rot. For the next five days we'll be averaging almost 50 miles a day, a distance I have managed only twice in my life. On both occasions, my butt hurt for days, and on one of those occasions I reached the point of muscle exhaustion at which the legs simply refused to work anymore, a phenomenon that cyclists call bonking. We'll just have to see how it goes.

Day one: Bighorn sheep grazing along the highway near Lake Minnewanka. I stop to check him out; he ignores me. I edge closer, almost to arm's length. He remains impassive. I cluck and whistle to get his attention. Suddenly, he lowers his extravagantly horned head and feints a charge. I scramble back in terror.

Lunch at Johnston Canyon, a sculptured limestone slot surging with whitewater. We hike to 100-foot-high Upper Falls, which sends a maelstrom of spray into our faces. After lunch, there is more spray in our faces, in the form of a cold, stinging drizzle. Castle Mountain is up there in the fog somewhere, our guide, Lois, assures us in her sweet southern drawl.

Nothing to do but don the rain suit, put down the head, grit the teeth, and keep pedaling. I haven't ridden in the rain since fifth grade. After a while, it's almost fun splashing through puddle after puddle, kicking up a constant rooster-tail of spray. Almost.

We arrive cold, wet, and exhausted at our lodgings, a huddle of rustic log cabins in a pine forest.

Today's mileage: 45
Condition of legs: Surprisingly good
Condition of crotch: Fair

Day two: More cold rain and gloomy fog, but it's only 9 miles to Lake Louise and our posh Post Hotel. The rain stops mid-morning, so my friend Howard and I set out on a grueling uphill 8-mile side trip to Moraine Lake, which glows an impossibly brilliant blue-green under the dull overcast. Two-hour hike along a soggy trail to Consolation Lake.

En route back to Lake Louise, we see four or five rental cars pulled over to the side of the road. The people inside gesticulate wildly and aim video cameras out the windows into the woods. Grizzlies? A herd of moose? We pedal up to find a lone whitetail deer grazing several hundred feet away, barely visible. One deer. This is almost certainly less than the number of deer eating my garden back in suburban New York at this very moment.

Mirror-smooth Lake Louise unfortunately reflects only gray clouds and the truncated lower halves of the surrounding peaks. A few of us make the two-hour hike up to a wooden tea-house that overlooks the six glaciers feeding Lake Louise. There we order Earl Grey with scones and strawberry jam and listen to the rumble of avalanches from the melting ice.

Today's mileage: 27
Total mileage: 72
Condition of legs: Good
Condition of crotch: Poor

Day three: No rain, but the low clouds persist. The view is like riding underwater; some pretty stuff down here, but I wonder what it looks like up above? We have yet to see the sun on this trip. Our American Rockies may be scenically deficient, but by God you don't have to wear rain slickers and thermal underwear in July.

A strong headwind kicks up. Our normal long-distance cruising speed on level ground is about 15 miles an hour, but Howard and I struggle into the gale at 10 or less. Neck and back ache from crouching. We take turns slipstreaming each other, tucking in close behind to catch the wind shadow. Riding in front, I lean forward, rest my elbows on the handlebars, and stare straight down at the white line as it blurs by the front wheel. This position, although unstable and precarious, presents less frontal area to the wind and takes the pressure off my back. When I glance back after a few minutes, I have left Howard a half mile behind. All praise to the Allah of aerodynamics.

Soon we pick up the Columbia Icefields Parkway, a smooth rolling road with vast broad shoulders as wide as the car lane itself. The headwind dies, and we cover 37 perfect miles before lunch. Lois, driving the van ahead, has a picnic waiting for us beside Bow Lake. We voraciously consume both the food and the warmth of the campfire.

Drizzle resumes. Brief stops at a number of lakes and waterfalls, and to read a huge sign: "Bear Warning. All bears are dangerous. If bears are encountered stay in your vehicle." Noted.

Day's mileage: 62
Total mileage: 134
Condition of legs: Hanging in there
Condition of crotch: Funky

Day four: Feeling solitary, I depart early while the rest of the group lingers over breakfast. There is no traffic whatsoever; I am totally alone on this ribbon of concrete. Just past the Weeping Wall, a cliff cascading with springs, looms the 9-mile 2,500 foot climb to Sunwapta Pass. Geared down and grinding, I am nearly to the top when Steve, the muscular young cycle stud of the group, pulls alongside. We ride together to the lunch stop at Athabasca Glacier, a massive river of ice that spills over from the Columbia Icefield and reaches almost to the highway.

In the distance we hear the grumble of the Sno-Coach, a huge buslike contraption with Caterpillar tires that takes tourists for rides along the glacier. Self-powered and proud of it, we sneer in disdain and don spiked boots to make the walk out onto the ice ourselves. A ranger tells us that every year three or four hapless tourists slip into the gaping crevasses that lace the Athabasca. (One fellow plummeted clear down out of sight into the subterranean river that flows beneath the glacier. Miraculously, he was swept downstream through a dark icy tunnel to the glacier's terminus, where he was spit out, chilled but quite alive.) Most crevasse-fallers are eventually retrieved, the ranger adds reassuringly, but particularly small or skinny victims sometimes slide so far down the wedge-shaped cracks that rescuers cannot reach them. Being built along the lines of a bicycle pump, I give the crevasses a wide berth.

This afternoon's ride is otherworldly in its effortlessness—a steep 5-mile downhill followed by a dead-level 21-mile stretch

blessed today with a strong tailwind. Howard and I, delighting
in our wind payback from day two, sit back tall in our saddles,
arms dangling, spinning the pedals effortlessly in top gear. The
wind blows in precisely the same direction and at the same
speed that we are pedaling. Our relative airspeed is thus zero,
and the familiar wind-rush in the ears disappears. As we race
along in the eerie stillness I can smell my own sweat. We cover
the 21 miles in fifty-eight minutes.

> Today's mileage: 61
> Total mileage: 195
> Condition of legs: Not quite rubber
> Condition of crotch: Getting funkier

Day five: Pleasant riding along the winding, deserted
Athabasca Parkway. Clouds seem to be lifting, and we can ac-
tually see the summit of Mount Edith Clavell, named for a
Canadian nurse executed by the Germans during World War I.
Yet another thundering waterfall sends spray drifting across the
road.

South of Jasper there is a traffic jam, a dozen cars pulled
over, people milling around. Approaching it, I fear there has
been an accident, that one of our group has been flattened by a
Winnebago. The hubbub, however, is due to a grizzly bear for-
aging among flowers just off the road. I snap one quick photo
and ride on, glancing over my shoulder.

The final run into Jasper is nicely downhill. We pull into a
parking lot, load our bikes onto the waiting van, and flop
wearily into our seats for the return trip to Banff. Outside the
window, the clouds are evaporating, and a bright sun begins to
flood the crystalline air.

Today's mileage: 34
Total mileage: 229
Condition of legs: Recovering
Condition of crotch: Stable but guarded

OUTFITTERS

The *Backroads* route from Banff to Jasper follows the Bow River Parkway, Icefields Parkway, and Athabasca Parkway. The basic route, which includes three full days and two half-days of riding, is 208 miles. There is a van-assisted short option of 120 miles, and longer routes available to the hard-core—a two days' increase to a total possible mileage of 229. Backroads also offers a camping trip along the same general route for $749.

The *Imagine Tours* trip starts in Jasper and proceeds south along the same general Backroads route, but in reverse, to Banff. After a rest day in Banff, you'll continue an additional two days and 80 miles eastward across the prairie to Calgary, along Route 1A. Total mileage is about 300. Lunches and most dinners are not included in the price, and groups may be as large as twenty. (Other outfitters include all meals and limit group sizes to about fifteen.)

Rocky Mountain Cycle Tours is based in Canmore, Alberta, the gateway to the Canadian Rockies. Its inn-to-inn trip starts in Jasper and finishes in Banff. RMCT says the north-to-south route makes for a quicker climb over Sunwapta Pass. Total mileage is 188, with van assistance available. Instead of two half-days of rest, riders get a full day off in Lake Louise, which gives the opportunity for an optional whitewater rafting excursion. RMCT, like Backroads, also offers a camping trip over the same route, in the northbound direction.

WHAT TO EXPECT

A full day's distance typically varies from 40 to 60 miles over rolling terrain. Sunwapta Pass, at 2,500 feet vertical, is no small challenge. Cyclists should have solid—and recent—long-distance experience. This is no trip to discover that 40 miles a day is your limit. Your butt should be in just as good a shape as your legs; anyone who attempts this trip without some well-established callouses on his rear end will be one hurtin' puppy after three or four days.

A sag wagon is always available, so it's not necessary to ride the full mileage each day.

You'll stay in hotels and B&Bs that range from comfortable to luxurious, and a support van hauls all the luggage. On the road, however, there's the potential for modest suffering: rain, cold, sore butts, long steep hills.

Camping trips, of course, are a bit more rugged. It takes a certain type of person to ride a bicycle 60 miles and then happily go showerless, eat outdoors, and set up a tent to sleep in. I clearly recall saying to myself, as the frigid rain beat on the roof of my comfy lodge every night, "Thank you, God, for not letting me choose the camping option."

The roads are smooth and untrafficked, and for most of the route the shoulders are as wide as the car lane, so little in the way of technical riding skill is required. You should know how to pace yourself, shift gears efficiently, and stay properly hydrated.

Trips run June through September, starting in Banff, Jasper, or Edmonton, Alberta, depending on the outfitter.

IN BRIEF

Backroads, 800-462-2848: 6 days, $1,298
Imagine Tours, 800-228-7041: 8 days, $975
Rocky Mountain Cycle Tours, 800-661-2453: 6 days, $1,095

Physical challenge, 3; Mental challenge, 2–3; Skills, 2.

FLORIDA
paddling the
everglades

After all those years, Totch Brown still lived on Chokoloskee Island, in a surprisingly reputable-looking house shaded by a tamarind tree. The lady at Smallwood's store said he still talked to visitors now and then, but when I knocked on his door, there was no answer.

It figured. In this remote southwest corner of Florida known as the Ten Thousand Islands, a vast wilderness maze of mangroves and sawgrass swamp that stretches from Everglades City down to Key West, folks don't pry too closely into other folks' business. Never have. A man can disappear into the landscape down here without a trace, and for that reason it's always been a sanctuary for outlaws like Totch Brown.

The serious outlawing in these parts commenced around the turn of the century, when fancy New York ladies wore big hats covered with bird feathers. The price of Everglades egret plumes went to $35 an ounce, same as gold, and the plume hunters and bird wardens began killing each other with some regularity. Later on, when the moonshiners and rumrunners took over, additional citizens on both sides of the law ended up cut, shot, and occasionally dead. But juries of local people, many of whom had more than a nodding acquaintance with plume-hunting and moonshining themselves, showed a marked reluctance to convict.

The most famous Everglades outlaw of them all was Ed Watson, a handsome, charming man with hard eyes who, it was whispered, was on the lam from two states. He'd supposedly killed the outlaw cowgirl Belle Starr in Oklahoma, and later two men in northern Florida. Watson came to the Everglades and built a fine wooden house on the Chatham River, deep in the mangroves south of Chokoloskee. There he grew sugarcane and raised the biggest hogs anyone had ever seen. Watson was a hard worker, a good neighbor, and paid his bills, but he had a mean streak in him, and the local folks noticed he never sat with his back to a door, not ever. Pretty soon two people turned up dead in Chatham River—a squatter couple living on a piece of land Watson had just bought. The two bloated bodies floating among the mangroves shook up the local folks pretty bad, and a couple of do-gooders decided they would bring Watson in. One of them, approaching Watson's dock in a small boat, got his left mustache shot off, a development that caused him to reconsider his plans.

Then, in 1910, just after the worst hurricane on record in the Everglades, three more dead bodies turned up in the Chatham River—workers living on Watson's farm. The corpses were gutted like gators and weighted down with scrap iron. When Watson came by Smallwood's store on Chokoloskee for supplies, he was met by a group of island men with guns. But Watson had guns of his own, and charm and bravado as well. He insisted that his no-good foreman, Leslie Cox, had done the killings, and promised to bring back Cox's head. The island men, buffaloed, let him go.

A few days later, Watson returned to Smallwood's carrying

not Cox's head but his hat. He found virtually every able-bodied adult male on the island—about twenty of them—waiting for him, guns at the ready. Watson calmly explained that he'd killed Cox, but the body had fallen into the river and sunk, leaving only the floating hat. The men of Chokoloskee didn't buy the story, and ordered him to hand over his double-barrel shotgun. Watson hesitated for one frightful moment, then fired point-blank into the crowd. Fortunately for the townsfolk, both shells, waterlogged from the recent hurricane, misfired, and Watson died instantly in a hail of return fire. The coroner removed thirty-three slugs from his body.

By the time Totch Brown was born—1920—things had cooled down a little in the Ten Thousand Islands. When the Depression came along, Totch's family set up a homestead camp on Possum Key, a speck of an island 8 miles south of Chokoloskee, near Watson's old place at Chatham Bend. Like virtually every other inhabitable spot in this part of the Everglades, Possum Key was an old Indian shell mound, built up out of the muck by Calusa Indians with centuries' worth of crushed oyster shells. It was one of the few places for miles around where a man could stand without getting his feet wet.

The Browns made ends meet with a little bit of everything—gator and coon hunting, mullet fishing, growing vegetables. And moonshining. By the time Totch was eleven, helping his dad with the still, Totch was well versed in the art of dodging the law. What little respect he had for government authorities declined still further when three agricultural officers showed up unannounced one day and killed Totch's pet bull because it hadn't been dipped for ticks, as state regulations required.

Totch grew into a young man and married Estelle, a shy fourteen-year-old from nearby Sand Fly Island. Totch mainly made an honest living fishing for mullet and pompano, but he couldn't resist a little gator poaching now and then. Nothing serious, of course, just enough to keep the rangers on their toes in what by then had become Everglades National Park.

Totch on gator poaching: "After a gator's been shot he'll flop around for hours, scaring away the others I'm trying to slip up on. I take the gator by the snout, pull his neck up over the side of the boat, push down on the snout, and then chop the spine in two in the back of the neck. If the gator is very lively, I chop him a second time on the back between the hind legs.

"The problem with this trick," he continues, "is the blood. Alligators have more blood than any animal I've ever shot. Cutting the head completely off makes no difference either, they don't even slow down. In fact, there's only one way to quiet down a gator you've just shot. After you've chopped the backbone in two at the four legs, run a small wire or reed down its spine. All hell is gonna break loose for a little while, but by damn that's the way to stop him."

Totch would set up camouflaged gator-skinning camps literally within earshot of the National Park guided tour boats. He was careful to keep his carcasses submerged, so as not to attract vultures, whose flocking might tip off the rangers. He built special gator-poaching boats called pans, very small, with flat bottoms for shallow water. The boats were made of plywood and screwed together, not nailed, so they could be disassembled and smuggled into the gator lairs in bigger, more innocent-looking deep-water boats, then quietly assembled under cover of darkness back in the mangroves.

In all his years of gator poaching, Totch never once got caught by the rangers in Everglades Park. Outwitted those Smokey Bears every time. "I never met a ranger in the woods while I was hunting, day or night, who wasn't shaky," he wrote contemptuously in his autobiography. "I even saw a park ranger drop his revolver once."

Totch became the nemesis of one particularly persistent

ranger. "Some park rangers do their job, let well enough alone, then go home. But Little Eddie was different. The more I outdone him, the harder he tried. He'd set up all night fighting mosquitoes just to get a peep of me coming in from gator hunting."

Little Eddie was laying for Totch one night as he came sneaking back from the Hamilton Lakes with eighty gator skins aboard. Eddie threw a spotlight on him and gave chase. But Totch knew every nook, crook, and stump of those islands and backwaters, even in the dark. After tossing his rifle overboard into shallow water, Totch headed straight for a sandbar with Little Eddie right on his tail. Totch swerved at the last second, but the ranger didn't. "Sure enough, Little Eddie piled 'er up, high and dry," Totch recalls with undisguised glee.

While Little Eddie struggled to get his boat off the sandbar, Totch hightailed it for home. After stashing his hides and gator boat up a little creek nearby, he cruised back to his dock on Chokoloskee, lights on, all nice and legal. Little Eddie showed up a few minutes later, mad as hell, and searched Totch's boat. Didn't find a thing, of course.

Now, it happened that Totch's dock was about 75 yards outside the park boundary, so Totch complained to the chief ranger about the search. The next day, Little Eddie came to Totch's house and apologized. That night, Totch retrieved his hides, gator boat, and gun. The hides brought about $2,000. "I always got my best kicks outwitting the rangers," says Totch. "Especially Little Eddie."

By the late 1970s, Totch found a new way to get his kicks: smuggling marijuana. A few of his pals had been making good money hauling pot in from "mother ships" anchored offshore, and they cut him in on the action. Totch's first pot run got botched up pretty bad. An engine quit, a couple of boats sank, the pot got soaked, and he almost got nabbed by the DEA. He ended up barely covering expenses. But Totch found that drug-running was "so exciting it could make a sick man well."

Over the next few years, as he learned more about the smuggling trade, Totch expanded his operations and began making his own runs from Colombia. He had his share of screw-ups and double-crosses, but finally managed to orchestrate that "one perfect run from the Colombian mountains to the creeks back home." He'd reached his goal. The thrill was gone. Totch retired, figuring he'd beat the lawmen once again.

But then came July 7, 1983, and the biggest excitement in Chokoloskee since Ed Watson got killed. Hundreds of state and federal agents swooped down on Chokoloskee and nearby Everglades City. Cutting off the only road into town, agents searched from house to house and boat to boat. They uncovered half a million pounds of marijuana and arrested two hundred people—nearly half the population of the town. According to a local newspaper account, Totch posted his bond of $1.3 million and walked out of the courthouse to the cheers of the townspeople.

But Totch couldn't wiggle out of this one. He served fifteen months in prison and was fined all the money he'd made smuggling, and more. Once he got out, things were pretty quiet for Totch, and that's the way he and Estelle preferred it after he had the heart attacks and the quadruple bypass operation.

Totch wouldn't trade his life in the Everglades for anyone's, but he's got a few regrets. The poaching, for one. "Remembering those piles of gators I shot and the bunches of birds I killed to eat, I wonder if I did right by Mother Nature. . . . God, I'm sure, knew when He built the Glades that the cup would not run over forever. I don't believe he thought it well of me to take the lives of the real owners."

Totch Brown died a few months after I knocked on his door. He won't be remembered as a genuine outlaw like Ed Watson.

His friends and neighbors would probably say that Totch was just a guy trying to make a living in the Everglades.

OUTFITTERS

Based across the road from National Park headquarters in Everglades City, *Huron Kayak Adventures* runs six-day trips by canoe or sea kayak into the Ten Thousand Islands area. Precise itinerary depends on water and weather conditions, but paddlers typically camp on sandy beaches on small islands such as Tiger Key, Comer Key, and Panther Key. Huron features ocean-going kayaks with spray skirts (owner Maks Zupan is a former Olympic kayaker), but also has canoes.

Nantahala Outdoor Center, the country's largest kayak school and outfitter, uses one-man sea kayaks for its eight-day Everglades journey. From Chokoloskee Island, you'll paddle out for overnight stays at Sunday Bay Chickee, Watson Place (where both Totch Brown and the notorious E. J. Watson lived for a spell), Mormon Cay, and Pavilion Cay. During two rest days, paddlers have the option of local day trips or just hanging out on the beach. First and last night spent at the historic Rod & Gun Club in Everglades City.

North American Canoe Tours, based in Everglades City, runs a one-week Gulf Coast Loop with a mixture of protected inland water and more exposed coastal routes. Precise itinerary depends on wind and weather conditions, but paddlers typically put in upstream on the Turner River, then follow the river and various creeks downstream to Sunday Bay. The route then picks up the Wilderness Waterway south to Lostmans River and out to the coast. Paddlers then head up the coast back to the Ten Thousand Islands and Everglades City. Campsites are about equally divided between chickees (wooden platforms built on poles over the water) and beach camps on the outer islands.

NACT also offers, on demand, one-way guided trips along the entire 99-mile Wilderness Waterway, from Everglades City to Flamingo. This is a more difficult trip, with long days of hard paddling.

NACT uses 17-foot aluminum canoes with 6-horsepower outboard motors to help out in strong headwinds or tidal currents. Sit-on-top sea kayaks are also available. Both trips pass by or stop at Chokoloskee, Watson's Place, Possum Key, and other old haunts of legendary Everglades characters.

WHAT TO EXPECT

People generally tend to think of canoeing as a languid, low-key activity—you get tired, you let your partner do the paddling. But when wind and tide are against you, as they often are in the Ten Thousand Islands, the game changes. Even with strong paddling, progress can be frustratingly slow. Single kayaks are a bit easier to paddle, but there's no partner to take over if you poop out. The small motors North American Canoe Tours puts on their canoes are a godsend for the faint of bicep but an affront to purists.

Camping in the Everglades runs the gamut from sandy beaches to Indian shell mounds to chickees. Space is often quite limited, and you may get a trapped feeling of being surrounded by water with nowhere to go. Wind and weather can make paddling frustrating and difficult. You can get unexpectedly cold.

And then there are the bugs. Trips are scheduled for the low-bug season, November through March, but mosquitoes and sand flies can occasionally be voracious. Everglades veteran Totch Brown offers this advice about "swamp angels," the local moniker for mosquitoes: "Once you get to the point that you expect 'em to be there, it's no longer a surprise, and that seems to help. The worst times are at daybreak, just before black dark, and at big moon-up. Mosquitoes are also bad in drizzly, overcast weather.

"A lot depends on what you have to do, or want to do in the mosquitoes. For instance, playing cards wouldn't be any fun. But the skeeters probably wouldn't seem too bad if you were counting up a bunch of found money or making love to your new bride."

Paddling in the bow of a canoe takes no skill at all, but captaining from the stern requires a bit of technique that can easily be learned and/or figured out by the quick-witted. Paddling a kayak in protected waters is dead easy.

All trips begin in Everglades City, Florida.

RECOMMENDED READING

Totch: A Life in the Everglades by Totch Brown. The old swamp rat's autobiography.

Killing Mister Watson by Peter Matthiesson. A novelization of the notorious outlaw's life in the Everglades, as "told" by the local inhabitants.

IN BRIEF

Huron Kayak Adventures, 813-695-3666: 6 days, $490
Nantahala Outdoor Center, 704-488-2175: 8 days, $895
North American Canoe Tours, 813-695-3299: 7 days,
$750–$800

Physical challenge, 2; Mental challenge, 3; Skills, 2.

MEXICO
climbing the
volcanoes

At 17,800 feet, just below the summit of Popocatepetl, it seemed as if we'd blundered into the midst of some cosmic quarrel between Lucifer and Thor. Dark clouds swirled. The sulfurous stench of brimstone bubbled up from the steaming crater. A blue-white bolt of lightning shattered the air 50 feet ahead. Cowering facedown in the snow as hailstones rattled my parka, I pondered the irony of what had attracted me to Popocatepetl in the first place: the sweet staccato of its name. Popo, mountaineers call it. A benign, jovial, favorite-uncle sort of name. But Uncle Popo had suddenly turned nasty.

No problem. Sergio would get us out of this one. Sergio Fitch-Watkins, legendary climbing guide and mystery man, who'd made the first of his two-hundred-odd Popo ascents at age eleven. A stocky, swarthy, handsomely bearded Mexican who, by all indications, was utterly fearless—the only mountain climber I've ever met whose cheating-death stories have nothing to do with mountains.

Sergio story No. 1: He is a philosophy student in Mexico City in 1968. The Mexican army, responding to massive student protests during the Olympic Games, sprays a demonstration with machine-gun fire, killing hundreds. Sergio, badly injured, lies semiconscious among the dead and wounded. A platoon of soldiers walks among the fallen, dispatching those still alive with .45-caliber bullets to the head. Sergio watches the executioners approach. Just as they reach him, he passes out.

He wakes up under a pile of corpses in the back of an army truck driving through the back streets of Mexico City. He claws his way to the top of the pile, and when the truck stops at a traffic light, he climbs off the back and crawls away. His head hurts where the bullet had somehow glanced off.

Sergio story No. 2: By now a heavily armed revolutionary streetfighter, he is walking past a bar in a dangerous part of Mexico City. He hears a scream inside. Soldiers have kidnapped a young American woman and are preparing to rape her. Sergio kicks down the door, sprays the bar with machine-gun fire, kills several soldiers, and rescues the woman. They flee in a hail of bullets.

Out of ammunition, they're eventually captured by a pursuing soldier, whom Sergio recognizes as a senior commander he knows from previous skirmishes. The commander tells Sergio to start walking away so that he can shoot him in the back. Sergio refuses, saying he prefers to look in the eyes the man who kills him. The commander obliges and puts the gun to Sergio's head. Sergio stands calmly. The commander pauses, smiles, and lowers the gun. You are a worthy enemy, he says. I prefer to kill you under more honorable circumstances. Get out of here. Sergio and the girl walk away unharmed.

To such a man as this, a mere electrical storm on an icy, exposed precipice 3 miles in the sky was a trifle. With only the faintest hint of urgency, he led our retreat through the fog and hail as the thunder boomed around us. Every couple of minutes we would feel our hair begin to rise and crackle as sparks jumped from our ice axes and ski poles. At the first crackle of sparks, we would hit the deck like soldiers under fire. After each ensuing explosion, we would jump to our feet and resume our urgent shuffle around the crater rim to our descent route.

Just as we started down the steep, icy slope, Howard's right crampon fell off. A novice outdoorsman who'd signed up for the Popo trip on the most ethereal of whims, Howard had equipped himself for the expedition by dropping off the outfitter's recommended equipment list and his American Express Gold Card at the local REI store the day before departure. Howard had never before seen a crampon much less used one, and had apparently failed to tighten its adjustment screws properly. Several had fallen out, and the crampon now dangled uselessly from his boot. Below us stretched a smooth, 2-mile-long 35-degree slope of icy crusted snow on which many careless or unlucky people have slipped and perished over the years.

My cold-numbed fingers fiddled woodenly with Howard's crampon to no avail. But I remained calm. Sergio would get us out of this one, too. From his lead position a few yards ahead, Sergio backtracked to see what the problem was. He briefly inspected Howard's dangling crampon. We looked at him expectantly, like children.

"You're afraid, aren't you," he said to Howard softly. Howard admitted that, well, yes, of course he was afraid.

"Death is nothing to be afraid of," Sergio replied. "I am not afraid to die." To demonstrate, he raised his steel ice ax over his head into the teeth of the storm. He held it there as the lightning crashed around us.

Sergio's stories are often sketchy, the details hard to verify. Huddled in base camp or sitting around a table in some dark little third-world restaurant, he'll tell you how, after leading a climb of Russia's Mount Elbrus, he accompanied a commando group of Russian soldiers, armed with machine guns and bazookas, on a night raid against smugglers. Or about his stint as a bodyguard for the children of the president of the Bank of Mexico. (He doesn't dwell on the irony of the former radical student revolutionary protecting an icon of the capitalist establishment.) Or the time he ran the Mexico City marathon without drinking any water, to prove his toughness. He'll show you the scars from his bullet wounds.

But press him for details, and you'll come up empty. Whatever happened to that American girl in the bar? How can it be that Russian soldiers allow foreign civilians to accompany them on secret missions? Some things you probably shouldn't know, Sergio will say. I have a dark side.

The dark side. A climbing companion describes watching Sergio beat up three South American taxi drivers who had tried to rip off the climbing group by charging too much. Another climber recounts Sergio's self-proclaimed training regimen from the mountains: "I go to bars and get in fights." A friend, after finally persuading a reluctant Sergio to demonstrate his martial-arts skills on him, subsequently spent a month in the hospital with a ruptured spleen.

The snow was swirling, and the lightning still crashed around our heads. As Howard contemplated the one-crampon descent of the icy slope before him, he felt his fear drain away. "Somehow I figured that nothing bad could happen as long as Sergio was looking out for me," he later recalled.

Sergio removed Howard's dangling crampon, and then took a climbing rope from his pack, looped it around Howard's waist, and secured it to his own climbing harness. He instructed Howard to start hopping down the slope as best he could on the one remaining crampon, while Sergio walked behind, keeping tension on the rope, ready to arrest Howard's fall in case of a slip.

They slowly worked their way down the mountain, like a man walking a lame hound on a long leash. The thunder receded, the sky lightened. After perhaps three hours, we reached the lower slopes, free of ice and snow, where we removed our crampons and continued the long trudge back to the base lodge over soft, black volcanic sand.

That night, over a dinner of soup at the base lodge, Howard said to Sergio, "I'll bet I can guess who your favorite philosopher is. Nietzsche." The former philosophy student, in perhaps his biggest show of emotion of the day, smiled faintly. "You're right," he said.

OUTFITTERS

Mexican volcano-climbing expeditions typically include some combination of three peaks: Orizaba (18,851 feet), Popocatepetl (17,887), and Iztaccíhuatl (17,343). All three lie within 100 miles of Mexico City; the latter two can be seen from downtown on the rare smog-free day.

At this writing (early 1997), Popo is closed to mountaineers because of a series of eruptions that began in 1995. In April 1996, five climbers who defied the ban were killed by an explosion at the summit. Volcanic eruptions are notoriously fickle, of course; the mountain may return to its normal quiet state at any time. Or it could blow its top tomorrow.

The itineraries listed below assume that Popo is open for climbing. Obviously, if it remains closed, all bets are off. Call your outfitter for Popo's current status.

Alpine Ascents International offers a relatively short nine-day trip that includes Orizaba and Popo. *American Alpine Institute*'s itinerary includes Popo, Izta, and Orizaba. AAI is a technical climbing–oriented company that requires some basic mountaineering experience for this trip. No beginners. *Condor Adventures* and *Mountain Travel-Sobek* also include all three mountains. Sergio Fitch-Watkins is Mountain Travel's long-time senior climbing guide, although he no longer leads the Mexican volcano trip. The current leader is Ricardo Torres Nava, who can't tell you many gun-battle stories but happens to be the first Latin American to reach the summit of Everest.

WHAT TO EXPECT

Although not technically difficult, Popo and the other Mexican volcanoes are serious physical challenges: six- to ten-hour climbs up steep snow slopes from 12,000 to over 18,000 feet, followed by descents that are only a bit less strenuous. Although you'll carry only a light day pack, the high altitude dramatically saps strength and energy.

Despite their tags as "beginner" mountains, the Mexican peaks cannot be taken lightly. You can die up there. You can also get a miserable headache from the altitude. The weather can be rotten, even dangerous, as Howard and I discovered. Gastrointestinal distress is a distinct possibility. And the vehicle ride to the base camps, Orizaba in particular, can be long, rough, and dusty.

You'll need to know basic mountaineering techniques: use of an ice ax, crampons, and rope. These aren't difficult, however; your guide can teach you the basics on the spot in an hour or two, and you'll practice them on the way up. Popo in particular is a good training ground for beginners. As noted above, American Alpine Institute is the one outfitter that requires previous technical mountaineering experience.

Trips typically run October through March. Mexico City is perhaps the world's most convenient staging city for a major mountain climb.

IN BRIEF

Alpine Ascents International, 206-378-1927: 9 days, $990
American Alpine Institute, 206-671-1505: 15 days, $1,790
Condor Adventures, 800-729-1262: 12 days, $1,050
Mountain Travel-Sobek, 800-227-2384: 13 days, $1,650

Physical Challenge, 4; Mental challenge, 4; Skills, 3.

UTAH

mountain-biking to

the maze

Edward Abbey, the revered and irascible chronicler of the American Southwest, offered this opinion about the ideal way to see Utah's canyon country: "You can't see anything from a car; you've got to get out of the goddamned contraption and walk, better yet crawl, on hands and knees, over the sandstone and through the thornbush and cactus. When traces of blood begin to mark your trail, you'll see something, maybe."

Abbey wrote those words in 1968, about six years before a California bicycle tinkerer named Gary Fisher found a rusty one-speed clunker in a chicken coop and cobbled on a fifteen-speed gearshift and some junked motorcycle brakes. He took the odd device out on the dirt roads of nearby Mount Tamalpais and had a blast. Fisher called it a mountain bike.

Would Abbey have approved of the mountain bike as a way to see what he called "this monstrous and inhuman spectacle of rock and cloud and sky and space"? Probably. Mountain biking, like walking, is a muscle-powered, wind-in-the-face, sweaty, dusty mode of transport. Ed would dig that. Like crawling, mountain biking can result in bloody knees and elbows. He'd love that, too. Best of all, a strong, skilled rider can easily outdistance a goddamned contraption car—even the four-wheel-drive kind—over the hideously rough dirt roads typical of canyon country.

In the spirit of Abbey, then, we're standing astraddle our mountain bikes on the edge of a precipice 60 miles from the nearest paved road, looking out over a juniper-bush valley sprinkled with buttes and ringed by burnt-orange cliffs. At the end of the valley, 20 miles distant, lies a labyrinth of sandstone canyons that Abbey called "closer to anything else in the 48 United States to being genuine terra incognita": The Maze.

Amid this stupefying vista, I am thinking about how much I love uranium miners. If not for these erstwhile merchants of death and rapists of Mother Earth, the journey from here to the Maze would require wings. Or at least a surefooted mule train. But in the mid-1950s (remember the Cold War, the missile gap, the arms race?), mining companies began to snoop around these parts for deposits of radioactive bomb material. They carved out what might loosely be called a road down the steep talus slope below us and on into the valley, so that prospectors could bring in their Geiger counters on jeeps instead of mules.

They didn't find any uranium, but the road is still here. Thank you, God.

We mount up and begin to pick our way down the road, now known as the Flint Trail. Forty years of erosion have turned it into a tortuous avenue of rocks, ruts, and switchbacks. I lower my seat, stand spring-kneed on the pedals, and shove my butt back until it practically rubs the rear tire. We'll soon see how far my very modest technical riding skills—and my new Quadra 10 suspension fork—will take me. I try to remember Todd-Dude's three rules of technical riding.

Todd, our assistant guide, is a long-haired kid in his early twenties who looks like a cross between a surfer and a rock musician. He tends to address others as "dude," apparently without irony or sense of self-mockery. He rides a mountain bike the way Stephane Grappelli plays the violin, with a consummate ease and playful abandon that leave mere mortals gasping in awe. He has already disappeared from view down the Flint, hopping fluidly over the ruts and around the rocks. Earlier this morning, rather than blast through a long mud puddle in a rooster-tailing, sunglass-spattering, yee-ha plunge like the rest of us, Todd casually leaned back, lifted his front tire to waist level in a flawless wheelie, and pedaled the 20 yards through the quagmire on the rear wheel alone, emerging dry and spotless.

Here are Todd-Dude's Three Laws of Technical Mountain Biking:

1. Pick your line early. The sooner you know what you have to do, the better you can do it.

2. Pedal smoothly. Don't pump the pedals, spin them. Rapid changes in the power stroke cause loss of traction at critical moments.

3. Learn to use momentum. Instead of powering up a short, steep grade or over an obstacle, build up speed in advance and use the bike's momentum to finesse the bike up and over. "The Big Mo will change your life, dude," he tells me.

I apparently have not yet come to a full understanding of the Big Mo, for my life on the Flint Trail is unfolding pretty much the way it has unfolded on all the other difficult, technical terrain I've tried to ride: haltingly and with scant pleasure. I'm still too cautious, too scared, unable to get into that Zen-like zone where one puts aside the fear and simply rides without thinking. Downhill mountain-bike racers refer to this exalted mental state as "No brakes, no brains."

Equipped with both brakes and brains, however, I can't help but notice a particularly steep, rocky section coming up. The front tire judders over the ruts, and the rear tire skids intermittently in the dust as I try to stay in control. My hands clench the bucking handlebars; my mouth is dry. I'm scared. I think how, at any moment, I may inadvertently follow Abbey's recommendation about marking one's trail with traces of blood.

Enough. I stop, get off, and walk the bike through the rough, steep section. It is a scene that will be repeated a number of times on the 4-mile descent of the Flint. Sorry, Todd. Sorry, Mo.

The sun is low in the October sky as we round the corner of Elaterite Butte and approach our camping spot at the Maze Overlook. There's no hint of what is to come; as we pedal through rolling juniper country, the ground simply falls away without warning into a surreal jumble of geology that stretches to the horizon: deep, narrow canyons twisting and turning and branching off and doubling back onto each other so tightly that it seems there's more air than rock down there. In the middle distance looms a line of four dark monoliths. On the horizon, at the far edge of the network of canyons, is a smattering of spires and needles. It is a tableau, intimate and richly textured, that makes the Grand Canyon seem lackluster by comparison.

Not even Todd-Dude could ride a mountain bike down into the Maze, so the next morning we begin our descent on foot. At first glance, the idea of getting to the bottom without a helicopter or a very long rope seems preposterous. To the untrained eye, there is no break in the canyon walls anywhere. But our trip leader, Anne-Clare, knows the way; she has explored the Maze for years and spent ten months living in a trailer as a volunteer ranger in the Maze District of Canyonlands National Park, often going out on five-day solo foot patrols into the heart of the labyrinth.

A consummate outdoorswoman who guides rafts down the Colorado during the bike-tour off-season, Anne-Clare is fiercely protective of the desert. If you ask, as I haplessly did, whether it's okay to fling an apple core out into the infinity of sand and rock, you'll get a steely-eyed "no." (Hey, an apple core is biodegradable, right? And at least I asked.) Comment on the beauty of Waterhole Flat, a sweeping grassy plain two days' ride south of the Maze, and she'll respond that it looks that way only because cows and sheep have long since grazed out the native desert species. "What you see is mostly cheat grass and Russian thistle, both exotic species." She spits out the word *exotic* with a special venom. Well, okay, but Waterhole Flat still looked mighty pretty to me.

Whoever laid out the foot trail down into the Maze was either a route-finding genius or very lucky. The descent hinges entirely upon four or five freakish geological features—a tiny slot, through which one can slither down to the next level; a certain handy arrangement of knobs and outcroppings, over which one can clamber down to a ledge; a fortuitous fan of dirt, down which one can slide on one's fanny—that allow a reasonably adept hiker to pass without the aid of ropes or rock-climbing skills. If not for these quirks of geology—and the perceptive fellow who first linked them all together—the nearest unaided route down into the Maze would be a 40-mile ride from here.

A snapshot taken from the Maze floor would appear little different from one taken in thousands of other canyons around the Southwest: red sandstone walls and cottonwoods. It's not the here that makes the depths of the Maze remarkable, it's the getting here. We've been rolling and bouncing and walking and scrambling for nearly three days. The nearest permanent human habitation is perhaps 60 miles away. Some of the side canyons that twist about us may not have been gazed upon by any human being since the Ancient Ones, hunter-gatherers who lived here two thousand years ago. Abbey makes a modest claim that he and a companion, scrambling down into the Maze in the mid-sixties, could have been the first humans to set foot in the labyrinth since the Ancient Ones.

But thanks to uranium miners and that guy Fisher, here we are. It's enough to change your life a little.

OUTFITTERS

All the Maze bike-tour companies follow the same general five-day itinerary, although there are variations in trip start and finish points and time spent hiking in the Maze itself. The cycling routes generally start at the Hans Flat ranger station and proceed down the Flint Trail to the Maze Overlook. After hiking down into the Maze, riders pedal south to a campsite at Teapot Rock, from which there's an out-and-back day ride to Standing Rocks. The last day is a long, smooth, "cruisy" ride down to the dusty hamlet of Hite. Total distance covered is about 120 miles.

The route *Kaibab Tours* takes is slightly different from the others; instead of riding from the Maze Overlook to Standing Rocks, you'll get there by walking through the Maze itself. The bikes are transferred by pickup truck. In three days of riding, you'll cover about 75 miles. The $725 price includes charter plane transfers to and from Moab at both ends of the trip. The itinerary of *Nichols Expeditions* includes only a half day of hiking in the Maze. Trip participants meet in Hanksville. Riders with *Rim Tours* meet in Moab or Green River and proceed by van to Hans Flat, where the riding begins. A six-day option adds an extra day of hiking in Horseshoe Canyon. This is the company that I traveled with. Anne-Clare has in the meantime left Rim and how works for *Western Spirit Cycling,* which offers

a six-day Maze trip that includes an extra day of hiking at
Golden Stairs.

WHAT TO EXPECT

You'll ride 25 to 35 miles per day over dirt roads that, at times,
are quite rough. Terrain is generally rolling, with some short
steep sections, but there are no long, grinding killer hills. Hot
weather can make this trip far more grueling. If you get totally
exhausted, the four-wheel-drive pickup support vehicle and
"sag wagon" is always available.

The pickup truck carries all the food, water, and gear. You'll
carry only a light day pack or small pannier. All meals are prepared for you, but you'll be responsible for putting up and taking down your own tent, and washing your dishes. Outfitters
typically provide full mechanical support—spare tires, parts,
and such.

The weather is highly changeable, especially in the fall. Temperatures can range from blistering to bone-chilling. Rain and
high winds are possible. (On my trip, a 60-mile-per-hour gust
blew down a couple of tents and sent the lunch awning flying.)

Minor injuries—scrapes and bruises—are common among
aggressive riders. A serious mishap would require a long, slow,
bouncy evacuation. Saddle sores are a common malady of the
unprepared.

The Maze route is a more technically challenging trip than,
say, the popular White Rim Trail in the nearby Island in the
Sky district. Although much of the route follows smooth dirt
roads, parts are quite technical. (The entire trip is on dirt roads;
there is no single-track.) You should be adept at rapid shifting,
picking a line, weight transfer, and lifting the front wheel over
small obstacles.

Raw mountain-bike beginners probably shouldn't take this

trip. With some off-road experience, basic technical skills, and a modicum of courage, you'll do okay—although you'll often find yourself walking your bike for short stretches. Riders with intermediate technical skills will find this trip a bracing challenge and skill-builder. Advanced riders will rarely be challenged but will have a lot of fun.

Maze trips run in April, May, September, and October.

RECOMMENDED READING

Desert Solitaire by Edward Abbey. An account of a lonely but rewarding year Abbey spent as a ranger in Arches National Park in the 1960s, when it was primitive and rarely visited.

IN BRIEF

Kaibab Tours, 800-451-1133: 4 days, $725
Nichols Expeditions, 800-648-8488: 5 days, $725
Rim Tours, 800-626-7335: 5 days, $725; 6 days, $835
Western Spirit Cycling, 800-845-2453: 5 days, $825; 6 days, $925

Physical challenge, 3; Mental challenge, 3; Skills, 3.

WYOMING
ski-touring in
the tetons

Leaning wearily on our ski poles, we stood at the crest of Beard Mountain, a smooth, rolling 10,500-foot summit in Wyoming's Jedediah Smith Wilderness. My friend Ted, an accomplished backcountry skier, grinned like a madman in anticipation of a dream run: vast expanses of feathery, untracked, knee-deep powder and a brilliant blue sky, with the jagged peaks of the Grand Teton Range as a picture-perfect backdrop. Best of all, there was not another human being within miles— a just reward for the grueling four-hour climb from our tent in the valley below.

I, on the other hand, could manage only a tentative smile. A neophyte backcountry skier, I was a long way from the gentle packed cross-country trails I'd happily shuffled for years around my home in New York's Hudson Valley. I suspected that my usual technique to avoid onrushing trees—fall down as quickly as possible—might not suffice out here. "Just stay crouched and bounce up and down to get a feel for the powder," our guide, Glenn Vitucci, assured me. "You'll be fine."

Perhaps he was right. An expert skier, naturalist, and a

fifteen-year veteran of the Teton backcountry, Glenn had inspired confidence from our first meeting three days earlier. Carefully inspecting the mountain of gear we'd brought along for the winter camping/skiing expedition, he nodded approvingly at Ted's monstrous assemblage of exotic moisture-wicking undergarments. But he told me to leave my jeans behind. "No cotton," Glenn said firmly. "Loses most of its insulation value when it gets wet."

My upper-body habiliments were also found wanting. Glenn advised a visit to Mountaineering Outfitters, just across the state line in Driggs, Idaho, a cluttered and friendly establishment that seemed to have been transplanted directly from Canal Street in New York City. There, from the bottom of a large cardboard box, I dredged out the requisite moisture-wicking Capilene undershirt to go under a heavy wool shirt and Gore-Tex wind shell.

I'd already acquired several new pieces of gear for the trip. In place of my normal cross-country skis and boots, I'd rented backcountry equipment more suitable for downhill runs in deep snow: wider skis that tapered in the middle, stout ankle-high boots, and skins—long strips of furlike material that attach to the ski bottoms for traction on long climbs. I'd also bought a body-hugging internal-frame backpack, which allows better balance and free movement of the arms while skiing.

While planning for the trip, Ted and I had considered two backcountry lodging options offered by Glenn's company, Rendezvous Ski Tours. The first was a string of three Mongolian-style yurts that Rendezvous sets up each fall under the watchful eye of the U.S. Forest Service. Each yurt is 20 feet in diameter and has a canvas roof, wooden floor, bunks, a kitchen, wood-stove, and even a sauna.

Option No. 2 was a large portable nylon tent in the shape of a tepee, complete with a lightweight breadbox-size wood-burning stove. Its sole attribute was flexibility—we could put it up anywhere we wanted.

To me, and to any rational human being, the choice was obvious. But Ted happens to be a notorious outdoor masochist and equipment fetishist. The lure of cramped, primitive quarters and a newfangled piece of outdoor gear—the tiny woodstove expressly designed for the tent—was simply too much for him. And so the tent it was.

Ted, Glenn, and I set off the next morning from a remote farm road a few miles out of Driggs, lugging 30-pound packs and accompanied by a porter, also on skis, who hauled a sled loaded with the bulky tent. Our goal for the day: establish a base camp about 4 miles up Leigh Creek, a tributary of the Teton River.

Our route along the creek, winding alternately through the pine trees and meadows of Targhee National Forest, fortunately did not overwhelm my modest Hudson Valley skiing skills. My backpack, although it caused me to sway like a top-heavy drunk at times, was surprisingly comfortable. Upon arriving at our campsite—a small clearing overlooking the creek, just at the edge of the wilderness area—we stomped down a tent-sized area in the snow, first with skis, then with boots. To venture afoot off this hardpack was to sink instantly to the crotch in soft snow. With skis off, we were islanders in a vast sea of white fluff.

Once the tent was erected, we carved ourselves an interior out of the snow base: a center platform for the stove, a walkway around it, and three sleeping ledges. I carefully sculpted my bunk to fit my body contour (if I couldn't have a cozy yurt, I would at least luxuriate in my own icy Barcalounger). After seeing off the porter and taking a brief exploratory late-afternoon ski, we returned to fire up the tiny woodstove. Disappointingly, the hot air rose immediately into the upper reaches of the tepee, well above our heads. Moreover, it required virtually constant feeding with twigs. My hopes for warm, pleasant evenings around the fire were dashed.

The stove did serve well as a dinner warmer, however, supplying copious amounts of boiling water for our mostly freeze-dried fare. My staple was instant rice and beans, but Ted, who revels in camp chores, fried up some pepper steak. After dinner we inevitably confronted that perennial problem of winter camping: how to pass the cold, dark hours between dinner and bedtime. After a few halfhearted attempts to read by flashlight, we eventually acquiesced to the usual solution: move up bedtime to eight o'clock.

By dawn, the thermometer read 2 below, so we waited for the sun to warm the tent before emerging from our sleeping bags. Living outdoors in the winter is a labor-intensive undertaking; simply gathering up twigs to get the coffee boiling required the following procedure: put on frozen boots, put on skis, affix skins, shuffle to woods, duck awkwardly under low-hanging branches, fall down, disentangle skis from saplings, gather twigs, fall down, disentangle skis from saplings, gather more twigs, shuffle back to tent.

Housekeeping chores completed, we got on with the day's mission: an 8-mile round-trip ski trek farther up the Leigh Creek valley, a warmup for the ascent of Beard Mountain the next day. We discovered, to my dismay, that a gang of snowmobiles had illegally entered the wilderness area and fouled the pristine snow along the trail.

We glided easily along the snowmobile tracks—okay, so they're not all bad—winding over mostly gentle terrain, through meadows and pine forests, under a perfect blue sky. It was an extraordinary day of skiing, but back in our tents that evening, we were ready to move beyond mere shuffling and gliding. Up where the snowmobiles couldn't go, we would face a sterner test.

With Glenn leading the way the next morning, we left the

Leigh Creek trail and began picking our way through the trees along Beaver Creek, a trickling tributary. Donning skins, we pushed upward through glades of pine and aspen. Skins prevent the skis from sliding at all, effectively turning them into long, skinny snowshoes. I plodded along, feeling more like a climber than a skier. After an hour or so among the trees, we broke out into a broad meadow with a view of the entire Teton Basin behind us.

Ted and I are running buddies, and our conditioning paid off as we puffed steadily upward along Commissary Ridge. The warm sun had pushed the temperature into the 20s, and the heat of our exertion soon had us shedding layers of clothing. We aimed to reach the top by early afternoon, when snow conditions on the west-facing slope would be ideal for the descent. If we dawdled, the cool air of late afternoon would freeze the snow's surface, creating the backcountry skier's nemesis: breakable crust, a fiendish substance that is not strong enough to support a skier, but strong enough to jab and batter the ankles and send skiers flipping out of control.

Glenn, a student of snow physics, had assured us that avalanches were no threat today. But on two occasions, I heard muffled cracks and felt the snow shift suddenly below my skis. "Just normal snow-settling this time of day," Glenn reassured us. "The slope along the ridge here isn't steep enough to worry about." I dubiously kept plodding upward, and we eventually reached the summit unscathed. There was little cause for celebration, however. The hard part—for me, anyway—was still to come.

Glenn was the first to start down, arcing effortlessly through a series of tight S-turns. Ted followed, alternately dipping his knees in the classic telemark style and carving a series of wide, sweeping curves.

Uncertain of my ability to telemark in the deep snow, I began a timid traverse across the hill. After several hundred yards, I stopped, kicked my downhill ski around the other way, and then traversed anew in the opposite direction—a crude zigzag that unfortunately marred the elegantly scalloped tracks of my companions. Aesthetic failures aside, I nevertheless got thrills aplenty from my hissing straight shots in the glorious sunshine, skis slicing invisibly beneath the surface while my knees plowed through the powder like the prow of a ship on a glassy sea.

Whooping steadily and stopping occasionally to rest, we worked our way down below tree line, where my inability to turn presented more than just aesthetic problems. But, by relying on the aforementioned tree-avoidance technique, I eventually arrived at the bottom intact, an exhausted and disheveled but gamely smiling snowman. Shuffling back along the creek trail, we returned to our humble tent in the woods. Now it seemed a palace, and the dinner of rice and beans a feast.

OUTFITTERS

Jackson Hole Mountain Guides offers a six-day Teton Crest Tour, a sort of American Haute Route trip that starts from Highway 22 at Teton Pass and proceeds generally along the Teton Crest trail to Cascade Canyon. Skiers carry full packs. The route may change due to weather and snow conditions. On the first night, skiers typically stay in a large semi-permanent tent, with woodstove and kitchen, called Mount Glory Hut. On the other four nights, you'll be winter camping in small take-along tents. Because you must carry your tent and food supplies, your pack will weigh 50–60 pounds.

Rendezvous Ski Tours, the company run by guide Glenn Vitucci, operates three yurt-style wilderness huts with kitchens, woodstoves, and bunks for eight. Various custom trips are available, but the most common long itinerary is an eight-day trip with six days of skiing and five nights in the yurts. After a night in Rendezvous's base guest lodge, you'll do a day trip in the local area to get muscles limbered up and a feel for local snow conditions. On the second skiing day, you'll climb 5 miles and 2,000 vertical feet to Baldy Knoll Yurt, then spend day three exploring the area around the yurt, choosing whatever terrain and snow conditions you prefer. On day four, you'll proceed to Plummer Canyon Yurt (down 1,800 feet, then up 1,200). After another day's skiing around Plummer Canyon Yurt, you'll ski 4 miles and 1,800 feet down to Moose Creek and the trailhead. Because all supplies have previously been hauled into the yurt, you need carry only a light pack with clothing and personal gear.

WHAT TO EXPECT

Skiing uphill with skins is aerobically more difficult than hiking the same terrain because of the soft snow, bulky equipment, and use of the arms. But once into a smooth rhythm of shuffling and poling, a reasonably fit person should have no problems with a light day pack. On the Rendezvous trip, daily elevation gains range from 1,400 feet to 2,100 feet, but the grades are generally modest. Overall, the aerobic challenge is equivalent to a difficult hike.

The Jackson Hole Mountain Guides trip is tougher, because of the 50- to 60-pound packs required.

The yurts used by Rendezvous (and the similar semipermanent hut employed by JHMG for one night) are quite comfortable—roomy and warm, with woodstoves, bunkbeds, and kitchens. Once everyone has gone to bed and the woodstove dies out, though, temps inside the yurt will fall well below freezing. Fortunately, one of the guide's duties is to get up first and get the stove going.

Skiers who choose the JHMG Teton Crest tour, however, will do some real winter camping, just the sort of thing my masochistic pal Ted prefers. This is a sterner mental challenge than the comfy yurts.

How cold will you get out on the trail? Not very, as long as you dress properly and keep moving. Daytime temperatures will typically range from 10 to 40 degrees. Backcountry ski-tourers generally have more problems with overheating and sweating than keeping warm. There is always the chance of a blizzard to make things interesting. Avalanches are a possibility, but outfitters pay close attention to such things, and you won't be permitted to ski in avalanche-prone areas. But just in case, you'll wear an avalanche transceiver, a radio beacon that helps rescuers find you under the snow.

How hard is ski-touring? It all depends. Shuffling along level, packed snow is almost as easy as walking, but it takes a near-superman to swoop gracefully down steep slopes in waist-deep powder, like you see on the ski videos. Rendezvous will take beginning skiers, who generally stick to gentle slopes around the yurts. But some basic cross-country ski experience is highly recommended; you should at least feel comfortable on groomed trails before tackling the challenge of off-track skiing. And, obviously, the more accomplished you are at backcountry skills like telemark turns and skiing deep powder, the more fun you'll have.

JHMG requires some free-heel skiing experience for the Teton Crest tour but says that no backcountry experience is necessary.

The ski season runs from December to mid-April. December and January have good snow and weather but are cold and have the least daylight. February and March are warmer and have more daylight, but snow and weather conditions are variable.

Both trips depart from Jackson Hole, Wyoming.

RECOMMENDED READING

Deep Powder Snow by Dolores LaChapelle. A memoir of a backcountry skiing life in the Wasatch Mountains in the 1940s and 1950s, when nobody did that sort of thing.

IN BRIEF

Jackson Hole Mountain Guides, 307-733-4979: 6 days, $1,100
Rendezvous Ski Tours, 208-787-2906: 8 days, $800

Physical challenge, 3–4; Mental challenge, 3–4; Skills, 3–4.

SOUTH

AMERICA

ANTARCTICA
cruising the
peninsula

We are embarking on a voyage to the greatest of all wild places, a place where light, water, and ice make colors found nowhere else on earth, and where one can stroll among 8,000-pound-predators. Only one thing is on my mind: vomit.

To reach Antarctica, our puny ship—the 237-foot M.V. *Professor Molchanov,* a Russian polar research vessel converted to carry thirty-eight passengers—must traverse the Drake Passage, the windswept 600-mile gap between Cape Horn and the Antarctic Peninsula that is the roughest stretch of water on the planet. As the *Molchanov* leaves the protection of Tierra del Fuego's Beagle Channel and bravely heads out into the open sea, we begin the rhythmic, wallowing pitch and roll that will continue for the next two days. The sky is leaden and the wind whips the whitecaps.

Clinging to my bunk, I read the words of Antarctic explorer Ernest Shackleton, who described these waters as "supreme strive . . . a seething chaos. . . . So great were the seas that often our sail flapped idly in the calm between the crests of two waves. Then we would climb the next slope and catch the full

fury of the gale." One enormous rogue wave nearly crushed
Shackleton's vessel. "During 26 years of experience of the ocean
in all its moods," he wrote, "I have not encountered a wave
so gigantic. It was a mighty upheaval of the ocean, a thing
apart. . . ."

I stroke the scopolamine antiseasickness patch behind my
ear like a talisman, feeling both fear and the shame of my fear.
Whimpering in my bunk, I am a cowardly maggot compared
to Shackleton and his men, who, after their ship was trapped
by pack ice in the Weddell Sea, spent seventeen months drifting helplessly through an Antarctic winter, dragging sleds
across ice floes, and finally rowing and sailing a tiny lifeboat
870 miles through these same waters to a whaling station on
South Georgia Island. And they did it all without patches.

Fortunately, both God and Ciba-Geigy are on my side this
day, for the seas are moderate by Drake Passage standards—
waves no more than 10 feet, with winds of only 20 knots—and
the patch works its chemical magic. Fighting the drowsiness
that is a side effect of the drug, I sit on the ship's bridge, watching the rain spatter on the windows and the gray ocean roll by
at 12 knots. I try to imagine myself out here in Shackleton's 22-
foot open lifeboat, the *James Caird*, instead of a snug, glass-
enclosed room warmed by the glow of the ship's instruments
and the Slavic murmurs of its Russian crew.

On the second day, as I semi-doze on the bridge in my
scopolamine stupor, Captain Maximoff calls over and points to
the ocean temperature gauge, which has in the past couple of
hours dropped suddenly from 6 degrees C. to one degree
(about 33 degrees F.). We have crossed the Antarctic Conver-
gence, the beginning of true polar waters. A few hours later, we
sight our first iceberg, a massive floating mesa of ice a half mile
square and 200 feet high, big and flat enough to land an F-14.
(Of course, ten times that volume of ice lies beneath the sur-

face.) Penguins appear off the starboard bow, leaping out of the water like tiny porpoises.

First landfall is Deception Island, a volcanic atoll about 40 miles off the Antarctic Peninsula. Its inner caldera is connected to the sea by a channel barely wide enough to accept our ship. Safely inside the bay, we don knee-high rubber boots and ineffectual-looking life preservers, then board small inflatable Zodiacs for a shore excursion. (Life preserver or not, anyone who falls overboard will be dead from hypothermia in four or five minutes.) We put ashore on a broad, smooth beach of black volcanic sand; the sensation of solid ground is intoxicating. As snowflakes flurry in the 35-degree air, the brave and high spirited among us—it is perhaps superfluous to mention that this group does not include me—strip down to bathing suits and plunge into a geothermal upwelling of hot water just off the beach, their heads faintly visible in the thick steam. The rest of us hike up a nearby ridge, where the wind tears at the red-hooded parkas Mountain Travel has issued us for our shore excursions.

We meet our first penguins the next day at Cuverville Island. These comical creatures quickly charm us with their earnest waddling and astonishing indifference to our presence. All of a penguin's predators—mainly killer whales and leopard seals—live in the water, so when a penguin leaves its ocean habitat to nest on a small pile of pebbles ashore, it loses all wariness. A human can quite easily sidle up to a nesting penguin and pat it on the head. We were forbidden to do so, however—it seems that despite the penguins' outward calm, an Antarctic researcher has discovered that their heart rates increase noticeably when humans approach. But considering that the penguins in question were chased down by the researcher, captured, put in a bag, carried squawking back to the laboratory, anesthetized, and surgically implanted with a heart-rate monitor, one perhaps cannot blame them for subsequently being a bit jumpy around the red-parkaed aliens.

The rules do allow us to sit motionless and let the penguins approach us as close as they like, sometimes within a foot or two. Such close encounters can be risky for humans, however, as penguins are given to sudden bursts of horizontal projectile defecation. Their nests are decorated with shit streaks radiating from the center in all directions, like ejecta from lunar craters. Penguin guano is pink and smells of fish, and once dried, sticks tenaciously to our rubber boots.

By the time we visit our sixth or seventh rookery, going eyeball to eyeball with penguins has lost its novelty. On Paulet Island, home of an estimated 1.2 million Adelie penguins, I am satisfied to sit on a small rise and look out over the vast totality of them: a squawking, braying, fish-smelling sea of black and white and pink that stretches to the horizon. The usual joke comes to mind about penguins dressed in identical tuxedos, each indistinguishable and interchangeable. Then I notice my compatriots wandering among them, each dressed in a bright red North Face parka and green L.L. Bean Wellington boots, indistinguishable and interchangeable.

Fortunately, just as penguin apathy begins to set in, we land at Livingston Island, inhabited this day by a herd of elephant seals. Hundreds of the 15-foot-long, 4-ton living mounds of blubber bask on the beach, sprawling lazily upon each other in large and small piles, snorting, barking, belching, farting, and smelling very bad indeed. One enormous pile contains about seventy-five seals, an agglomeration of blubber that must weigh half a million pounds. Like penguins, the elephant seals ignore us entirely, and we walk close enough so that our camera viewfinders overflow with eyes, noses, and whiskers.

For all their sleek agility in the water, elephant seals are ponderous and awkward on land (think of a quadruple-amputee hippopotamus). The flippers, too small and weak to walk upon, serve mainly to prop up the animal's front end if necessary. To actually move on land, the elephant seal must, with great heaving effort, hump itself along on its huge jelly-belly a foot or so at a time, its blubber rippling in a wave from tail to head with each awkward lunge. This mode of locomotion leaves a pair of odd-looking knobby streaks in the sand, and the beach at Livingston appeared to have recently hosted a dune-buggy meet.

Male elephant seals, otherwise so flaccid and blubbery, can boast of unflagging rigidity in one location: the penis, which contains a 2-foot-long retractable bone. This arrangement has certain advantages, particularly for the more elderly bulls, but comes at a price. A marine biologist on board the *Molchanov* told how he had once observed an enormous bull elephant seal busily engaged in mating when a smaller rival brazenly approached an idle member of the Big Fella's harem. Roaring in jealous rage, he disengaged in mid-stroke and flopped off to attack the intruder. Unfortunately, the Big Fella had neglected his retraction procedure, and as he lunged forward, his Brobdingnagian dick caught in the sand, bent backward, and broke under the behemoth's weight. The snap of the bone was clearly audible from 100 feet away.

Much of Antarctica consists of broad featureless plains of windswept snow and ice, but the Antarctic Peninsula is ruggedly mountainous. As we pick our way through the loose pack ice of the Lemaire Channel, the hull grinding and clunking, snowcapped granite peaks tower on both sides, and glaciers creep down to the sea. The effect is that of cruising through the Himalayas with sea level unaccountably risen to 18,000 feet and the light turned eerily crystalline.

The light of Antarctica is like that of no other place, an ever-changing panorama of sun and sea and snow and cloud. Sunlit icebergs float in matte-black seas, the contrast so great that the eye cannot cope. A cloud of high-altitude ice crystals glows like a rainbow. I stand on the foredeck of the *Molchanov* for hours at a time, gazing in wonder at the water and the distant shores as the sun plays through low-hanging stratus, my camera dangling unused because I know this light can never be captured by film. If Monet could stand beside me now, he would weep.

This unique Antarctic light is the result of several factors. During the summer, the sun orbits the sky never far from the horizon, providing twenty-four hours a day of the "golden hour" so treasured by photographers, when the sunlight turns orange and soft, and long shadows bring out detail and texture. (My *Molchanov* cabin mate, a professional photographer, shot eight hundred rolls of film during our trip.) Because the air is so cold, it is quite dense, and thus refracts light more powerfully, giving rise to mirages and other optical illusions. Moreover, Antarctic air is surreally clear. For an eye that has spent a lifetime seeing more distant objects as progressively hazier, such clarity is disorienting. A large iceberg we pass in the Gerlach Strait could be 5 miles away or twenty-five; it is quite impossible to tell.

Shackleton made note of the optical trickery of Antarctic air. "Mirages are continually giving us false alarms," he wrote. "Icebergs hang upside down in the sky; the land appears as layers of silvery or golden cloud; cloud-banks look like land; icebergs masquerade as islands . . . worst of all is the deceptive appearance of open water, caused by refraction, or by the sun shining at an angle on fields of snow." Antarctica—where reality and illusion blur together, where night does not always follow day—is a place that reminds us: The things you take for granted are not always so.

As the *Molchanov* ends her Antarctic sojourn and turns due north back toward Tierra del Fuego, the mystical light begins

to fade and the spray once again flies in plumes over the plunging bow. If Monet could stand beside me now, he would puke.

OUTFITTERS

Perhaps more important than the outfitter is the ship you
choose. The choices range from thirty-eight-passenger converted Russian research ships like the *Molchanov* to the monster eight-hundred-passenger *Marco Polo,* a Love Boat–style
cruise ship.

In choosing a ship, the adventure traveler's motto should be
"Less is more." Although smaller ships may get tossed around
in the Drake Passage, the rewards once in Antarctica are great.
Smaller ships have the intimate feel of an expedition rather
than a mass-market cruise; you'll actually get to know all of
your shipmates. Smaller ships are more maneuverable and have
less draft, which allow more flexibility in picking landing spots.
Smaller ships also provide more time ashore; because rules pro-
hibit landing more than a hundred passengers at a time, larger
ships must ration their shore excursions.

Converted Russian research ships, which now make up the
majority of Antarctic cruise boats, have great appeal. The ships
themselves have an exotic air about them, and the Russian
crews, in addition to being the world's premiere polar navigators,
are invariably jolly and eager to meet Americans. More than a
few of my fellow *Molchanov* expeditioners were soundly defeated
by off-duty crew members in vodka-swilling competitions.

In 1996–1997, American outfitters operated twelve vessels
to the Antarctic Peninsula. Most outfitters offer a variety of
itineraries that include various combinations of the Antarctic
Peninsula, the Falkland Islands, South Shetland Islands, and
South Orkney Islands. Travelers typically fly either to Santiago
or Buenos Aires, and then to Ushuaia, Argentina, where the

ships are based. Itineraries that include the Falklands usually have a flight to Stanley. Cruises typically run from thirteen to twenty-one days, with prices ranging from about $3,000 to $10,000, depending on trip length, accommodations, and season.

Abercombie & Kent operates the *Explorer,* the venerable 105-passenger expedition liner built in 1969 by Antarctic cruise pioneer Lars-Eric Lindblad. Refurbished in 1992, the *Explorer* was the first ice-protected passenger vessel specifically designed for Antarctic waters.

Marine Expeditions, the largest Antarctic tour company, operates five ice-protected former Russian polar research ships converted for passenger use, plus one built-from-scratch polar cruise ship. The *Livonia, Multanovski,* and *Golitsin* are thirty-eight-passenger sister ships to the *Molchanov,* with some upgrades. The *Akademik Ioffe* and *Akademik Sergei Vavilov* carry seventy-nine passengers, and the *Alla Terrasova* is a true cruise ship that carries a hundred passengers. For its own marketing purposes, Marine Expeditions calls these ships by bland corporate-speak names like *Marine Adventurer.*

Mountain Travel-Sobek, the outfitter I used for my Antarctic trip, now uses a spiffed-up sister ship of the *Molchanov,* the thirty-eight passenger *Livonia,* which it charters from Marine Expeditions and staffs with its own trip leaders, along with a biologist, historian, and so on.

Orient Lines operates the huge eight-hundred-passenger *Marco Polo,* although only four hundred people will be aboard for the Antarctic cruises. A good choice for Love Boat types, perhaps, but most adventure travelers will prefer a smaller ship.

Along with Marine Expeditions, *Quark Expeditions* is the other major player in the Antarctic arena. It operates two thirty-eight-passenger converted Russian polar research vessels, the *Professor Molchanov* and *Professor Khromov,* plus a mammoth 434-foot, helicopter-equipped, 24,000-horsepower Russian icebreaker called the *Kapitan Khlebnikoff*. Quark's itineraries include the usual Peninsula and southern islands circuit. For the hardy of spirit (and bank account), Quark also offers a sixty-six-day circumnavigation of Antarctica on the *Khlebnikov*. Price ranges from $30,000 to $50,000, depending on accommodations.

Society Expeditions operates *World Discoverer*, a 138-passenger cruise liner that, along with the *Explorer*, was the mainstay of Antarctic cruising until the Russian ships came along in the early nineties. Fitted out like a true cruise ship, it lacks the intimate, expeditionary feel of the smaller boats. On the other hand, in the 40-foot seas of the Drake Passage, a big ship has certain advantages.

WHAT TO EXPECT

There is little physical challenge on a typical Antarctic cruise. Even nonathletes may at times get a bit restless for lack of exercise. Shore excursions demand only leisurely walking, but vigorous hikers may make longer walks on Deception, Paulet, and Cuverville Islands, among others. (In fact, the three-hour climb a few of us made to the summit of Paulet Island was quite challenging.)

Seasickness is the main discomfort you'll face. If the Drake Passage is in an especially foul mood, you may have a wretched two days indeed, and the mental-challenge rating of 2 might rise to 3 or even 4. But despite the Drake's fearsome reputation, smooth trips are not at all unusual. A scopolamine transdermal patch, worn discreetly behind the ear, is strongly recommended. (Production of the patches was temporarily suspended in 1995 due to quality control problems, but was scheduled to resume in 1997.)

Shipboard accommodations, although perhaps not luxurious by cruise standards, are quite comfortable. On the *Molchanov*, the bathroom was usually down the hall, but other ships have private or semiprivate baths. For the long hours in the Drake Passage, there are libraries, videos, and bars on board all of the above-mentioned ships.

Surprisingly, being cold isn't much of a problem on Antarctic cruises. On my trip, the temperature never got out of the 30- to 35-degree range, and one young woman created an on-board sensation by briefly sunbathing in a skimpy bathing suit. The weather is extremely changeable, however, and storms blow in and out with amazing speed.

Reasonable agility is required to get in and out of the Zodiac inflatable boats used for shore excursions, particularly in rough water. And in rough seas out in the Drake Passage, just getting around the ship could be difficult for the elderly or fragile.

The Antarctic cruise season runs from November through February, the austral summer. December and January expeditioners will experience twenty-four hours of daylight.

RECOMMENDED READING

Endurance by Alfred Lansing. The classic narrative of Ernest Shackleton's incredible voyage of survival after his ship was crushed in pack ice in 1915. Quite possibly the best adventure tale ever told.

IN BRIEF

Abercombie & Kent, 800-323-7308: 14–19 days, $4,495–$7,595
Marine Expeditions, 800-263-9147: 13–23 days, $2,890–$5,490

Mountain Travel-Sobek, 800-227-2384: 14–21 days, $4,995–$7,995

Orient Lines, 800-333-7300: 10–19 days, $3,320–$4,460

Quark Expeditions, 800-356-5699: 15–24 days, $2,400–$5,995

Society Expeditions, 800-548-8669: 15–21 days, $4,990–$7,440

Prices listed are for low season and least expensive double-occupancy cabins. A number of other travel companies buy wholesale block space on the trips of the above outfitters. Some provide a separate staff for their "group within a group," others merely book space. Among these suboutfitters are Geographic Expeditions (800-777-8183), International Expeditions (800-633-4734), Intrepid Tours (formerly Linblad Travel, 800-558-2522), Overseas Adventure Travel (800-221-0814), and Zegrahm Expeditions (800-628-8747).

Physical challenge, 1; Mental challenge, 2; Skills, 1.

ARGENTINA

trekking the northwest
frontier

Jackie Steakley was thrilled when an Argentine couple came into her jewelry gallery in Carmel, California, one day in 1995. A veteran Nepal trekker and world traveler, Steakley had just signed on for a three-week Andes trek in the remote northwestern corner of Argentina, in the frontier province of Jujuy. The outfitter's catalog had rhapsodized about isolated, austerely beautiful mountains and amiable local people little touched by modern ways. Eagerly she pumped the Argentine couple for information. Have you ever been there? How's the scenery? What are the people like?

The Argentinean couple looked at her aghast. Jujuy? You're going to Jujuy? Nobody ever goes there, they told her. There's no reason to go there. Nothing to do, nothing to see—just Indians. Go to Bariloche, they advised. Go to Fitzroy, see the beautiful parts of our country. Don't waste your time on Jujuy. We're ashamed of that place. That's not Argentina, that's Bolivia!

Steakley shakes her head and laughs when she recalls the incident today. "They were right about one thing—nobody ever goes there—but totally wrong about everything else. I've been all over the world, and that's the only place I ever cried when I had to leave," she says.

Mostly it was the people. Descendants of the Inca, the Collas Indians live in the end-of-the-road town of Iruya and twenty-five surrounding mountain villages reachable only by foot. Almost from the moment of their arrival in Iruja, Steakley and her trekmates were overwhelmed by the friendliness of the Collas. Children clambered about them, smiling and laughing with sparkling dark eyes. But unlike the well-practiced beggar children of Nepal, who mob trekkers with shouts of "Rupee!" "Bon-bon!" and "Pen!," the Collas ragamuffins demanded from their visitors only the chance to hold hands and talk.

Steakley remembers two girls, six or seven years old, who walked to an orchard outside of town, picked a basket of small white peaches, then walked back to the stoop of the local guest house, where they sat down to wait for the trekkers to emerge. An hour later, when Steakley appeared, the girls pushed the basket of peaches into her hands and ran off giggling.

On another occasion, when the outfitter's Renault van broke down on the dirt road to Iruya, children with outstretched arms surrounded the group, offering necklaces and other local handicrafts. When the trekkers reflexively pulled wads of pesos from their pockets, the children shook their heads. Don't you understand, Americanos? We want nothing from you. These are gifts!

The Collas villages are populated mainly by women and children; the men spend most of the year in distant sugarcane fields and towns, working for cash wages. When the men do come home, they like to celebrate. One group of trekkers happened into the village of San Juan during the Day of the Cross celebration and found every male in town dead drunk.

Constitutionally incapable of selfishness even in their alcoholic haze and horizontal repose, the men, upon seeing their visitors, offered up from the gutters their remaining corn whiskey. There were no takers.

There were many takers, however, for the coca leaves that the trip leader, the perpetually smiling Luis Aguilera, handed out to group members in moments of duress. Whatever the complaint—jet lag, altitude sickness, fatigue, agoraphobia on the precarious trails—Luis's reply was always the same: "Suck on this." He would pull from his pack a fistful of coca leaves, to be either brewed up in tea or inserted 'twixt the cheek and gum like a wad of chewing tobacco.

Coca leaves, which are, of course, the raw material for cocaine, have been used for centuries by Andean mountain people for strength, endurance, and to make the wretched days of poverty go by a little faster. "I felt euphoric," reported one trekker. "It took the edge off," commented another. Jackie Steakley, phobic about riding in vehicles on narrow, twisting, mountain roads, chewed on coca and found an eerie inner calm. "A miracle," she says.

The coca leaves did not, however, cure a hacking cough that Steakley developed in the dry, dusty air. For that, Luis took her to a village market, where a *bruja*—a female witch doctor— mixed up a custom cure. The *bruja,* an elderly woman with piercing eyes and a limited number of teeth, listened intently as Luis described Steakley's symptoms. Then, as Steakley tells it, "she started grabbing stuff from various bags around her." The final mix included several varieties of dried leaves, a chopped-up llama fetus, and a number of "weird shriveled-up carcasslike things with eyes and beaks." The *bruja* ordered Steakley to brew tea from the mixture and drink three cups of it. Steakley nodded politely but, in the end, could not bring herself to comply.

Most nights the group camped near villages, often in schoolyards. The local women would drift by the camp before dinner to say hello to Luis, who has been roaming these canyons for fifteen years and always brings gifts of tools, food, and medicine. The women usually stayed for dinner and talked late into the night about the hardships of life in these valleys: avalanches, flash floods, child-eating pumas, witches. They revealed methods for improving their husbands' fertility (get a special magic pebble from the *bruja* and slip it into bed) and their opinions of the local Catholic missionaries. ("They're gossips, so in confession, we never tell them the truth. We make up all sorts of wild stuff to keep them occupied.")

The stark terrain of northern Jujuy is remarkable for its bands of alternating colors. Oranges and reds mix with sandy pastels and a rainbow of greens—gray-green, blue-green, green-green. "Never have I seen such colors," reports one trekker, a connoisseur of the American southwest. "There is no way these colors can be captured on film, or even by a painter. And any attempt to describe them with words would be ludicrous." In that case, let's move on to the condors.

The hot sun and steep valleys of northern Jujuy create powerful atmospheric updrafts, which happen to be the main habitat requirement for *Vultur gryphus,* the Andean condor. At 25 pounds the world's largest flying bird, the condor is too heavy to fly under its own power for more than a few seconds, and therefore must ride rising currents of air to stay aloft. (A condor hates to flap; it will walk 100 yards to jump off a cliff rather than take off under its own power.) Once aloft, however, the Andean condor is a superb soaring machine, effortlessly riding updrafts for hours. Scientists have measured the condor's lift-to-drag ratio, a measure of aerodynamic efficiency, at 14 to 1— 40 percent better than a single-engine Piper Cherokee's.

If the air is quiet as you walk along the trail, you will hear a condor coming before you see him; the hiss of vibrating wingtip pinion feathers is audible 100 yards away. While the bird's other feathers slip cleanly and silently through the air, these wingtip feathers deploy slightly askew to the wind, disrupting the vortex of air that spins off the tip of the condor's wing as it cruises along at 35 miles per hour. By "untwisting" this drag-producing vortex, the condor increases its overall aerodynamic efficiency by 3 or 4 percent. (Boeing and Airbus have only recently discovered this drag-reduction strategy; they now put vortex-killing upturned vanes on the wingtips of their 747-400 and A340 jetliners.)

If the approaching whoosh of pinion feathers is drowned out by the wind or the scuff of hiking boots, the condor will announce his arrival overhead by blotting out the sun. "You kind of jump when the shadow suddenly goes over you," reports one trekker. "It's huge. At first you think it's an airplane." The condor's 10-foot wingspan is second only to that of the great albatross, and its total wing area of about 20 square feet— the size of a CEO's desk—is the largest of any bird.

Condors often follow trekking parties for some time, swooping down as low as 20 feet above their heads. "They seemed to be checking us out," reports Steakley. Such low-level flybys are most likely mere curiosity about a new species of biped. But the darker possibility of preprandial reconnaissance cannot be discounted. "We kept yelling up at them, 'Hey, man, we're alive! You can't eat us,'" reports one trekker. Villagers have seen condors dive-bomb lambs on clifftops, in hopes of distracting them into a fatal slip and then dining on the ensuing carrion.

Man and condor have had a tumultuous relationship over the centuries. The Incas revered them as gods, and credited the great birds with moving the sun across the sky. More recently, however, men have treated the condor rather more shabbily.

Some Andean villagers still shoot and trap condors for meat and medicine; they believe ground-up condor bones cure rheumatism and paralysis, and that condor feathers under the blanket ward off nightmares. Condor blood is traditionally prized as a life-extension tonic.

A few Andean villages still carry on the condor-bull festival, in which a captured condor is lashed to the back of a furious bull by a rawhide strap that pierces the bull's skin. When released, the bull bucks frantically, trying to dislodge the giant bird, while the condor tears at the bull's flesh with its powerful beak. After ten minutes of frenzy, both animals collapse in exhaustion. The condor is then untied from the bull, draped with necklaces and fed a bowl of *chicha,* a local corn beer. Then, quite drunk, the condor is carried in a solemn procession to a nearby precipice, from which it is set free in wobbly flight.

Even more brutal is a traditional Peruvian Indian ceremony in which a captured condor is hung suspended by its feet in the village plaza. Horsemen with white-painted faces take turns charging at the helpless bird and pummeling it with their fists. Finally, one man grabs the battered condor by the throat and bites its tongue out. The carcass is then lowered into the waiting crowd, which tears it apart in a frantic struggle for talismans. Performed publicly into the 1970s, the "condor-*rachi*" (literally, "the tearing of the condor to pieces") is now outlawed, though it may still be secretly carried out in remote villages.

But certainly not in the northwest frontier of Argentina, home of the gentle Callos. "They are the kindest, most unspoiled people I've ever seen," sighs Jackie Steakley. "I still can't figure out why nobody ever goes there."

OUTFITTER

Above the Clouds starts its "High Andean Argentina" trek with a day of sightseeing in Buenos Aires. From there you'll fly to the northwestern frontier town of Jujuy; then it's an all-day drive through a picturesque valley to Iruya, a village at 8,700 feet. Following a warm-up day of local hiking, you'll meet your burro pack train and spend seven days hiking through rugged valleys surrounded by high peaks, overnighting at trailside campsites and in the villages of San Juan, Matancillas, Cuesta Azul, and Nazareno.

Trekkers then say good-bye to the burros and hello to Renault minivans for three days of overland touring to the Bolivian border town of La Quiaca, the salt lake at Pozuelos National Monument, the village of Pumamarca, the Mountain Cloud Rainforest, and the ancient city of Salta. From Salta, trekkers fly back to B.A.

WHAT TO EXPECT

The first two days of trekking are half-days, but thereafter you'll walk for six or seven hours a day, sometimes steeply up and down. Maximum one-day elevation gain is 2,800 feet. Altitude is moderate, ranging from about 10,000 to 12,800 feet.

Burros carry the loads and your guides take care of all the camping chores. Altitude sickness is a possibility, especially in the latter overland section of the trip, where you'll drive over passes as high as 18,000 feet. The weather is hot and dry, and the trail occasionally narrow and precarious, with steep drop-offs. Several river crossings require a certain amount of sure-footedness and balance.

Prime time for trekking in this part of Argentina is October through March.

IN BRIEF

Above the Clouds Trekking, 800-233-4499: 16 days, $1,950

Physical challenge, 3; Mental challenge, 3; Skills, 1.

BELIZE
kayaking the
off-shore islands

We'd been paddling for almost four hours, our oceangoing kayaks slicing through wind-riffled seas under a fierce tropical sun. Dead ahead, a speck on the otherwise unbroken horizon, lay Laughing Bird Cay, a solitary quarter-mile sliver of sand 12 miles off the coast of Belize in the Caribbean Sea.

We were seeking that most enduring of travelers' fantasies, the deserted tropical island in the middle of nowhere—a place to be a castaway, to sleep in a hammock under the stars and the palm trees, to eat fish you catch yourself, to drink coconut milk from the husk, perhaps to find romance. My own personal desert-island fantasy had been nurtured by 1950s-vintage Virgil Partch cartoons in the *Saturday Evening Post*. (Example: Guy and buxom, scantily clad girl are marooned on a desert island. The moon is just rising in a starry sky, a gentle breeze riffles the palm trees. Guy says to girl, "What do you mean, 'Not here, not now'?")

There may be no better place to pursue the desert-island fantasy than Belize, where the world's second-longest barrier reef parallels the coast about 20 miles offshore, creating hundreds of small uninhabited coral islands and atolls. Moreover, the reef protects the waters around the islands from big waves, so they are easily accessible to small man-powered craft.

Our voyage had begun in Placencia, a sleepy fishing village whose main "street" is a sidewalk that meanders through the sand. Our group of eight, which ranged in age from twenties to fifties, and in fitness from lean triathlete to pudgy sloth, arrived from Belize City via chartered twin-engine bush plane and outboard launch. We pitched our tents on the beach and inspected the waiting kayaks, which were laid out on the sand like a string of giant mackerel. Our trip leader, Clark Jones, a crinkly-eyed riverman from Moab, Utah, delivered the pretrip briefing. The primary hazards, he warned, would be sunburned lips, sea urchins, and falling coconuts. And well, yes, there was a slight chance of encountering a shark while swimming or snorkeling. "If you see one, just don't act like shark food," he advised reassuringly.

The next morning, Clark and our assistant guide, David, a wiry, irrepressibly wisecracking Belizean, checked us out in the kayaks. At 6 feet 2, I found it awkward to scrunch down into the tight cockpit, and my knees and feet were jammed into the narrow snout. An elastic spray skirt, which stretched around the perimeter of the cockpit to keep out breaking waves, held me in even more tightly. The word *sardine* came to mind.

After a lesson in basics of paddling, we moved to the so-called wet exit exercise, an outfitters euphemism for "practicing how to get the hell out of a flipped kayak before you drown." Unlike tippy whitewater river kayaks, sea kayaks require a rather extreme tilt to capsize. To my relief, once flipped, I was easily able to release the spray skirt and wriggle out of the cockpit while ingesting a minimum of saltwater. It is surprising how quickly and decisively the human body reacts when suddenly placed underwater and upside down.

The packing up was a painstaking ordeal that took almost three hours. Tents, sleeping bags, cooking equipment, first-aid kit, hammocks, snorkeling gear, and food for six days had to be stuffed into waterproof dry bags and crammed through small watertight hatches into the crafts' innards, along with huge jugs of fresh water.

At last, around midafternoon, the final dry bag was shoe-horned into place, and we were ready to get under way. Lips balmed with SPF 40 and cosseted in place by our spray skirts, we set off into the gentle swell. The day's destination was Bugle Cay, a mangrove island just visible in the distance, about 5 miles away. Not a particularly inviting place, it would serve only as an overnight stop and a place to top off our water supply.

Because of my long legs, I had switched to one of the roomier two-seaters. My front-seat crew member, Ursula, due to certain unfavorable marital dynamics, had elected not to paddle with her husband. A novice kayaker, she seemed nervous and claustrophobic as we set off. But after fifteen minutes of paddling without mishap across the warm, sparkling seas, she reported giddily, "This is great! I feel totally comfortable." Our armada of eight—six singles, two doubles—cruised along in loose formation, stretched out over several hundred yards. We reached Bugle Cay after a pleasant two hours.

Unfortunately, not much about our sojourn there was pleasant. As Clark had warned, the bugs were voracious, forcing us into long pants and sleeves almost immediately. Then, just after we'd made camp on the island's one small corner of dry sand, a drenching thunderstorm roared in, flattening two tents and flooding another. The resulting improvised sleeping arrangements did much to promote a feeling of group unity.

The next morning we set off under ideal conditions—smooth water and a slight tailwind on the 9-mile run to Laughing Bird Cay. We quickly fell into the languid Zen-like rhythm of long-distance paddling across the open sea. After two hours, the speck on the horizon looked pretty much the same as it had when we set off, the tops of the palm trees barely visible over the curvature of the earth. But with an eerie suddenness, the slender trunks and the beach popped into view. Our fantasy had at last taken form, and the sight of it renewed flagging energy. One by one, we nosed onto Laughing Bird's beach of white coral sand. No other sign of human presence intruded.

Within minutes, Hal the Math Professor, a paunchy, sedentary fellow who viewed kayaking as a lamentably arduous means of transport between hammocks, had assumed his favored horizontal position. The rest of us quickly set up our tents, taking care to avoid potentially lethal coconut drop zones. Bursting with energy and enthusiasm, we felt smugly superior to our lethargic comrade. Little did we know what was to come.

Our major task for the rest of the day was to catch dinner. David quickly organized a spearfishing party, which swam out several hundred yards wielding three-pronged spears and towing empty kayaks as giant floating creels, into which bleeding, flopping fish were tossed as quickly as possible in the hope that passing sharks would take no notice.

A peaceful sort, I chose not to join the bloodthirsty hunting party. (I did not hesitate for an instant, however, to later scarf down my share of the spoils.) Instead, I snorkeled, unarmed, a few yards offshore amid the phantasmagorical underwater landscape of Belize's barrier reef. Cartoonishly decorated fish drifted among forests of elkhorn coral. Clouds of minnows flashed and billowed. Floating just above a spherical brain coral that must have been 12 feet across, I felt as if I were orbiting Ganymede.

Back on shore, as the sun dropped below the horizon, we lounged in our hammocks, sipped rum and coconut milk, and watched an egret perch on a reef, motionless against the copper sky. My energy level seemed to be inexorably declining. The palm trees rustled in the breeze. Wavelets lapped at the sand.

There wasn't a bug anywhere. Yes, we agreed, this was a rather good approximation of paradise.

For dinner, David steamed up the day's catch—hog snapper, French angelfish, mackerel, and parrotfish, along with side orders of crab, conch, and lobster—in Ricardo sauce, a spicy Belizean specialty. After-dinner entertainment consisted of a palm-frond bonfire, David's off-color jokes involving various tropical fruits, and the seven o'clock radio news broadcast from Belize City. The lead story was the graduation of twenty students from a Red Cross training course. I fell asleep in my hammock just as the full moon came up.

We had planned a one-day layover on Laughing Bird, but high winds kept us pinned down a second day, by which time we began to fall irrevocably into the grip of tropical ennui. The pace of island life soon approximated that of an unair-conditioned old folks' home in August. Trivial matters loomed large from the languorous vantage point of the hammock. Hey, Hal, you think that coconut up there is fixin' to fall any time soon? (Hard to tell, we'll continue to monitor the situation.) Should I make the five-minute walk to the end of the island now or later? (Later; I don't feel like expending the effort just now to brush the sand off my feet and find my sandals.) Time to snorkel? (Nah. The underwater light is better in the late afternoon.)

The hyperactive David, failing to recognize that the entire group had by now become firm acolytes of Hal, at one point actually tried to rouse us with a game of coconut bocce ball. But the sentiment of the hammock-bound was unanimous: Sorry, David. Not here, not now.

OUTFITTERS

On the seven-day *Ecosummer Expeditions* itinerary, kayakers begin at Lighthouse Reef and paddle sail-equipped double kayaks south along the barrier reef to Half Moon Cay, camping on small islands along the way. Ecosummer also offers a fourteen-day trip that includes three days of kayaking out of a base on Ranguana Cay, a two-day trip by sea kayak along the Chiquibul River, a half day of paddling on the Monkey River, and a week of nonkayaking activities on the mainland of Belize.

The point-to-point ten-day trip of *Island Expeditions* starts at Coco Plum Cay and works south along the reef, camping on various islands along the way and finishing at Big Creek. A fourteen-day itinerary follows the same route, but paddlers then proceed up the Monkey River for four days. A third alternative is a ten-day base-camp trip out of Southwest Cay on Glover's Reef, well outside of the main barrier reef. Paddlers are a bit more pampered, staying in big stand-up tents with cots and making day-trip excursions to nearby reefs and islands.

Slickrock Adventures, the outfitter I traveled with, has since changed its itinerary. Like Island Expeditions, Slickrock now runs a base-camp trip out of Glover's Reef. The camp is on Northeast Cay, about 6 miles from the Island Expeditions camp. Paddlers stay in cabanas or large stand-up tents and make day trips around Northeast Cay or to the four other islands in the atoll. Windsurfing and scuba diving are available.

Wilderness: Alaska/Mexico follows the same basic route I took with Slickrock—five or six days of island-hopping out of Placencia. Paddlers stay in small two-man tents. There's plenty of opportunity for snorkeling, but no scuba diving or windsurfing.

WHAT TO EXPECT

Paddling a kayak can weary the arms of the unpracticed, but the pace of these trips is leisurely. Typical daily paddling distance is 5 to 10 miles.

No previous kayaking experience is necessary. Sea kayaks, stable and equipped with rudders to aid in turning, are far easier to handle than tippy river kayaks, although less maneuverable. Paddling in smooth conditions is child's play, and the basics can be learned on the spot in a half hour or so. Unexpected winds, however, can kick up rough water and quickly turn a languid float into a grim ordeal for the uninitiated. Kayaks can feel claustrophobic at first, and the wet exit exercise required by some outfitters can be scary for waterphobes.

Prime time for these trips is December through May. The staging city is Belize City.

RECOMMENDED READING

The Life and Adventures of Robinson Crusoe by Daniel Defoe. The classic desert-island story that's been spawning fantasies for generations.

IN BRIEF

Ecosummer Expeditions, 604-669-7741: 7 days, $1,195; 14 days, $2,295
Island Expeditions, 604-325-7952: 10 days, $1,039; 14 days, $1,429; 10 days, $1,129
Slickrock Adventures, 801-259-6996: 10 days, $1,350
Wilderness: Alaska/Mexico, 907-479-8203: 8 days, $1,175

Physical challenge, 2; Mental challenge, 3; Skills, 2.

CHILE

rafting the

futaleufu

One day in 1989, as Eric Hertz's rented Toyota van bucked along a dirt road through the remote mountains of southern Chile, he looked down from a bridge and saw what appeared to be a narrow tongue of the Caribbean Sea, a ribbon of bright aquamarine blue foaming with whitecaps.

Hertz, the owner of a small whitewater rafting company called Earth River Expeditions, had paddled down wild and scenic rivers all over the world, but he'd never seen anything like this. He stopped the van, walked over to the railing, and stared down at the rushing water. "I knew in an instant that this was the most beautiful river I'd ever seen," Hertz recalls. "No other river has ever affected me like that. Not the Colorado, not even the Bio Bio. It was like God had designed the perfect whitewater river and laid it at my feet."

According to the tattered map in Hertz's glove compartment, the river flowed from a glacial lake in the Argentine Andes to the Gulf of Corcovado on Chile's Pacific coast. There was not a single human settlement along its entire 150-mile length. The map said that the river was called the Futaleufu.

In those days, virtually no one in the whitewater rafting business had even heard of the far-off blue river with the melodic name, pronounced FOO-ta-lay-oo-FOO. Three daring kayakers had run it in 1985, encountering a gauntlet of Class IV and V rapids—the biggest and most powerful that can be run—through deep granite canyons past meadows, temperate rain forest, glaciers, and eerily spiked summits. A year later, an exploratory three-raft expedition had given up halfway down, emerging wet, bedraggled, and without one of its rafts, which had flipped in a vicious Class V rapid, danced upside down in a whirlpool for several hours, and eventually flushed into a lake 30 miles downstream.

Unfazed by the horror stories from the previous raft attempt, Hertz returned to the Futaleufu in 1990 with a group of expert river guides and two lightweight self-bailing rafts. Despite some scary moments—inevitable when you don't know what's around the next corner—Hertz's crew completed the first full raft descent of the river. The whitewater and scenery turned out to be every bit as dramatic as he had imagined, and the water still ran that astonishing blue.

Hertz was hooked. He bought some land along the river from local farmers, set up temporary camps, and in 1991 began taking a handful of paying customers down the river. His clients raved. He began to make a little money. And the best part was that he was spending two months a year on the most beautiful river in the world.

Then came ENDESA—Empresa Nacional De Electricidad Sociedad Anonima. In March of 1994, Hertz's partner in Earth River Expeditions, Santiago native Robert Currie, was chatting with a friend in Chaiten, a coastal fishing town that serves as the last jumping-off spot to the Futaleufu put-in, four hours away. "So how are you guys going to run the Fu after they put in the dam?" the friend inquired.

Currie was stunned. The friend showed him the legal notice in Chaiten's weekly newspaper: ENDESA, a huge, privately owned energy company based in Santiago, was planning to build three hydroelectric dams on the Futaleufu and sell the power to Argentina. The first dam alone would create a lake 20 miles long, submerging the world-class whitewater and the scenic heart of the river.

Industry-friendly Chilean law allowed citizens opposed to the dam only forty-eight hours to respond to the legal announcement. Currie rushed to the provincial governor's office to register his objections. Waiting to see the governor, he struck up a conversation with a real estate developer. "The Futaleufu dam is a billion-dollar deal," the developer told him. "I'd advise you not to try to fight it. Your life is probably worth less than a billion."

ENDESA had already steamrollered opposition to a series of hydroelectric dams on the Bio Bio, a wild and glorious river 300 miles to the north that had become a favorite of whitewater connoisseurs during the late 1980s. At this writing, construction of one dam on the Bio Bio is well along, and a second is under way. About a third of the river has been lost to rafting, and all whitewater operations are expected to cease there by 1998. ENDESA plans to eventually build three more dams on the Bio Bio, essentially destroying the entire river, as well as the ancient culture of the Pehuenches Indians who live along its banks. The Bio Bio, it seemed, was the grim blueprint for the Futaleufu.

Hertz and Currie decided to fight the Futaleufu dam their own way. A former playwright, Hertz knew the power of emotion. "You have to get the local people and the decision-makers involved in a very personal way," he says. "You do that by taking them down the river on a raft. Once they see the extraordinary beauty with their own eyes, run the rapids, get wet, catch trout, maybe see a condor, it's no longer just a matter of kilowatt-hours and dollars. What was abstract is now in their hearts."

Hertz had already employed that philosophy to good effect on Quebec's Great Whale, an untouched wilderness river on Cree Indian land that was to be flooded by the vast James Bay hydroelectric project. In the late 1980s, New York State signed two twenty-year contracts to buy $19 billion worth of James Bay electricity starting in 1995, a deal that provided the project its major financial impetus. Hertz, who'd been commercially running the nearby Magpie for several years, organized a series of raft trips down the Great Whale for New York officials. The politicians and bureaucrats spent a week in virgin wilderness, sleeping in tepees on pine-needle beds, listening around the campfire as Cree elders talked of their sacred lands that would soon be inundated.

State Senator Franz Leichter was one of those who accompanied Hertz down the Great Whale. "Seeing it with my own eyes brought home to me in a very dramatic way what a shame and a tragedy it would be to dam that river," says Leichter. He and Assemblyman Bill Hoyt, who also spent a week on the Great Whale with Hertz, subsequently held public hearings on the power contracts, which were scheduled to come up for renewal in 1992 and 1994. Faced with an outcry from environmentalists, as well as changing economic conditions, New York decided not to renew the power contracts. Without its prime customer, the James Bay project was put on indefinite hold.

But the situation in Chile was different: Unlike the politically savvy Cree, most of the people who lived near the Futaleufu had no idea how a big dam would change their lives. The nearest village, also called Futaleufu, was 2 miles from the river and well upstream, out of sight of the first proposed dam and lake. Most of the river valley itself was wilderness; the few inhabitants were farmers whose houses for the most part lay well away from the river. The farmers might lose some grazing acreage to the rising water behind the dam, but surely there would be a hefty check from ENDESA in compensation. And wouldn't a dam create jobs and boost the local economy?

"The only time most local people ever noticed the river was when they went over the bridge," says Hertz. "To many of them, it was a place you drowned." Hertz knew he had to grab the farmers and villagers by the heart. "If they didn't care enough to fight for this river, there would be no fight at all. It didn't matter how good the fishing was or how wonderful the rapids were."

Hertz and Currie approached farmers who owned land along the river and offered to drive them up to the Bio Bio to take a look at what happens when a wild river is dammed. Ten landowners accepted. For many, it would be their first trip more than 50 miles from home.

Currie and the farmers piled into two vans and headed north. Hertz, not wishing to appear the meddling gringo, stayed behind. The farmers' first surprise came when they rolled into the town nearest the Bio Bio dam to find the main guest house strangely empty. The owner, surprised by the unexpected influx of customers, had to rustle around and make up the beds as they waited. "No tourists come here anymore since they started building the dam," she apologized. "My business is just about dead."

At the dam site the next morning, the Futaleufuians saw a scene of devastation: newly gouged roads, blasted granite, canyon walls stripped of trees, massive piles of rubble, trucks, machinery, and mud. The farmers looked stunned, Currie recalls. "They had no idea you could do such things to a river."

The farmers saw that the ENDESA workers had their own self-contained town. Without identifying themselves, they walked up to one of the workers and began to quiz him. Do you buy your food and supplies from the local merchants?

Oh, no, came the answer. The company ships everything down from Santiago. We don't buy the junk they have around here.

Do you hire local people?

Of course, replied the dam worker. To clean the toilets.

At a town meeting back in Futaleufu, Nedea Dicares, a fifty-six-year-old woman whose family farm lies along the banks of the river, stood up and told her neighbors what she'd seen at the Bio Bio. Her impassioned, tearful speech stirred shock and outrage.

That same month, Hertz and Currie organized a cultural-exchange raft trips for kids. Six ninth-graders from Smyrna, Delaware, and two young girls from the village of Futaleufu paddled and splashed and screamed and giggled their way down the easier sections of the river. Along the way they met a Chilean woman who roasted them a lamb and knitted each of them a pair of wool socks. On the last night, as the kids snuggled into their sleeping bags around the campfire and the river rushed by in the darkness, one of the Chilean girls on the trip, a pretty dark-haired twelve-year-old named Suj ey, stood up and announced that she had something to say.

With Currie translating, she told her new friends how she'd never really thought much about this river till now, that she had been a little frightened of it at first, and that her parents almost didn't let her come on the trip because they were afraid of it, too. But she'd had a wonderful time, and had seen what a beautiful river it was.

Suj ey said that she was amazed and grateful that the other kids would travel halfway around the world just to see this river in her backyard, and to help save it. "I didn't even know about the dam until recently," she said. "My father thinks it will be a good thing. But now I feel very strongly that it shouldn't be built, and I'm going to tell him exactly how I feel."

Hertz, listening in the darkness, made himself a promise: Every kid in town, and every Futaleufu farmer's son and daughter, was going to get a ride down the magical blue river.

OUTFITTERS

Earth River Expeditions staff meet rafters in Puerto Montt, a small port city in Chile's lake region 600 miles south of Santiago. After a day's sightseeing—including a two-hour raft ride down a Class III river, it's a charter flight farther south to the coastal village of Chaiten. Next comes a three-hour drive on dirt roads—with a stop along the way for a hike to a glacier—to Earth River's Futaleufu base camp on the banks of the river.

The first day on the river is a training day from the base camp, with a swim test and several short practice runs through Class IV rapids. (Rapids are rated I through V, with V being the most difficult and dangerous.) Day two begins with a van ride upstream to the put-in, just below the Argentinean border. You'll proceed downriver through Inferno Canyon to Campo Casa de Piedra, another Earth River camp set in a cave just below Zeta, a monster Class V+ rapid. (Zeta and another V+ rapid, Throne Room, are considered too dangerous to run commercially. Rafters will walk around them while the empty rafts are floated along the shoreline attached to ropes.)

During a rest day at the cave camp, rafters may hike, rock climb, ride horses, fish, swim, or kayak in a large spring-fed pond. After another night in the cave, you head downriver to the base camp. The last day is a long, hard run that Hertz calls the best day of Class V rafting in the world. From the takeout, you head directly back to Chaiten, thence to Puerto Montt, Santiago, and home.

You'll cover a total of forty miles on the river, in the process traversing thirty-three Class IV and V rapids.

Bio Bio Expeditions, a part-time venture of three California river guides, ran three commercial trips on the Fu in 1997. Rafters stay in tents in a rented field, with one night in a hotel in the village of Futaleufu before tackling Inferno Canyon. Bio Bio uses 16-foot rafts, which are very maneuverable but may not be suitable for certain high-water conditions. For safety, Bio Bio employs one cataraft and one kayak for each raft. The company's introductory $1,600 price for 1998 will rise to $2,000 for the 1999 season.

WHAT TO EXPECT

This is no float 'n' bloat trip. Because of the difficult rapids, all participants must paddle energetically, sometimes for extended periods. This kind of upper-body exertion can be surprisingly strenuous—check the statistics for heart attacks suffered while shoveling snow—and requires good overall cardiovascular fitness. In addition, you'll need to have your upper-body muscles in good shape. Weight training before the trip is a good idea, especially for pectorals and lats.

With its ten Class V rapids, the Futaleufu is more technical and difficult than, say, the Grand Canyon. There are various definitions of a Class V rapid, but Hertz's criterion is that a capsize and subsequent swim have serious or potentially fatal consequences without immediate rescue. In 1993, in fact, two people on another outfitter's trip drowned in the Fu when their rafts flipped in high water just minutes after launching on the first day.

None of the guides on that fatal trip, however, had paddled the river before, and some had never even seen it. Earth River, which made the first full descent of the Fu by raft in 1990, uses only veteran Class V river runners who know the Fu intimately. They employ a fleet of rescue kayaks and ultra-stable "catarafts" to quickly pluck out swimmers in case of a capsize. Earth River uses custom-built 18-foot Sotar self-bailing rafts specifically designed for the Fu. For better maneuverability, they carry no supplies. Hertz says that raft capsizes on the Fu are rare, but it is not unusual for paddlers to be washed or catapulted overboard in big rapids. So far, all Earth River swimmers have been quickly pulled out unharmed, although not unshaken.

If all this sounds a bit intimidating, there's an out: a horse trail that runs virtually the entire length of the river. The faint of heart can walk, or ride a horse supplied by Earth River, around every big rapid.

Novice raft-paddlers are accepted for this trip, but only the very fit, strong, and fearless. Preferably, you should have paddle-rafting experience on Class V rivers such as the Gauley in West Virginia or California's Tuolumne. Although guides in each raft command all maneuvers, you must be able to respond instantly and correctly with great vigor and proper paddling technique. Mistakes or hesitation on one paddler's part may jeopardize the safety of everyone aboard.

Earth River's two camps are about as plush as you can get and still call it camping. The main base camp has a large open-air gazebo for sleeping, plus a sixteen-person hot tub atop a cliff overlooking the river. Campo Casa de Piedra is a large stand-up cave with a sandy floor and natural venting for a campfire. Both camps offer the services of Juaquina, a comely Chilean masseuse. (Sorry, massages are extra, not included in the price of the trip.)

The rafting season runs from January through March, the austral summer.

RECOMMENDED READING

Travels in a Thin Country by Sara Wheeler. A woman's off-the-beaten-path wanderings through Chile.

IN BRIEF

Earth River Expeditions, 800-643-2784: 10 days, $2,100.
   Earth River's trip may also be booked through Mountain Travel-Sobek (800-227-2384), which ran its own trips on the Fu for a year but found it could not compete with Earth River's sumptuous base camps. If three or more Sobek clients are booked on one Earth River trip, Sobek will supply one of its own guides.
Bio Bio Expeditions, 800-246-7238: 10 days, $1,600/$2,000.

Physical challenge, 3; Mental challenge, 4; Skills 3.

DOMINICA

mountain-biking the
rain forest

From the first glimpse of Dominica out the window of the Twin Otter, I can see it is like no other Caribbean island: no broad white sandy beaches; no big resort hotels; no cruise ships. Cliffs rise straight out of the water. Mountains disappear into the clouds. And instead of the multihued patchwork of red and green and blue roofs that typically dot Caribbean islands, there are vast expanses of wild, unbroken green.

Ian, the tour guide, is waiting at the airport. We drive the half hour to Soufriere, the fishing village (pop: 998) where he and his wife, Barbara, live and run their mountain bike/scuba diving/sea kayaking business. The bike tour doesn't start until tomorrow, but I have an itch to break a sweat and unlimber leg muscles withered by a long day of sitting in cars, planes, and airports. So instead of cadging a lift from Ian to my quarters, I decide to pedal there.

Petit Coulibri, an isolated guest cottage on a 260-year-old plantation estate, lies 3 miles and 1,000 vertical feet up a rutted dirt road at the head of the Soufriere Valley. Vehicle-bound visitors dread the rough, slow ride up and down, but mountain bikers look at the world from a different perspective. Bone-jarring bumps? Vertiginous switchbacks? Unrelenting 12 percent grades? Perfect.

Pedaling away from Ian's shop, I pick up Soufriere's main street, which runs along a narrow beach of pebbles and dark volcanic sand. A gentle surf rocks the village fleet of anchored fishing boats as I try to remember to stay to the left side of the road. The locals regard me with some curiosity, but generally smile and offer the standard Dominican greeting: "Okay!" or "All right!" A plump housewife sweeping her sidewalk sings at the top of her lungs to no one in particular. Old men sit together along the street on small bleachers hammered together from tree branches, communal stoops on which to gossip and watch the world go by. After all, one can never tell when something truly bizarre might happen along—like a white guy wearing Lycra shorts and a fluorescent yellow helmet.

A furious pickup basketball game is under way on the village court. To my surprise, the players are quite skilled, with graceful jump shots and serviceable crossover dribbles. (How dare these foreigners play our game as well as we do!) Unlike American playground hotshots, however, these young men seem to relish a good pass as much as a good shot. I briefly consider joining the game—I've played basketball all my life, and usually don't embarrass myself—but then a spring-legged 6-footer rises with a rebound for a rim-rattling two-handed dunk. Way out of my league. I ride on.

Down the street, near the Slow Corner Cafe, four old men play dominoes. They bang their tiles onto the table with resounding thumps, the geriatric equivalent of a slam dunk. The rules of the game are explained to me, and appear so simple— one merely puts down a domino with a number matching that of the last domino played—that there seems to be no room left for skill or strategy. But one small, slender fellow, an iconoclast who slides his dominoes quietly into position, wins three games in a row with a knowing look. I still can't figure out what the skill or strategy is. Out of my league again.

As I'm about to pedal on, a wild-eyed man wearing a bright blue robe approaches the domino game. In a loud, raspy voice, he berates the players. "Hear my words!" he shouts in the lilting accent of the Caribbean. "You are doomed to burn in hell unless you accept my Lord Jesus Christ into your life, as I have!" The players don't even look up. It's just Tisson, the village madman, they tell me. Harmless, lives alone, spends his days wandering the streets in brightly colored robes, incessantly delivering high-decibel sermons to anything that moves, and some that don't. The townspeople, although clearly weary of his preaching, look out for him and keep him supplied with food. After ranting at the domino group to no avail for some minutes, Tisson drifts away down the beach, where he is soon haranguing a coconut tree.

Just outside of town, I pedal by the village schoolhouse. It is dismissal time, for the road is packed with children walking home. The crowd of kids has an eerie homogeneity; the girls are dressed in identical yellow blouses and brown skirts, while the boys wear yellow dress shirts and brown pants. As I weave the bike through the sea of chattering yellow exuberance, I ponder how odd it is that these children, whose family incomes average perhaps $3,000 a year, have all the appearances of wealthy, refined young men and women. The schoolkids in my home town—average family income $75,000—in their ripped jeans, Oakland Raider T-shirts, backward baseball caps, and unlaced Air Jordans, look like grubby cretins by comparison.

Beyond the last house in the village—with all the distractions, the half-mile journey has consumed twenty minutes—the road to Petit Coulibri narrows and turns to ugly dirt. The big, sharp, embedded rocks make me long for my own bike, which has a front shock absorber; the rigid-fork model I've rented from Ian is a truck by comparison. (Suck it up, dude; you'll just have to pick your line a little more carefully.) The road winds up through fields of banana and coconut trees. Another reason to wear one's helmet: Falling coconuts are a leading cause of accidental death in the Caribbean. At one particularly narrow spot, a cow standing in the road blocks my way. After an initial staring contest, we negotiate the terms of my passage: The cow will stay put, and I will dismount and carry the bike through the forest around her. Deal.

A cleverer writer than I once noted that, when it comes to travel by mountain bike, God is in the detours. I have come to embrace that philosophy. So when a side road and a small sign ("Sulfur Springs") appear, I veer off without hesitation. There is suddenly the stench of rotten eggs, and then a burbling creek unusual in two respects: It is bright orange, and it steams. A dip of the hand reveals that its temperature is about that of a Jacuzzi. Farther upstream is a small clearing of barren, yellowish dirt. The ground is hot to the touch, and wisps of steam drift out of small holes. (I later learn that there was a small volcanic eruption here last year, complete with red-hot molten lava.)

Back to the "main" road. The grade steepens, and I shift to the small chain ring. The surface turns seriously rough, forcing me to unleash my modest technical riding skills and horse the front wheel up and over occasional big rocks and ledges. A couple of abrupt switchbacks add variety. In the tropical heat and humidity, the sweat is suddenly flowing in rivulets. I grind up past gnarled lime trees, wild guavas, and a massive chatagnier tree with flying buttress roots that look like fins on a rocketship. A view down the valley reveals a broad swath of jungle, a wall of cliffs, and the white gash in the greenery that is the Sulfur Flat.

It begins to rain. The shower is intense and brief, and in my overheated state, quite welcome. As it passes, a rainbow glows beyond the far ridge. Ahead on the road, a shabbily dressed man is walking toward me with a 2-foot-long machete. A product of my culture, I cannot suppress a brief, reflexive frisson of fear. As he nears, I see that he is smiling broadly, perhaps at my outlandish attire. He gives me a hearty "Okay!"

His name is Otto, and he lives in Soufriere, but most days tends a field of dasheen up at the head of the valley. He's been cutting weeds today. There's an old abandoned stone plantation house up ahead, he tells me, and I should bear left there. When he learns that I will be riding back down to the village from Petit Coulibri tomorrow morning, he says, "Then perhaps I will see you again, my friend. Have a safe journey." As he walks away, I am filled with the hope that fear can be unlearned as easily as it is learned.

Just past the abandoned plantation house, the road suddenly turns to cobblestones, and once again I miss my shock absorber. (You can't pick a line through cobblestones.) The overhead canopy of trees thickens, and with the sun now well down behind the surrounding mountains, I am juddering through a gloomy tunnel of green.

Another sidetrack into the forest appears, once again impelling me to follow. It soon dead-ends at the tin-roof shack of a goatherd, where the gobbling of a turkey announces my arrival. The goatherd, apparently in the middle of dinner, gives a wave from his front porch. Not wishing to intrude, I retreat to the road.

Almost immediately another intriguing branch presents itself. This one dead-ends after a mile at a large iron gate guarding what appears to be a millionaire's mansion. I glimpse red bougainvillea bushes and a perfectly manicured lawn as two nasty dogs race toward the gate in full voice. I make a hasty departure, contemplating the irony that an impoverished goat-herd and a reclusive millionaire are next-door neighbors.

Out of the tree tunnel now, a long traverse up the side of a hill, a sharp left turn, and suddenly there is the Atlantic, crashing into the rocks 1,000 feet below, almost straight down. Hazy on the horizon lies Martinique, 23 miles distant. The road parallels the precipice for a few hundred yards, then turns abruptly straight up the hill at an impossible angle. I shift to first gear, stand up, and give it my best shot. Not good enough. After 100 yards, I come to a gasping halt.

A brief, humiliating trudge, a left turn through another green tunnel, a final push up a rough, rocky stretch, and at last I burst out onto a level green lawn, with an imposing stone-and-wood house and sweeping veranda on one side, a swimming pool on the other, and the ocean spread out below, where the sun is just now setting. It is Petit Coulibri. I am home.

After a swim and dinner, I hit the sack early, for tomorrow begins my mountain bike tour of Dominica. It should be fun.

OUTFITTERS

Nature Island Dive is primarily a scuba-diving operator, but its owner, a thirty-year-old Canadian named Ian Collumbin, is a mountain-bike fanatic as well. NID runs guided, vehicle-supported day rides in five different parts of the island. Price variations depend on group size; the low price is for six or more people, the higher for two or three. Prices include guide, shuttle, lunch, and bike rental (Giant Rincons). Rentals for independent riding are $30 a day, or $20 for a half day.

Trips are run on demand, with no set schedule. Any of the one-day trips that make up the five-day package may be taken separately. Price is $55–$80 per day, depending on group size.

Nature Island Dive also offers scuba diving (one-tank dive,

$40; two-tank dive, $60; resort course, $80), sea-kayak rentals ($10 per hour, $25 per half day, $40 per day), and two-day guided sea-kayak trips. Lodgings are not part of the trip package, but NID can book any number of lodgings.

It would be hard to imagine a better place for a mountain biker than *Petit Coulibri* (809-446-3150), with its beautiful, rugged 3-mile dirt-road ride in and out. Perched on a bluff 1,000 feet above the ocean, the view framed by dramatic mountains, this former lime plantation is run by Barney and Loye Barnard and their daughter, Emie. Refugees from Florida, they bought the plantation thirteen years ago to raise aloe vera plants. But a series of natural, bureaucratic, and business disasters finally persuaded them in 1993 that tourism might be the way to make a go of it up here. They built four cottages along the forested ridge behind the main house, each a stone and wood masterpiece with stunning views of the Martinique Channel on one side and the Soufriere Valley on the other. To say this place is romantic is a wild understatement; the Barnards' very first guests decided to get married on their third day here.

Petit Coulibri has three two-bedroom, two-bath units with full kitchens at $200 per night. There's also one studio room, with two beds and a bath for $90 per night. Discounts are available for long-terms stays. Home-cooked dinners in the main house are $25 per person, breakfast $10.

If you prefer not to be so isolated, Nature Island Dive has a two-bedroom cottage just outside of Soufriere, right on the ocean, with full kitchen, for $100 per night. For those on a budget who want a taste of local village life, there's Gachette's Seaside Lodge (809-448-4551) in Scott's Head, just down the road from Soufriere.

WHAT TO EXPECT

Your small chain ring will get a serious workout. Dominica is the most mountainous island in the Caribbean (several peaks approach 5,000 feet), and long, steep grades are commonplace, both on paved roads and off-road trails. Be prepared for serious quad burn.

You'll be staying in lodges or cottages every night, so weather during the ride will be your biggest mental challenge. The heat and humidity can be withering. On the other hand, it rains often, particularly in the interior mountain areas, where most of the riding takes place. Most showers are brief, ranging from two minutes to thirty.

Injury is always a possibility on a mountain-bike trip. (On my trip, in fact, trip leader Collumbin did an over-the-handlebars faceplant onto broken asphalt. He was picking rocks out of his chin for days.) However, a support vehicle and basic medical facilities will always be reasonably nearby.

Beginning mountain bikers can do this trip by simply opting out of the more difficult technical single-track routes. A significant portion of the riding is nontechnical, on semi-paved and dirt roads. But to take advantage of the more challenging routes—the Galion Trail, for example, or the single-track descent to Petit Savane—at least intermediate technical skills are necessary.

The mountain biking is good in Dominica year-round. The semi-dry season (January through June) is slightly hotter; the semi-wet season (July through December) is a bit cooler because of greater cloud cover. Cool or dry, take your pick; you can't have both. But virtually any day of the year, you'll get hot and sweaty, and you'll get rained on.

The staging city is Roseau, Dominica.

RECOMMENDED READING

The Orchid House by Jean Rhys. A novel of island life by Dominica's most prominent literary figure.

IN BRIEF

Nature Island Dive, 809-449-8181: 5 days, $250–$375 plus
food and lodging
Petit Coulibri, 809-446-3150: $90–$200 per night

Physical challenge, 3; Mental challenge, 1; Skills, 3.

PATAGONIA

crossing the
ice cap

Two or three minutes into Southwind Adventures' promotional video for its Continental Ice Cap Traverse, the sound begins. For the next forty-five minutes it virtually never ceases. As the trekkers on the TV screen pick their way with ski poles across the desert of ice and snow, there's the sound. As the camera pans vistas of jagged peaks and saucer-shaped clouds, there's the sound. Even as the trekkers huddle in their tents and talk of the day's progress, there's the sound. At times it is a locomotive's rumble, at others the howl of a jet engine, or, as Paul Theroux described it, the rasp of sand in a chute. But always it is there—the sound of the Patagonian wind.

According to the *World Survey of Climatology,* during the summer months in inland Patagonia the average reported wind speed from nine reporting points—day, night, week after week—is just under 8 meters per second, about 18 miles per hour. Average summer afternoon wind in Rio Gallegos, southern Patagonia's largest town, is 23 miles per hour. Twenty-three percent of the time, the wind in Rio Gallegos exceeds 31 miles per hour. The *Survey* authors note, however, that "the published values of wind speed in the interior of Patagonia are certainly not representative," due to the location of most reporting stations in villages or towns, which naturally tend to be in the most sheltered places. Newer stations in less sheltered areas, they report, register average wind speeds in some cases more than 100 percent higher than the published numbers. A 1994 study revealed hourly mean wind speeds of up to 56 miles per hour on the Pampa del Castillo in east-central Patagonia.

The wind has been remarked upon by virtually every traveler to the bottom of South America. "Grant tempefte" were mentioned in the first written dispatch from Patagonia, the journal of the adventurous young Italian Antonio Pigafetta, who as a lark joined Ferdinand Magellan's three-year round-the-world expedition in 1519. Charles Darwin wrote of the "constant succession of gales" that assaulted the H.M.S. *Beagle* during his 1834 Patagonian expedition.

George Gaylord Simpson, a young naturalist on a 1932 journey to Patagonia for the American Museum of Natural History, wrote in his journal, "Justino awoke me this morning by shouting that the wind was blowing, which is like telling a sailor that the sea happens to be salty this morning. . . . The fact that the air is in rapid motion becomes almost as elemental as the fact that there is air. It is a condition of life here. . . ."

On another occasion, Simpson noted, "The strongest wind I have ever seen was blowing on the barranca today. To climb over the crest, I had to crawl on my belly, and in a less cautious moment was knocked down and almost blown over the cliff. Going into the wind down a slope that was too steep to stand on at all ordinarily, we could walk leaning forward at an apparently fatal angle, supported by the constant gale in our faces. There could hardly be a more curious sight or a stranger sensation. Just there the wind was blowing such large pebbles that we had to remove our goggles for fear of their being hit and broken."

Lady Florence Dixie, an adventurous and wealthy Victorian

woman who toured Patagonia in 1880, noticed that after some weeks "a most disagreeable metamorphosis had taken place in our faces. They were swollen to an almost unrecognizable extent, and had assumed a deep purple hue, the phenomenon being accompanied by sharp itching. The boisterous wind which we had encountered during the day, and which is the standard drawback to the otherwise agreeable climate of Patagonia, was no doubt the cause of this annoyance. . . . After a few days the skin of our faces peeled off completely, but the swelling did not go down for some time. I would advise any person who makes the same journey to provide themselves with masks; by taking this precaution they will save themselves a great deal of the discomfort we suffered from the winds."

None of these travelers, however, ventured into the really windy part of Patagonia: the ice cap that runs 200 miles down the spine of the southern Andes, along what is now the border between Chile and Argentina. Jutting up 5,000 feet above sea level, this great plateau of ice catches the full fury of the most powerful prevailing wind on earth.

The Patagonia Ice Cap was entirely unexplored, a blank on the map, until well into the twentieth century. The first march along its full length, by the British mountaineer and explorer Eric Shipton, was not made until 1961, four years after Sputnik. Shipton, a veteran of scores of climbs and expeditions in the Alps, Himalayas, and Karakoram, described his fifty-two-day slog with three companions as "an experience as completely satisfying as any I have known."

Wind direction alone determined the route of Shipton's expedition; to travel on foot, hauling a heavy supply sled, in any direction but downwind was clearly unthinkable. Shipton commissioned the design of special wind-resistant tents that weighed 60 pounds, and devised for them a high-wind setup procedure so complex that it required three men to perform and half a page to describe in his narrative of the expedition. "In moderate weather the whole operation took about an hour to complete," he wrote, "but in really bad conditions it took considerably longer."

Wind shapes the physical landscape of Patagonia. Shipton noticed a number of 100-foot-deep ravines in the ice that he at first took to be "melt pits," troughs created by melting from the heat of adjacent sun-warmed rocks. But he soon realized that the ice canyons had been scoured out of the glacier by the sheer force of the wind alone.

He also noted that "the most lovely feature of the mountains of southern Patagonia [is] caused by the winds, heavily charged with moisture, striking against exposed surfaces to form a coating of rime. It clings to vertical and even overhanging precipices . . . which results in wildly improbable shapes on the faces of the peaks, and of immense cornices along the wind-ward side of their summit ridges." Less lovely were the sastrugi, wind ridges in the snow "rather like giant sand ripples." The alternating bands of ice and fluff exhausted Shipton and his men and battered one of their sleds to destruction.

Shipton's report of his encounters with a williwaw—a sudden swirling wind phenomenon that tends to form over glaciers—echoes Simpson's account. "Without any warning, the tornado struck with incredible violence. . . . I was blown off my feet by the first blast." Trying to reach the shelter of a rock outcrop above, "we needed only to allow ourselves to be hurled up the slope towards it. There, funneled by the gap, the wind was stronger than ever, and we had to crawl through on hands and knees until we reached a steep gully beyond."

On the ice cap itself, Shipton was spared the ordeal of wind-flung pebbles that had bedeviled Simpson, but he had to contend with a new airborne hazard. "The wind whipped the snow from the surface of the glacier and hurled it along as a dense cloud of spray," Shipton recounts. "As the temperature was well above freezing, the snow had melted by the time it reached us and in a few moments we were entirely drenched, as though we had been subjected to the concerted aim of a fireman's hose."

On another occasion, dragging their sleds over the snow in near-zero visibility and a gale-force crosswind, Shipton and his men unexpectedly trod upon an area of wind-scoured ice, hard and smooth as a skating rink. Shipton, in the lead and staring down at his compass, failed to notice the change of surface and was instantly blown off his feet. In the process he dropped the compass, which went sliding away like a curling stone. He got up, tried to chase the windblown compass, and was hurled to the ice again. He eventually retrieved it by scrambling in pursuit on all fours. "I learnt later that my antics looked extremely funny," Shipton recounts. "By his repeated references to the incident, [my companion] Eduardo evidently came to regard it as one of the highlights of the trip."

With the wind still slanting across their line of advance, Shipton and two companions resumed pulling the larger sled, which weighed several hundred pounds. As soon as its runners reached the icy section, it was blown sideways, dragging the three men with it. "After that, Eduardo hitched his trace to the back of the sledge and pulled to windward. Even so it was very difficult to keep a straight course, and we went along in a crab-like fashion, with repeated falls, for a couple of hours, [until] we found ourselves on snow again."

Shipton's narrative continues: "The wind was too strong for us to stop for lunch, and in the early afternoon it increased to such violence that at 2:15 I decided we had better pitch the tent while it was still possible. Our drill came in for a severe testing. Fortunately, before we reached the most delicate part of the operation, it began to moderate." Miraculously, by five P.M. there was absolute calm.

"As with the sudden cessation of an artillery barrage, the silence was uncanny, almost oppressive," Shipton wrote. "It took some time to become accustomed to the strange tranquility, and even when I awoke the next morning I had a sense of unreality, as if a fundamental part of life were missing."

OUTFITTER

Trekkers on *Southwind Adventures*'s sixteen-day Continental Icecap Traverse fly first to Buenos Aires, then to Rio Gallegos, the Argentine gateway to southern Patagonia. From there it's a four-hour drive across barren plains to Calafate, on the shores of Lago Argentina. You'll spend a day visiting Moreno Glacier, which regularly calves great thundering chunks of ice into the lake. Then comes a three-hour drive on dirt roads, around the lake and north to El Chalten, a hamlet at the foot of Fitzroy Massif, the much-photographed gaggle of mile-high granite needles. The following day, after a short drive, you'll begin hiking along the Rio Electrico, continuing over rocky moraine to a camp at the foot of the Marconi Glacier.

There follow five or six days (depending on weather) of glacier trekking by foot, ski, or snowshoe, depending on conditions. The route circles the Fitzroy Massif by ascending to Marconi Pass, then turning south along the ice cap to Viedma Glacier and Paso de Viento (Windy Pass), then back down to El Chalten. Total distance covered on foot is about 50 miles, 20 of it on the glacier itself. If weather and time permit, trekkers will have the opportunity to climb Gorra Blanca, a 9,385-foot peak with grand views.

WHAT TO EXPECT

What separates this expedition from other treks is the fact that you'll be humping your own loads—no porters or pack animals once you get up on the ice cap itself. Expect to begin with a full expedition pack of about 70 pounds and cover an average of 10 miles a day. Largest daily elevation gain is 2,600 feet. The optional climb of Gorra Blanca requires a 4,500-foot climb but only a light day pack.

Normally, a carry-your-own trek such as this would rate a 4 in terms of mental challenge, but the potential for truly awful weather ratchets the misery level up a notch. Temperature is usually not bad—40–60 degrees F. during the day, nights typically in the 30s—but the incessant wind can drive the chill factor well below zero. And on top of that there is the almost daily rain, sleet, and fog. If you can, emulate Shipton himself, who accepted the vileness of the weather as a challenge and derived the major satisfaction of his trip from merely surviving it.

Add in the onerous camp chores required of all trip participants—setting up tents in the wind, melting snow for water, cutting ice blocks to make windscreens, and so on—and the potential for falling into crevasses, and this trip may be the sternest mental test of any in the book, save Mount Everest. Patagonia ice cap trekkers would be well advised to adopt the grittily upbeat attitude of Barney, one of Shipton's mates, who at one point "was blown off his feet and, in falling, injured his back. Though as a result of this he was largely crippled for the next few weeks, he continued to maintain that the trip had been one of the most enjoyable he had ever experienced."

Previous winter camping, backpacking, and backcountry travel experience are essential, and some mountaineering background is advisable. Depending on conditions, the use of skis and/or snowshoes may be required. The optional climb is mostly glacier-walking, but has a few moderately technical sections.

Trips run during the austral summer, November through March.

RECOMMENDED READING

Land of Tempest by Eric Shipton. An understated yet riveting account of Shipton's three excursions on the Patagonia Ice Cap, the last an epic fifty-two-day traverse of its entire length.

In Patagonia by Bruce Chatwin. The classic account of the author's wanderings through the plains of Patagonia and his philosophical and historical musings thereon.

IN BRIEF

Southwind Adventures, 800-377-9463: 16 days, $2,495

Physical challenge, 4; Mental challenge, 5; Skills, 3.

PERU

trekking to the
sacred city of
the incas

Gary Ziegler's obsession had its beginnings in 1964, when he and a friend, fresh out of college, spent a month tramping through the backcountry of Peru. To Ziegler's astonishment, the landscape was littered with archaeological relics in such profusion that the locals hardly took notice of them. The sight of 1,000-year-old clay pots lying untouched on the side of the road sparked in him a fascination with ancient Peruvian culture.

But his obsession didn't bubble to the surface until 1993, as Ziegler sat with his pal Barry Walker in the Cross Keys Bar, a raffish trekker's hangout in the Peruvian mountain town of Cuzco. By then a serious student of Inca history with a Ph.D. in archaeology from the National University of Peru, Ziegler had for years doubted the established scientific dogma about one of the great Inca mysteries: the location of Vilcabamba, the legendary sacred city and last refuge of the Inca emperors after they fled the Spanish conquistadors in 1535.

The Inca emperor Manco, realizing he could not defeat the invaders, gathered up the empire's remaining treasury of gold and its most sacred religious icons, and fled with his royal court to the city of Vilcabamba, a virtually impregnable stronghold in the remote, mountainous jungles north of Cuzco. There he established the Inca's spiritual and religious center. The conquistadors never reached Vilcabamba, and its location has never been pinpointed with certainty.

Throughout the nineteenth century, historians believed that the mystery city had been located at what is now called Choquiquirao (CHOKE-ee-ker-OW), whose name means "Cradle of Gold." A remote ruin on a 10,000-foot-high ridge overlooking the Apurímac River, it had been visited by a handful of treasure hunters over the centuries, but the way was so difficult—one vertiginous ridge upon another, blanketed in dense jungle—and the ruins so overgrown, that intruders rarely remained more than a few days. Little excavation had ever been done, and although local Indian legend says that the Incan gold is there, none has ever been found.

Then, in 1911, Yale professor Hiram Bingham discovered the breathtaking ruins at Machu Picchu. He returned with a team of archaeologists the next year and began excavation. Citing Machu Picchu's extraordinary stonework and architecture, and its numerous religious relics, Bingham made a convincing case that this, not Choquiquirao, was the sacred city of Vilcabamba.

Bingham's theory held sway until 1964, when maverick American explorer Bill Savoy uncovered expansive ruins at a place called Espiritu Pampa. Savoy claimed that Espiritu Pampa met the geographical requirements of Vilcabamba as described in ancient documents, and was much larger than Machu Picchu. And in the meantime, evidence had been mounting that Machu Picchu had been abandoned by the 1520s, and could therefore not have been Vilcabamba. Nowadays, it's generally accepted among archaeologists that Espiritu Pampa is the site of the lost Vilcabamba.

But for Gary Ziegler, the Espiritu Pampa theory just didn't

add up. For one thing, Espiritu Pampa lies in the hot, humid, lowland jungle. "The Incas are a high-altitude people," he says. "Their religion is focused toward the sun and the stars. Their shrines are typically in high places, with views of sacred mountains and rivers. Espiritu Pampa's lowland setting just didn't fit Inca theology or the lifestyle of the emperors."

And then there were the chronicles. In the 1560s, two Spanish missionaries, Friars Marcos and Diego, traveled to Vilcabamba from Vitcos, a city whose location is known with certainty today. In their journal, the friars describe a cold, high-altitude journey of three days. "A trek from Vitcos to Espiritu Pampa doesn't fit that description," says Ziegler. Although the distance is about right, the obvious route from Vitcos to Espiritu Pampa would follow a lowland river valley.

As Ziegler saw it, only one place matched both the Incas' high-altitude culture and the friars' chronicles: Choquiquirao, the "Cradle of Gold," whose identity as Vilcabamba had been out of fashion for a century. Sitting in the Cross Keys Bar, Ziegler and Barry Walker decided there was only one way to prove his theory: trek from Vitcos to Choquiquirao, using the friars' chronicle as a travel guide, and retracing what he hoped would be their steps.

Ironically, a member of Hiram Bingham's 1912 expedition, Assistant Topographer Heald, had journeyed to Choquiquirao from the same general direction. He had described the terrain thusly: "From a purely artistic point of view, the country was wonderful, with its splendid ranges of gleaming white peaks all covered by glaciers, and the jungle below leading down into straight-sided valleys with streams white with foam. However, from the point of view of one who had to travel through it, it was anything but lovely."

Heald's party reported numerous miseries. There was almost continuous rain and fog. The bites of green jungle-flies caused such swelling that "not a man of us could bend his wrists, the knuckles on our hands were invisible, and our eyes were mere slits that it cost an effort to open enough to look out of." Several men slipped and fell down the muddy, precipitous slopes, and were recovered, frightened but unharmed, only with considerable effort.

At one point, the Indian porters refused to go any farther. "They said that if they did, it would be merely to die of thirst; that the city of Choquiquirao was non-existent, and that they did not wish to die just because I did," wrote Heald. "I knew we couldn't make them work, but I thought we could make them travel. Giving the .22 to Tomas, I told him to shoot any man who tried to bolt, but to do it carefully, around the edges. . . ."

So motivated, Heald's party eventually reached Choquiquirao. But they did little excavation, and the focus of Bingham's expedition, and his search for the lost Vilcabamba, remained on Machu Picchu. For eighty years, Choquiquirao lay virtually untouched.

Ziegler and Walker recruited a motley team for their expedition to Choquiquirao: two friends, eight paying customers, and, in the manner of modern-day explorers, a two-man video crew to document the journey. Supported by a team of horses, mules, and eleven Indian wranglers, the expedition set off from the ruins at Vitcos, walking steeply uphill on a muddy dirt road. Ziegler clutched the accounts of Friars Marcos and Diego to his chest as a mother carries a child.

The chronicles did not promise an easy journey. Local Indians had advised the friars that the route to Vilcabamba was "practically impassable, and the difficulties so great as to leave no hope of reaching it unless one had the wings of a bird."

The expedition's difficulties began almost at once. The four-wheel-drive truck that was to have carried supplies for the first half day soon bogged down in the mud. By the time the load had been shifted to the mules, the group was well behind schedule. To make camp that night, the trekkers had to walk in darkness for several hours, groping their way up steep, slippery trails. Altitude and dehydration took their toll; one burly trekker, on a weightlifter's diet that consisted entirely of tuna fish, had to be carried the final stretch by mule, with a wrangler on either side propping him up. The friars had described the way to Vilcabamba as "a terribly . . . tiresome journey." By this measure, at least, the expedition was clearly off on the right foot.

On previous hikes in the area, Ziegler and Walker had seen, from several miles away, a faint wrinkle in the landscape, a crease leading up to a 15,000-foot pass in the general direction of Choquiquirao. They suspected it might be a section of an old Incan highway running between Vitcos and Choquiquirao, which would be strong evidence for Ziegler's Vilcabamba theory. Bushwhacking toward the faint crease, the group found an overgrown cobblestone road leading up and over the pass. His suspicions confirmed, Ziegler now believed more than ever that he might be on to something.

Going down the other side of the pass, into a broad, glacier-sculpted valley overhung with granite pinnacles, the trekkers sloshed through a long swampy stretch before reaching the second night's camp. The friars, in their chronicles, had described passing through a section of waist-deep water, where they slipped and fell repeatedly before finally emerging chilled and muddy. Once again, Ziegler seemed to be on the right track, for "chilled and muddy" was a pretty good description of the trekkers as they bedded down below the glaciers of Nevada Pumasillo, a 19,980-foot peak whose name means "Claw of the Puma."

For the next three days, the group struggled up and over two more steep forested ridges, uncovering Inca roads so densely overgrown at times that an advance team of Indian scouts had to be sent ahead to hack the way clear with machetes. As they neared Chiquiquirao, the expedition came upon a large, previously undocumented ruin of what apparently had been an agricultural town, with terraced fields, irrigation canals, and a number of small houses. The friars had reported just such a place on the outskirts of Vilcabamba, and in fact had stayed there during their visit. (The wary Incas, considering it a blasphemy to allow heathen Catholic sorcerers to see the temples and icons of Vilcabamba, had kept them out of the sacred city itself.)

When the expedition finally reached the central site of Choquiquirao, Ziegler found that it fit perfectly the Incan concept of sacred geography, with its holy mountains and rivers. From one particularly prominent, high, level place among the ruins, a single sweep of the eyes can take in five snow peaks and the mighty Apurímac River, all held in reverent esteem by the Incas. "It's hard to imagine a better site for a shrine," says Ziegler.

To his disappointment, however, he found the stonework at Choquiquirao to be rough and mediocre, much inferior to that at Machu Picchu. If this were indeed the sacred city, why was the stonework so poor? (Hiram Bingham had asked himself the same question nearly a century before, and had eliminated Choquiquirao as a Vilcabamba candidate primarily for that reason.) Ziegler examined the stone closely and found that it was primarily quartzite, a hard, brittle rock that simply cannot be cut into large blocks or carved into fine detail, as can the granite at Machu Picchu.

But poking around one crumbling wall, he found several sections covered by a smooth plaster into which intricate designs had been carved. Had the rough quartzite originally served merely as a base structure, to be covered with plaster and inscribed with decorative artwork worthy of an emperor? Ziegler believes so. If he's right, Bingham's main justification for eliminating Choquiquirao has been skewered.

The expedition remained only two days at Choquiquirao, barely scratching its surface. Although Ziegler's evidence is tantalizing, it is by no means conclusive. In the maddening manner of most scientific and historical inquiry, new questions arise as quickly as the old ones are dispatched. "I'll be back," he says. "The mystery is far from solved."

OUTFITTERS

American Wilderness Experience markets the trek, led by Gary Ziegler and Barry Walker, that retraces the route of their exploratory expedition described above. It includes two days of excavation work at Choquiquirao, during which trekkers dig under Ziegler's supervision.

From Lima, group members fly to Cuzco, then take the train to Machu Picchu. After a day of sightseeing, it's a jeep ride up a dirt road, then a hike to the Incan ruins at Vitcos. From there, the ten-day trek retraces the route Ziegler believes was followed by the two Spanish friars who, in the 1560s, traveled from Vitcos to Vilcabamba, the secret last stronghold of the Incan emperors.

The trek route follows trails and ancient Incan highways over Choquiticarpo Pass, to Colamachay, Yanama, San Juan Pass, and finally to Choquiquirao. After two days at the site, the group descends to the Apurímac River, and then by bus to Cuzco for the flight back to Lima. AWE offers a shorter, easier version of the trek to Choquiquirao for those who don't wish to retrace the original route of the friars.

Wilderness Travel gets to Choquiquirao by a different route, but trekkers hit many of the same spots. In addition to Choquiquirao, Vitcos, Yanama, and a post-trek visit to Machu Pic-chu, Wilderness Travel's trek includes a visit to the ruins at Puncuyoc, known for their highly ceremonial architecture.

WHAT TO EXPECT

This is a physically demanding trek. The route crosses several steep ridges, and there are two days that include ascents of 4,000 and 5,000 feet, plus two days with 6,000-foot descents. Some of the route requires bushwhacking with machetes. (The trek staff does most of the hacking, but you can help if you want to.) Where trails do exist, they are often muddy and slip-pery and demand a modicum of surefootedness. Altitude ranges from 4,000 to 15,000 feet.

Horses are available to ride if the going gets too tough. But of course that opens up all sorts of new possibilities for pain; if you have not ridden recently, your first two hours on a horse will leave a very distinct impression on your backside.

The weather in upland Peru is very changeable and can lead to great misery if you're not prepared. Temperature changes of as much as 60 degrees are possible on some days, and drench-ing rains are commonplace. At the end of the trek, there's a thrilling (or scary, depending on your point of view) ride across the Apurímac River in a cable-supported two-person basket.

Ziegler schedules his trek in October. Wilderness Travel has two departures a year, in June and August. Both trips begin in Lima.

RECOMMENDED READING

Lost Cities of the Incas by Hiram Bingham. The pioneering explorer's account of his discovery and excavation of Machu Picchu.

IN BRIEF

American Wilderness Experience, 800-444-0099: 18 days,
    $2,685. This trek may also be booked through Wildland
    Adventures, 800-345-4453.
Wilderness Travel, 800-368-2794: 21 days, $3,095

Physical challenge, 3; Mental challenge, 4; Skills, 1.

VENEZUELA
living with the
fierce people

Visitors to the Yanomamo Indians, the isolated tribesmen who inhabit the tropical upper reaches of the Orinoco River basin, invariably return with astonishing observations of ritualistic violence, sorcery, even mild forms of cannibalism. Bolder adventurers do more than just watch; on occasion they join the Yanomamo to eat tarantulas, trek naked through the jungle, snort hallucinogens, hunt caimans, and sleep elbow-to-elbow in the huge, smoky, raucous common village living quarters called *shabonos*. It all makes for great stories to tell the folks back home.

Herewith, selections from the Yanomamo tales.

Tales of Testosterone

The Yanomamo are renowned for their personal ferocity and warlike culture. One-on-one duels by fist, club, and spear typically result in only moderate injuries, but these highly orchestrated rituals sometimes escalate into all-out wars between villages, often with fatal results. Some years ago, an American anthropologist counted twenty-five raids on one village in fifteen months. He estimates that a quarter of Yanomamo males die violently.

What's all the fighting about? Basically, women. One anthropological theory primly ascribes the Yanomamo's penchant for violence to a protein deficiency, positing that they fight each other to protect hunting territories and hold down their population in a world of limited food supply. But if you ask the Yanomamo themselves, they laugh at the protein theory. "We do like meat," they told one researcher, "but we like women a whole lot more."

Indeed, most one-on-one conflicts among Yanomamo men arise from marital infidelity, suspected marital infidelity, or failure to deliver a promised wife to a suitor. Woman-abduction raids on nearby villages are commonplace, and even during raids launched for other purposes—to avenge a previous abduction, say, or to steal food—Yanomamo men make off with the enemy's women at every opportunity, viewing them as their rightful war booty.

Although the Yanomamo may occasionally allow a ritualistic chest-beating or club-fighting duel to play out in front of outsiders, real Yanomamo warfare is rarely glimpsed. Yet even on their best behavior for tourists, the Yanomamo are by no means Mr. Nice Guys; there is no toadying to the gringos in order to sell trinkets. "The first tribe we visited was pretty hostile," recalls Gary Richter, a forty-year-old California physicist on a trip organized by the American outfitter Turtle Tours. "They more or less drove us out of the village.

"When we first showed up, most of them stared at us very aggressively, very hostile and cold," says Richter. "They obviously didn't want us there. We went out hunting with a few of the friendlier guys, and as we were heading back toward the village, this weird howling started in the distance, like nothing I'd ever heard before. I couldn't imagine what sort of animals were making such a noise.

"But as we approached the village, I realized it was people. I mean there were a hundred guys howling like dogs in the center of the village. They'd gotten hopped up on yoppo, a hallucinogenic powder they snort, and started painting themselves and brandishing their weapons and giving us really mean looks. It was very scary. Our guide said we'd better get the hell out of there fast, so we grabbed our stuff and left.

"The second village we went to, things eventually warmed up. That's the way it is when you visit the Yanomamo. At first they're fairly hostile, but once they accept you, you're like a member of the family. You never quite know which way it's gonna go. You have to feel them out."

Richter's group spent several days living at the second village, eating and sleeping with the villagers. "It's about two A.M. and we're hanging there in our hammocks in the *shabono,* stacked up like cordwood, elbow-to-elbow with Yanomamo in all directions—let me tell you, you make any body noises and the whole village knows it—and all of a sudden some guy just starts screaming. I woke up with a start, and I figured that another village was attacking us. But it was just one of the villagers ranting and raving at another.

"Our translator later told us he was shouting something like, 'You goddamn son of a bitch, I saw you down by the river with my wife this morning. What's the matter, isn't your wife pretty enough? You've shamed yourself and the whole village!'

"Then the other guy started screaming back, something like, 'You blind old fool, that wasn't me, that must have been somebody else. What would I want with an old hag like your wife?' This went on for about an hour until the first guy finally petered out. And that was the end of it. The next morning, all was forgiven. It's their social system for resolving conflicts before they get fatal."

The Tale of the Taboo

Among the Yanomamo, it is considered disrespectful to say each other's names out loud, particularly the names of adult males and deceased relatives and friends. This name taboo proved to be a serious roadblock for American anthropologist Napoleon A. Chagron, who was attempting to construct a detailed genealogy of a Yanomamo village. Well aware of the taboo, he worked hard to earn the villagers' trust, and was eventually able to persuade a few of them to whisper to him, in private, the names and relationships of family and neighbors. Chagron put five months of painstaking work into constructing the genealogy, which would serve as the groundwork for the years of further study of the Yanomamo he planned.

But then one day, in a neighboring village, he was chatting with a group of Yanomamo and happened to mention the name of the headman's wife in the village he was studying. There was a stunned silence, followed by an explosion of hysterical gasping, choking, howling laughter. It seemed that the name he had been given for the headman's wife translated as "Hairy Cunt." Other villagers on his genealogy chart, he soon learned, were listed as "Fart Breath," "Eagle Shit" and—this was years before Clarence Thomas—"Long Dong." The villagers whose trust he'd worked so hard to earn had in fact perpetrated a stupendous hoax on him while maintaining the sanctity of their real names.

Tales of Yoppo

There's one story of personal interaction with the Yanomamo that doesn't always get told back home, a story that, when related for publication by one participant, began, "Well, I'd really appreciate it if you didn't use my name. People at the office might get the wrong impression about me." (It's not just the

Yanomamo who have name taboos, it seems.) We'll call our correspondent Melvin R. Crudley.

Crudley's tale concerns yoppo, the greenish hallucinogenic snuff powder that the Yanomamo grind up from the beanlike seeds of the hisiomo tree. Every afternoon, Yanomamo men paint themselves up, don feathers, and blow the powder into each other's nostrils through 2-foot-long tubes. According to Chagron, "the recipient grimaces, chokes, groans, coughs, gasps, and usually rubs his head excitedly as he duck-waddles off," his nostrils dangling long strands of green snot. The effect of yoppo on the inhibitions is no less remarkable than on the mucous membranes; when Chagron tried yoppo himself, he pranced about ecstatically, sang at the top of his lungs, and gave the finger to the local Catholic missionary.

"I'd read about yoppo," says Crudley, a participant in another Turtle trip, "and I figured if the opportunity presented itself, I'd give it a shot. I'll pretty much try anything once; I was a skydiver in my younger days, and I've always enjoyed dancing on the edge. Anyway, we were watching some of the Yanomamo men load up their blowpipes one afternoon, and I asked if I could join in, and they said no problem.

"So they sat me down, and one of them held me from behind. Through the interpreter, he told me that it would hurt a lot at first, but that I shouldn't panic. So they loaded the powder into this long tube, stuck one end of the tube up my nose, and one of the Yanomamo blew into the other end—not a quick hard puff, but a steady blast for quite a long time.

"Well, the first thing that happened was my brain caught on fire. There was serious, big-time pain. Then the mucus came flying out of my nose so fast that I felt like I was going to choke to death. There was more mucus coming out of me than I could have ever imagined was in my body. It was much worse than tear gas. I stood up and reeled around, trying to wipe off all this green gobby stuff that's pouring out of me. Then they sat me down and blew some more into the other nostril. Same effect."

Once the initial burst subsided, strange things began to happen. Says Crudley, "I'm not some sort of old hippie who can compare yoppo to other drugs. But I had this notion that it would be hallucinogenic, and that I'd be seeing things, colorful visions, like the Yanomamo shamans do. But it wasn't like that at all. After about twenty minutes, once the initial jolt had subsided, I started getting the strangest feelings. At one point, I had a distinct impression that my arms were not mine, and that they were extraordinarily hairy. I remember looking down at them, and rationally I knew that these were my arms, but I was flooded with the bizarre feeling that somehow I was wearing the arms of an ape.

"The next day, I decided to try yoppo again. This time I didn't have any of the weird feeling that my arms weren't mine, or anything like that. In fact, after the initial pain, I felt fine, very mellow, and lay down in my hammock.

"And then I began to feel extraordinarily good. This is very hard to explain, but do you know how sometimes your stomach feels queasy for a long time, and then finally you throw up, and afterward you feel terrific? Well, try to imagine if you were born with your stomach feeling queasy, and it stays queasy your whole life, and finally when you're thirty years old you throw up for the first time, and you never realized that it was possible for your stomach to feel that good.

"Well, the yoppo made me feel like I'd thrown up my brain, because all my life I had never realized it was possible to feel this good. It was a very powerful feeling. My brain had been sick all my life, and I'd finally purged it. That night I slept like a log and woke up feeling more refreshed and alive than I've ever felt. It was just amazing. I can certainly understand why the Yanomamo snort this stuff every day."

OUTFITTER

Irma Turtle, proprietress of *Turtle Tours,* has a personal fascination with so-called primitive cultures, and structures all of her trips to focus on them. Her Yanomamo trip begins in Caracas and proceeds by bush plane to Puerto Ayacucho, capital of the Venezuelan territory of Amazonas. From there it's another bush plane to the Yekwana Indian village of Culebra, on the Cunucunuma River. (The Yekwana are slightly more modernized neighbors of the Yanomamo.) After an overnight stay, you'll proceed by motorboat down the Cunucunuma to another Yekwana village, Akanana. Next day it's on to the Orinoco River and El Sejal, a Yanomamo village.

For the next five days you'll visit various Yanomamo villages along the Orinoco and Casiquiare Rivers, sleeping in hammocks in *shabonos,* the common living quarters, and joining the Yanomamo in their daily activities. (The itinerary is somewhat loose during this period, depending on how the Yanomamo are feeling about outsiders, and whether they are in the process of going on *wayumi,* a free-form hunting/gathering trek in which the entire village picks up and leaves for two or three months.) The trip concludes with two semiluxurious days on a guest ranch in the llanos, the plains region of southern Venezuela.

Turtle also offers a quickie eight-day version of the trip, with five days and four nights in various Yanomamo villages.

WHAT TO EXPECT

This is primarily a tour, not a trek. You'll be riding in small motorboats and will be required to do nothing more physical than take short walks in and around villages. But hard-core jocks may get a chance to flex their muscles and aerobic systems; one very fit trip participant reports total exhaustion after trying to keep up with a band of Yanomamo men on a dawn-to-dusk hunting party.

People with back problems may have trouble sleeping in hammocks; in that case, purchase an aluminum cot upon arrival in Venezuela.

A combination of the jungle environment and culture shock make this trip an invigorating challenge to the typical American psyche. The humidity is brutal, although most people are surprised that the jungle is not as oppressively hot as they expect; usual daytime temperatures are in the 80s and 90s. No-see-um bugs leave welts that last a week. Your only baths will be in the rivers. Your clothes will stink after a while. You'll sleep in hammocks in crowded, smoky, noisy Yanomamo sleeping quarters. (Privacy lovers have the option of sleeping outside in hammocks or on cots.) Your group will have its own Western-style food and cook, although you may partake of the Yanomamo staples of plantain and manioc if you wish.

Although the villagers are usually friendly once they get to know you a bit, they may be hostile at first, and may not fit your preconceived notions of idyllic, noble savages. Pacifists will deplore the violence. Feminists—and almost everyone else, for that matter—may be offended by the blatant subjugation, and occasional beating, of women in Yanomamo culture. (A Yanomamo woman was once overheard saying to a friend, "You have so many scars on your head; your husband must really love you.") Animal lovers will be offended by the Yanomamo's politically incorrect hunting and fishing methods. In short, this is a trip for flexible, open-minded people who do not rush to make value judgments on other people and cultures.

Trips run from November through March, the dry season. The staging city is Caracas.

RECOMMENDED READING

In Trouble Again by Redmond O'Hanlon. A hilarious account of a three-month expedition into Yanomamo country by an overweight British literary critic and his lazy, whining companion.

Yanomamo: The Fierce People by Napoleon A. Chagron. An anthropological case study, for the most part in layman's language, by a man who spent forty-two months living with the Yanomamo.

IN BRIEF

Turtle Tours, 602-488-3688: 14 days, $3,450

Physical challenge, 1; Mental challenge, 3; Skills, 1.

EUROPE
& THE
MIDDLE EAST

ENGLAND

walking coast

to coast

In 1972, a sixty-five-year-old retired accountant from Cumbria, Alfred Wainwright, undertook what he called "a harmless and enjoyable walk across England." Starting in St. Bees, a coastal town 40 miles south of the Scottish border, he dipped his boots in the Irish Sea, then set off on foot eastward through the Lake District, the Yorkshire Dales, and the North York Moors. Taking care to "commit no offense against privacy nor trample on the sensitive corns of landowners and tenants," he stuck to remote, high-ridge trails wherever possible and slept in hostels and village inns along the way. After 190 miles and a leisurely month of walking, he eventually arrived at Robin Hood's Bay on the North Sea, a resort town where he was delighted to find "ice cream, girls, and all that."

Wainwright subsequently published a small guidebook, hand-lettered and decorated with exquisitely detailed pen-and-ink drawings, and dedicated it to "the second person, unidentifiable as yet, to walk from St. Bees Head to Robin Hood's Bay." His intuition was spot on; Wainwright's coast-to coast walk has become a classic, undertaken by hundreds of hardy pilgrims each year.

A lifelong outdoor enthusiast, Wainwright had an unerring sense of what makes a good long-distance walk. "One should always have a definite objective, in a walk as in life—it is so much more satisfying to reach a target by personal effort than to wander aimlessly," he wrote. Toss in England's best scenery (mountains, lakes, dales, and moors), history (prehistoric ruins, medieval towns, and churches), physical challenge (climbs to numerous peaks), and respite (cozy pubs and inns with fireplaces) and one has the recipe for a superb route. Perhaps Wainwright can be forgiven his smug dismissal of the Pennine Way, the celebrated long-distance walkway that briefly intersects his route: "Spare a smile of pity for any poor wretches you see traveling thereon," he advises his pilgrims. "Your own route is so much better."

The walker starting out in Wainwright's footsteps from St. Bees may be forgiven for having a few initial doubts. Shortly after leaving behind the 300-foot sea cliffs of St. Bees Head, one immediately encounters a massive chemical plant. Resisting the temptation for environmental hand-wringing, Wainwright observes, "These works have added nothing of amenity or scenic values to the landscape. . . . But man must live, somehow—and here he has. . . ." A bit farther along the route, the walker is further insulted with a barbed-wire fence across his path, for which Wainwright offers this advice: "Place a coat or jacket across the top strand and stride over. Better a torn garment than impaled testicles or what have you."

Genitals intact, the hiker may look forward to immediate relief from this inauspicious start, for a mere 10 miles ahead lies England's scenic heart, the Lake District. For the next four days, the coast-to-coast walker will wander eastward through Lakeland's innumerable fells (defined as "an upland pasture, moor, or thicket; a highland plateau") not to mention its becks, tarns, scars, pikes, gills, riggs, pots, and nabs.

Nannycatch "a shyly hidden ravine" east of the village of Cleator, is merely the first of dozens of odd place-names along Wainwright's route. These richly idiosyncratic appellations are irresistibly charming to Americans, accustomed as we are to the pallid likes of "Rolling Sunny Hills Whispering Vista Estates." The geographical index in Wainwright's book includes such entries as Scugdale Beck, Jingling Pot, Puttering Holes, Nun Cote Nook, Crinkle Carr, Crackpot Hall, Flincher Gill, and Boggle Hole. He apologetically notes, "There is one inadvertent omission from the index, but this is of no importance, it being extremely unlikely that any reader will wish to refer to Great Tongue on page 31."

In the Lake District, the Wainwright pilgrim will walk the shores of Angle Tarn, described as "a dark and sinister sheet of water . . . often frequented by naked bathers." He'll pass by Ullswater, whose daffodil-lined banks were an inspiration for Wordsworth, a resident of nearby Grasmere. Along a smooth ridge called High Street, the coast-to-coast walker may tread the highest Roman road in England and tiptoe to the edge of Bleawater Crag, over which a dedicated nineteenth-century foxhunter named Dixon disappeared in pursuit of his prey. The poor fellow, Wainwright tells, "fell hundreds of feet over the escarpment, coming to rest on the scree far below, where he raised himself, pointed in the direction the fox had gone, and shouted excitedly to the horrified onlookers on the cliff-top, 'It's gone o'er theer! It's gone o'er theer!' and then dropped dead of his injuries, a victim of fanatical enthusiasm."

The foxhunting Dixons were apparently an accident-prone clan, for another Dixon fell to his death in 1858 during a chase along Striding Ridge, a narrow 300-yard knife-edge ridge that is perhaps the most exhilarating section of the coast-to-coast route. A small iron monument marks the demise. A second memorial along Striding Ridge, dating from 1890, commemorates the fatal fall of Charles Gogh, out for a walk with his dog. His body was not found for three months, during which time the faithful dog stood guard by the side of his dead master. The incident inspired both Wordsworth and Scott to write poems, but as Wainwright notes, they dwelled "more on the fidelity of the dog than on poor Gogh." Despite the grisly monuments, coast-to-coast walkers should have no fear of the scramble along Striding Edge; thousands of tourists traverse it every year without mishap, at times in such masses that queuing up is necessary.

Once past the rough, craggy Lake District, the walker will encounter the softer contours of the Yorkshire Dales, known to many Americans as the setting for James Herriot's *All Creatures Great and Small.* The bedrock in these parts is limestone, which makes for easy walking on smooth rock and velvety turf. A high point of the Yorkshire Dales—both literally and figuratively— is the Nine Standards, a series of house-high rock cairns atop a broad, smooth summit. In addition to commanding perhaps the most extensive and interesting viewpoint along the coast-to-coast route, the Nine Standards also mark the Pennine Watershed, the dividing line where rainfall flows either westward to the Irish Sea or east to the North Sea. (Male walkers are respectfully requested to refrain from straddling the line and ceremonially urinating from side to side.)

Oddly, in a region that has been well populated for more than a thousand years and prides itself in its history, no one seems to know who built the Nine Standards, or when, or why. Archaeological mystery is in the air here; near the village of Kirkby Stephen lie a series of very old earthen mounds known locally as the Giants' Graves. Five yards wide and 15 yards long, their origin and function also remain unknown. Learned authorities theorize that the mounds were either warrens to facilitate the breeding and capture of rabbits, or platforms for stacking bracken.

Walkers may well be puzzled by two graves in this area. A loose pile of rocks marks a place called Robin Hood's Grave, which, Wainwright explains cryptically, "is not the grave of Robin Hood." A bit farther down the trail, in the village of Bolton-on-Swale, are the remains of one Henry Jenkins, whose gravestone declares that he was born in 1500 and died in 1670. "A remarkable achievement," observes Wainwright.

East of the Yorkshire Dales is the only dull stretch of the route, a farming region of unimaginative terrain. ("Those who believe the earth is flat will be mightily encouraged on this section," notes Wainwright.) Moreover, the way is blocked by barbed wire, dykes, too-friendly bovines, and other obstacles. Consequently, the walker has little choice but to ignominiously take to the roads. Danby Wiske, the only village of this section, "is less attractive than its name. You might, with luck, get a bag of crisps at the inn, but certainly not a meal or a sandwich. You are tired and hungry and nobody wants to know."

But the walker's reward for his persistence lies just ahead: the North York Moors, a vast bleak plateau of rippling heather that has far-reaching views. When the fog rolls in, however, there is only grayness and the sound of squishing boots and wind. Fog-bound moor-walkers are well advised to step lively and not dwell on Doyle's fictional man-eating moor-roaming hound, nor on the grisly real-life "moors murders" that shocked England in 1965. (For the sake of the walkers' peace of mind, we shall not elaborate on them here.) You'll see no one out here; villages are sparse and unattuned to cross-country walkers. Wainwright warns that the inhabitants "are not unlikely to suspect, if you ask for a bed, that you are suggesting a sexual adventure, which, of course, is ridiculous (or is it?)"

The desolate gloom of the moorlands is not without its bright spots, however. A notice affixed to a gate near Beacon Hill reads: "Be ye man or be ye woman, Be ye going or be ye comin', Be ye soon or be ye late, Be ye sure to shut this gate."

And then there is the Lion Inn, dating from 1553 and reached only after an arduous day's walk across Urra, Farndale, and High Blakey Moors. The first human habitation for 16 miles, its fireplace has been a beacon of hope for a generation of Wainwright's cross-country walkers.

Suddenly, you are almost there. Across Danby High Moor, past the monuments to Old Ralph, Young Ralph, and Fat Betty, along river and woodland, you climb the burial mound at Flat Howe and catch your first glimpse of the North Sea, 5 miles distant. Try not to hurry past a splendid waterfall, Falling Foss, and resist the temptation to take the shortcut along the road directly to Robin Hood's Bay. Instead, proceed north to Maw Wyke Hole and then promenade gloriously along the sea cliffs in a proper entrance to Robin Hood's Bay. Following Wainwright's advice, "proceed with decorum to the bottom of the hill, to the limit of terra firma, where the tarmac ends at a shingly beach and the sea. Go forward and put your boot in the first salt-water puddle."

"Now you can rest on your laurels in the Bay Hotel with a pint (but let there be no mistake about this) you do so at your own expense. It's no use saying 'Charge it to Wainwright.'. . . No, sonny, that game won't work here. Pay for your own. I'm skint."

OUTFITTERS

Sherpa Expeditions, a British outfitter, offers a no-frills trip for purists who wish to cover every step of Wainwright's 190-mile route across England. The fifteen-day trip begins in St. Bees and ends in Robin Hood's Bay, with no rest days or side excursions. Except for breakfasts, the $1,675 price does not include meals.

A self-guided option, which may be taken any time, includes all accommodations, breakfasts, and luggage transfers but dispenses with the leader. In his place, you'll be given detailed route instructions and maps.

Sierra Club Outings generally follows Wainwright's route, but skips several sections due to logistical demands and to reduce daily mileage. The trip starts in St. Bees, and ends in York, with a rest day in Richmond. Total walking distance is 97 miles. In some cases, accommodations are distant from the starting and finishing points of each day's walk, requiring mini-van transfers.

Wilderness Travel's itinerary, although it skips some sections of Wainwright's route, covers 126 miles, a third more than the Sierra Club route. There is one rest day, during which you'll make a side excursion to Durham, and a day of touring in York after completion of the walk. The price also includes airport transfers to and from Manchester. For accommodation, WT uses the base-camp approach, staying for several nights each at inns in Kirkby Stephen, Keswick, and Pickering and minibusing walkers to and from the trailheads each day. Price does not include lunches.

WHAT TO EXPECT

The physical demands depend on the outfitter. Sherpa's trip averages a grueling 14.5 miles a day, with two flat days over 20 miles and no rest days. (Walkers always have the option, however, of skipping a day and riding in the van with the luggage to the day's destination.) Rate it a 3 on the physical-challenge scale. Wilderness Travel's itinerary averages 10.5 miles a day, with a maximum daily mileage of 13. Call it a 2 plus. Sierra Club averages a modest 9 miles a day, with only one day more than 10 miles. Call it a 2.

In all cases, there will be a number of days with a good bit of up and down, and elevation gains of up to 2,000 feet. Luggage is transferred by van, so walkers need only carry light day packs with snacks, rain gear, and camera.

Accommodations are in comfortable and often quaintly charming inns or bed-and-breakfasts. Wilderness Travel's choices tend to be the most upscale, followed closely by Sierra Club's and not so closely by Sherpa's. Sherpa does not stint on the quaintness, however; a number of its accommodations date to the seventeenth century and beyond.

Weather can be soggy; your enjoyment of the trip should not depend on blue skies. On the Sherpa trip, the unrelenting 15-mile days may be mentally taxing. Pick another trip if you're the stop-and-smell-the-roses type.

Trips run May through August.

RECOMMENDED READING

A Coast-to-Coast Walk by Alfred Wainwright. The sacred text itself, hand-lettered, with the author's maps and illustrations.

IN BRIEF

Sherpa Expeditions, 011-44-181-569-4101: 15 days, $1,650/$1,395. This trip may also be booked in the United States through Himalayan Travel, 800-225-2380.
Sierra Club Outings, 415-923-5588: 14 days, $2,770
Wilderness Travel, 800-368-2794: 16 days, $2,350

Physical challenge, 2–3; Mental challenge, 1; Skills, 1.

FRANCE

hiking in the cevennes

In 1878, Robert Louis Stevenson captured the ethos of adventure travel about as well as anyone ever has: "I travel not to go anywhere, but to go," he wrote in *Travels with a Donkey in the Cevennes*. "I travel for travel's sake. The great affair is to move; to come down off this featherbed of civilization and find the globe granite underfoot and strewn with cutting flints. . . . To hold a pack upon a pack saddle against a gale out of the freezing north is no high industry, but it is one that serves to occupy and compose the mind. And when the present is so exacting, who can annoy himself about the future?"

Stevenson, then twenty-seven years old, spent twelve days walking with his pack donkey, Modestine, 120 miles through the compact rugged mountains of the Cevennes, now part of France's largest national park. The book became a minor classic and over the years has inspired a number of people to retrace his footsteps. Sherpa Expeditions, a British trekking company, offers a ten-day walk along the Stevenson Trail, which includes overnights in most of the villages where RLS himself stayed. But no donkey. Admits Sherpa's brochure, "We

have taken the liberty of replacing Modestine with less trouble-
some methods of baggage handling."

That's a pity, for *Equus asinus* is in fact the most felicitous
means yet devised for the transport of a long-distance walker's
accoutrement. I say this with the authority of one who has, on
three occasions, spent a week in the wilderness with an aging
New Mexican burro named Jesus, a placid, reliable, and en-
dearing beast of burden who belongs to my sister. Carrying
without complaint 120 pounds of food and camping gear,
Jesus made us the envy of every sweating backpacker we met
along the trail. While they grunted under 60-pound loads, we
breezed with 10 pounds on our backs. While they, obsessed
with weight-saving, consumed freeze-dried space food, we ate
porterhouse steak. They drank iodine-treated water, we drank
beer. They lacked a warm snuffling velvet muzzle to stroke each
night around the campfire. We didn't.

Stevenson recognized the charms of the donkey at once.
Dismissing the horse as an "uncertain and exacting ally [which]
adds thirty-fold to the troubles of the voyager," he sought instead "something cheap and small and handy, and of a stolid
and peaceful temper." In the marketplace of the village of
Monastier, Stevenson, with the help of a crowd of kibitzing locals, bought Modestine, a "diminutive she-ass, not much bigger than a dog, the colour of a mouse, with a kindly eye and a
determined underjaw." Her price was 65 francs and a glass of
brandy—less than the cost of Stevenson's sleeping bag, which
had set him back 80 francs and two glasses of beer. (The relative value of donkey and sleeping bag, incidentally, seems to
have changed little in the intervening century. According to the
American Donkey and Mule Society, a "run-of-the-mill back-
pasture jack" goes for about $150 these days, while a Marmot
Sawtooth goose-down trekking bag rated to 25 degrees F.—
about what Stevenson would have needed for his fall walk—is
today priced at $200.)

Stevenson, a very green donkey driver, got off to an "uncouth beginning" with Modestine. For a man to whom the great affair is to move, the donkey's initial pace was excruciatingly slow, "as much slower than a walk as a walk is slower than a run; it kept me hanging on each foot for an incredible length of time; in five minutes it exhausted the spirit and set up a fever in all the muscles of the leg. . . . Of all conceivable journeys, this promised to be the most tedious."

The tedium was soon interrupted when, due to an insufficiently tightened pack saddle and a poorly balanced load, Stevenson's belongings took an ugly slew to one side and rotated around Modestine's belly to the ground, where they scattered across the road. The scenario was repeated a number of times that first day, to the great amusement of passersby. "I think I never heard of one in as mean a situation," Stevenson lamented of his despicable fix.

In the auberge the first night out, however, Stevenson found salvation. "Blessed be the man who invented goads! Blessed be the innkeeper of Bouchet St. Nicholas, who introduced me to their use!" he exulted. "This plain wand, with an eighth of an inch of pin, was indeed a sceptre when he put it in my hands. Thenceforward Modestine was my slave. A prick and she passed the most inviting stable door. A prick, and she broke forth into a gallant little trotlet that devoured the miles." Like almost everyone who lays his load on a donkey's back, Stevenson eventually developed a deep affection for the animal. Upon her sale at the end of the journey, he actually cried. "She was patient, elegant in form . . . ," he wrote fondly. "Her faults were those of her race and sex; her virtues were her own."

Stevenson found the local people along his route friendly and hospitable for the most part. "The people of the inn, in nine cases out of ten, show themselves kindly and considerate," he noted. That ratio seems to have held up over the years; by all reports the present-day residents of the Cevennes—some of them descendants of hosts to Stevenson himself—take kindly to strangers. But do not expect fawning obsequience; the farmers and villagers retain the fierce independence that has made the Cevennes a hotbed of resistance to authority for centuries. It was in the village of Pont de Montvert, near the end of Stevenson's route, that the Camisard rebellion, a revolt of Protestant zealots against the persecution of Louis XIV, broke out in 1702. Fifty-two Camisards stole into town under cover of night and set fire to the house of the Abbot Chayla, the despised chief inquisitor, who was well known to take pleasure in closing the hands of Protestants around red-hot coals and plucking one by one the hairs of their beards in hopes that they would be persuaded of the error of their beliefs.

Chayla, his leg broken during a desperate leap from the flaming second floor, was dragged to the public square. Each Camisard stepped forward in turn, shouted his personal grievance ("This is for my father, broken on your wheel! This is for my sister, imprisoned in your convents!") and plunged a dagger into Chayla. When the body had accumulated precisely fifty-two stab wounds, the Camisards kneeled and sang psalms till dawn, then fled back into the mountains.

Like its inhabitants, the scenery of the Cevennes has mellowed with time. Stevenson called the stretch between Cheylard and Luc, which had been cleared and heavily overgrazed, "one of the most beggarly countries in the world. It was like the worst of the Scottish Highlands, only worse; cold, naked, and ignoble, scant of wood, scant of heather, scant of life. . . .Why anyone should desire to visit either Luc or Cheylard is more than my much-inventing spirit can suppose." Today, however, thanks to a declining population and efforts by nineteenth-century conservationists, the forests have come back in many places. And, as the modern world has accelerated around them, Luc and Cheylard have taken on the charm of the outdated.

The scenery along the second half of the route, from Mont Lozère south to St. Jean du Gard, drew Stevenson's praise, as it does that of modern visitors. The 5,574-foot Pic de Finiels commands a view of all lower Langeudoc to the Mediterranean Sea, 65 miles away. Below it the river Tarn tumbles through a 300-foot-deep limestone gorge, the Grand Canyon of France. Stevenson found the Tarn Valley so beautiful that, attempting to sketch the scene, he laid down his pencil in despair. He was particularly taken with the ancient chestnut trees along the river. "To see a clan of old unconquerable chestnuts cluster like herded elephants . . . is to rise to the higher thoughts of the powers that are in Nature." The trees remain today, reduced somewhat in number but not at all in grandeur.

Stevenson, educated a Presbyterian but a self-described "heretic" deeply skeptical of organized religion, spent one night at what for him was a "strange destination": a Trappist monastery called Our Lady of the Snows. With a white statue of the Virgin Mary pointing the way, Stevenson approached the monastery, "driving my secular donkey before me, creaking in my secular boots and gaiters, towards the asylum of silence. . . . I have rarely approached anything with more unaffected terror . . . suddenly, on turning a corner, fear took hold of me from head to foot—slavish, superstitious fear." To Stevenson's surprise, however, he had a pleasant stay at Our Lady of the Snows, and even came to admire the monks' spare and regimented way of life. Nevertheless, Stevenson "blessed God that he was free to wander, free to hope, free to love."

Our Lady of the Snows still provides simple lodging for travelers willing to maintain silence within its walls. But do not expect calm outside; during the summer buses disgorge thousands of tourists each day to buy the monastery's wine, cheese, and honey. Yes, the contemporary wanderer along the Stevenson Trail must make certain concessions to the modern world.

But submitting to the luggage van is not necessarily one of them. "Well, yes, I suppose one could bring along one's own donkey," says a spokesman for Sherpa Expeditions when pressed on the matter. "That might be quite a bit of fun, actually."

OUTFITTERS

Alternative Travel Group, an upscale British hiking outfitter, lives up to its name on its eight-day walk through the Cevennes: It avoids the Stevenson Trail altogether. Instead the Alternative itinerary covers "everything that eluded Stevenson during his Travels with a Donkey." Alternative not only refuses to apologize for this omission but in fact brags about it: "Stevenson and his long-suffering donkey . . . might have envied our journey. . . . He should have come to the area we visit!"

Brochure hype notwithstanding, the Alternative itinerary lies to the southwest of the Stevenson Trail. The walking route begins in Pont d'Herault and heads northwest through L'Esperou, Meyrueis, and LeRozier, before turning south and finishing up in Millau. The terrain is high forested hills and open rolling plateaus and meadows, interspersed with the deep gorges of the Tarn and La Jonte. Hikers also visit several famous caves, including Aven Armand and Grottes des Demoiselles.

Sherpa Expeditions, another British company, calls its Cevennes trip "In Stevenson's Footsteps" and follows RLS's route as closely as possible. Start point is Monastier and the finish is St. Jean du Gard, with overnight stops in Le Bourg, Pradelles, La Bastide, Le Bleymard, Le Pont de Montvert, Florac, and St. Germain de Calberte. The route includes a climb to Pic de Finiels, highest point in the Cevennes.

A private self-guided trip, which can be taken any time by any number of people, costs $1,375. The price includes hotels, meals except lunch, baggage transfers, and detailed maps with trail instructions.

WHAT TO EXPECT

Both itineraries are fairly tough by the standards of European walking tours, which typically average 10 miles a day or less. Alternative's daily average is 13 miles, with a maximum of 19. Total distance covered is 64 miles. (One 10-mile day is optional.)

Sherpa's more difficult itinerary averages 15 miles a day, with one 22-miler. Total distance covered is 119 miles. The footsore or faint of heart may hitch a ride with the luggage van, of course, but that means missing an entire day; the van goes straight to the day's destination.

Both trips have significant ups and downs, with maximum altitudes of 5,000-plus feet.

Before the start of his journey in the Cevennes, Robert Louis Stevenson was warned by locals that he would be subject to "many ludicrous misadventures, and . . . sudden death in many surprising forms. Cold, wolves, robbers, above all the nocturnal practical joker. . . ." RLS, occasionally camping out, in fact encountered only cold. The modern-day Cevennes walker need not even put up with that; hikers stay each night in full-service hotels and inns, and eat in restaurants.

Alternative's accommodations, which include a couple of châteaus, typically rate three stars in the *Guide Michelin*. Sherpa's accommodations typically rate two stars. (Sherpa, incidentally, opts not to put up its clients at the Our Lady of the Snows Monastery, where Stevenson stayed one night, because it considers the accommodations there too rustic.) In either case the Cevennes hiker need not descend even a millimeter from the featherbed of civilization.

Both trips run from May to September. Alternative walkers start and finish in Montpelier; Sherpa clients show up at Monastier and are on their own again at St. Jean du Gard.

RECOMMENDED READING

Travels with a Donkey in the Cevennes by Robert Louis Stevenson. It would be unthinkable to make this journey without reading the book that inspired it.

IN BRIEF

Alternative Travel Group, 800-527-5997: 8 days, $2,050
Sherpa Expeditions 011-44-181-569-4101: 13 days, $1,595.
    This trip may also be booked in the United States through
    Himalayan Travel, 800-225-2380.

Physical challenge, 3; Mental challenge, 1; Skills, 1.

GREENLAND

sea kayaking the
eastern fjords

The story begins with ice. The east coast of Greenland—the far side, from the North American perspective—is one of the most inaccessible places on earth, hemmed in by the vast Greenland Ice Cap on the interior and, on the ocean side, by drifting pack ice that sweeps incessantly down from the Arctic Ocean. Despite being only 400 miles from Reykjavík, a city of 100,000 with a major international jetport, and despite mild summer temperatures that reach into the 60s, Greenland's 1,200-mile east coast is virtually uninhabited.

But about halfway up the coast, in a band between 70 and 74 degrees latitude, there is a breach in this barrier of ice. On the inland side, mountains rear up and hold back the Greenland Ice Cap from the shoreline. And on the ocean side, during six weeks in July and August the pack ice recedes slightly, leaving what is called a land-break opening—a narrow alleyway of open water along the coastline. In a coincidence of geography for which sea kayakers should get down on their knees and thank God, this temporary oasis of navigable water happens to occur in the heart of the largest system of fjords in the world, where sea canyons wind more than 100 miles inland and cliffs rise straight out of the water for 5,000 feet. "Nothing can be conceived more rugged," wrote the Scottish whaling captain William Scoresby, the first European to behold the East Greenland fjords, in 1822. "Yet nothing I have ever seen equals it in bold grandeur and interesting character."

Olaf Malver, a sandy-haired forty-two-year-old Danish adventurer, came 167 years later. In 1989, he and three friends were the first nonnative kayakers to traverse the East Greenland fjords. (The native Eskimoes, or Inuit, who, after all, invented the kayak, presumably paddled here centuries ago in their craft, carved from driftwood and whale bones and covered with sealskin.) Now, Malver leads kayak enthusiasts into the inner fjords of Scoresby Sound, the southernmost of the region's three major fjord systems. With an awe and enthusiasm reminiscent of William Scoresby, Malver declares flatly, "I have climbed and paddled all over the world, but nothing compares with East Greenland." It is not hard to believe that his words are unsullied by commercial intent.

Kayakers fly in via Twin Otter bush plane from Iceland, leapfrogging the pack ice that has for centuries blocked and bedeviled ships trying to reach the East Greenland coast. Off the right wingtip is the general area where, in 1777, fifty whaling ships were caught and crushed in the ice, leaving five hundred men shipwrecked on floes. Technically free from the command of their captains, the sailors celebrated drunkenly. When the rum gave out, they stayed warm by burning their ships. Most of the men eventually perished, but a few were able to trek across the ice to shore and, with the help of puzzled Inuits, make their way to Danish settlements on the west coast.

Malver's groups begin paddling at Gurreholm, a rarely visited scientific outpost consisting of a cabin and a level spot on the tundra for an airstrip. From there, the paddlers wander for eleven days among the fjords, camping out or sleeping in shacks left by hunters and explorers. (One night, paddlers sleep in bunks erected in 1891 by the Danish explorer C. Ryder, leader of the first party to fully explore Scoresby Sound and to winter there.) The precise paddling route is determined by weather and exploratory whim. And of course, by the ice.

Always there is the ice. It starts in the vast Greenland Ice Cap, five Californias in area, thicker than the Rocky Mountains are tall, a million cubic miles of ice. From it flow ice rivers, glaciers propelled by the pressure of the ice cap at breakneck speeds of up to 10 feet a day. When the glaciers reach the fjords, they break off, or calve, in building-size chunks, with mighty cracks and roars and stupendous splashes that send out long rolling swells. To sit in a kayak in mirror-smooth water in the shadowy depths of a narrow fjord, and to hear a ghostly rumble from somewhere around the corner echoing against the canyon walls, and a few minutes later to feel the water around you silently swell, is to be in the hands of a greater power.

The calved chunks of glacier, once in the water, become icebergs. In Scoresby Sound they tower to a height of 200 feet, with jagged, jumbled, surreal shapes that rival the sawtooth peaks of the Karakoram or the hoodoos of Bryce Canyon. At the waterline, they glow turquoise or green, depending on the light and the color of the sky. Floating serenely like cathedrals in calm water, these icebergs nevertheless have the potential for sudden violence against kayakers. The cathedral may tumble on its head at any moment, for as the underwater portion of the berg slowly melts away in the seawater, the center of buoyancy and gravity gradually shifts. At some point, it may become unstable and, like a delicately balanced boulder given a flick of the finger, tumble to a new equilibrium. (Any kayak that is nearby, of course, may be upended as well.) Tumbled icebergs have smoothly rounded tops, like Henry Moore sculptures, the jagged edges smoothed away by months or years of slow underwater melting. Some icebergs tumble repeatedly, and one can clearly see the previous waterlines etched in their flanks like geological strata gone askew.

Or an iceberg may explode. Melting water seeps into cracks, then freezes, prying apart the berg with enormous pressure. The inevitable shattering makes a report like a rifle shot and sends ice chunks flying. On Malver's 1995 trip, he and his fellow kayakers were sprayed with shrapnel from an exploding berg, fortunately without injury.

Not all the hazards of kayaking in Scoresby Sound are coldly inanimate. Polar bears graze and forage for berries ashore in summer, and hunt their primary food, ring seals, on the pack ice year-round. (The first polar bear den ever documented was found here in 1929.) Unlike grizzly bears, which are mostly vegetarian and attack humans out of fear or for territorial defense, polar bears are true carnivores. They attack humans because we are tasty and nutritious, although probably less so than a ring seal.

With this fact in mind, the expedition is accompanied by Boas Madsen, an Eskimo polar bear hunter from the nearby Inuit village of Ittoqqortoomiit, who carries a loaded rifle at all times. As an additional precaution, each campsite is ringed with a polar-bear alarm system, a 300-foot circle of electrical wire connected to sleeping bag–side beepers, whose activation sends Boas scrambling for his rifle. No polar bear has yet triggered this alarm system, but its effectiveness was inadvertently demonstrated by a bleary-eyed kayaker who left his tent for a midnight bladder evacuation. "For a moment there I thought I was going to die in the wilderness with a bullet in my head and my pants around my ankles," he recalls.

It remains to be seen whether polar bears will be able to outwit the alarm system; they are crafty, patient hunters of legendary resourcefulness. Inuits report watching polar bears push chunks of ice in front of them as cover while stalking seals. According to folklore, a polar bear on the trail of a seal will cover up its black nose with a paw to preserve its all-white camouflage. These behaviors have not been documented by credentialed biologists, but one researcher has reported evidence of tool use by polar bears: a 45-pound chunk of ice used to bash through the roof of a seal's snow lair. And biologists have observed oddly human behavior among polar bears: shading their eyes from the sun with a furry paw, pounding the ice in apparent frustration when a seal slips away after long, patient pursuit.

Chances of a polar bear encounter during the trip are slim, but kayakers are almost certain to see narwhals, the bizarre "unicorns of the sea," horned whales that, like the platypus or giant squid, appear to have been sprung from some fantastic mythical bestiary. No narwhal has ever survived in captivity for more than a few weeks, and the shy creatures do not migrate to warmer waters to breed, so scientists have had little chance to study them. (As the writer Barry Lopez has noted, "We know more about the rings of Saturn than we know about the narwhals.") Biologists hotly debate the evolutionary purpose of the narwhal's spiral stiletto, which may reach lengths of 10 feet. But kayakers on past trips, paddling among small herds of narwhals, have watched them probe loose-packed ice from below, waving their horns about like lances, right in front of the kayaks.

Walruses, although more commonly seen farther north, occasionally wander down to Scoresby Sound. Generally docile and lethargic this time of year, walruses can turn nasty when threatened. Malver describes an encounter with a walrus during his 1989 kayak expedition through the Greenland fjords: "The huge mammal raised its head and looked at us with startled reddish eyes. Suddenly he dove into the water with a thunderous splash, aiming for our midships. . . . We froze in fear and waited for the impact. Like a deadly one-ton meat torpedo with fangs, the walrus slid right beneath the boat, grazing his thick and scarred skin on the bottom of the kayak." Fortunately, the fanged meat-torpedo made only one pass, and the paddlers escaped unharmed.

Kayakers will certainly see musk oxen, for some fifteen thousand of these extravagantly horned and hairy mammals roam Northeast Greenland National Park, whose border transects Scoresby Sound. Contemporaries of the woolly mammoth and saber-toothed tiger, musk oxen are one of very few large mammal species to have survived both the last Ice Age and thousands of years of human predation. Perhaps this is a testament to their peaceful nature and strong instinct to act in the best interests of the herd. Perhaps there's a lesson there for us.

The musk ox's hair can reach 2 feet in length where it hangs down below the animal's chin in a protective skirt. Its fleecelike underfur is eight times warmer than sheep's wool, far superior to the most advanced microfiber synthetic insulations devised by man. The musk ox is so well insulated, in fact, that after a snowfall it may walk around with unmelted snow on its back for days. There is a story of a Greenland explorer who sought refuge from a blizzard in the lee of what he took to be a series of mounds of snow-covered dirt. As he climbed over one of the mounds, it stood up. Welcome to Greenland, land of surprises!

OUTFITTERS

Black Feather, a small Canadian outfitter that specializes in Arctic adventures, offers a slightly different trip than the one described above: nineteen days of paddling in and around King Oscar Fjord and Franz Joseph Fjord, to the north of Scoresby

Sound. The precise kayaking itinerary depends on weather and ice conditions, but will include a number of exploratory day hikes.

Paddlers fly in from Akureyri, Iceland, to the landing strip at Mestersvig in Northeast Greenland National Park. The trip is supported by motorboat.

The trip operated by *Mountain Travel-Sobek,* described above and led by Olaf Malver, starts in Akureyri. Guests fly by Twin Otter bush plane to Gurreholm, a flat spot with a dirt airstrip and hut about 90 miles up Scoresby Sound. Paddlers set off from there and spend eleven days exploring Gaase Fjord, Rode Fjord, Northwest Fjord, and the Bear Islands. The precise itinerary depends on weather and ice conditions, but the general strategy is to establish a series of base camps for two or three days, and take daily kayak excursions from there, as well as hiking trips along glaciers and up previously unclimbed mountain peaks. A Zodiac support boat carrying most of the camping gear and food proceeds directly to the camping spot each day, leaving the kayakers to dawdle in pristine silence.

The paddling finishes up in the Bear Islands, where kayakers are picked up by a boat and ferried to Ittoqqortoomiit for an overnight stay in a local guest house. From there it's back to Akureyri by Twin Otter.

WHAT TO EXPECT

A typical day includes about six hours of moderate paddling, with a three-hour run before lunch and another three hours in the afternoon, usually in smooth water. However, long crossings of open water, or passage through sheer-walled canyons without landing areas, may require runs of up to six consecutive hours of strong paddling. If the wind kicks up unexpectedly, short sprints to shelter may be required. On the plus side, the kayaks are lightly loaded, since the Zodiac carries most of the gear. There will also be moderately strenuous side hikes.

Weather-wise, these trips are not grim Arctic ordeals; summers in northeast Greenland are surprisingly pleasant. A stationary high-pressure weather system usually brings dry, clear days with temperatures ranging from 30 to 65 degrees. Showers and strong winds are possible but rare.

Accommodations are two-man tents, which you'll be expected to put up and take down yourself. Meals are also do-it-yourself. This is an expedition-style trip, with logistical and housekeeping chores shared among all trip members and staff.

Kayaking for hours on end can be painful if you do not paddle regularly. Lapsed paddlers will almost certainly get blisters and a sore back for the first few days. Some paddlers on this trip have developed tendinitis.

Two factors add the spice of real danger; polar bears and cold water. An Inuit professional polar bear hunter—and his rifle, of course—accompany the Mountain Travel trip, and a polar-bear alarm system is set up each night around the campsites. To reduce the possibility of a capsize into the 29-degree water, which would be fatal in a matter of minutes, Klepper expedition kayaks with stabilizing inflatable sponsons are used. In addition, paddlers may wear neoprene dry suits if conditions are at all risky. Icebergs and calving glaciers are given a wide berth, and paddlers always stay in close formation in case a rescue is necessary. According to Malver, "Everything we do on this trip is aimed at making sure no one goes into the water." But accidents happen, and a capsize in these waters is a serious matter indeed.

Advanced sea-kayaking skills are not necessary, but this is not a trip for beginners. You should have intermediate paddling skills, several sea-kayak trips under your belt, and feel quite comfortable in open water.

Trips run during the brief Arctic summer, in late July and early August.

RECOMMENDED READING

Arctic Dreams: Imagination and Desire in a Northern Landscape by Barry Lopez. Sharp observations and poetic musings about man and nature at high latitudes.

IN BRIEF

Black Feather, 800-574-8375: 22 days, $5,625
Mountain Travel-Sobek, 800-227-2384: 18 days, $3,950

Physical challenge, 3; Mental challenge, 4; Skills, 3.

ITALY
hiking the
dolomites

Walking alone below the 3,000-foot wall of the Sassolungo, with the sun-dappled Val Gardena spread out below, I puzzled over the absence of my countrymen from this splendid mountain tableau. In the course of a cool August morning, I had been showered with *buon giornos* and *guten Tags* from passing walkers, but had received not a single *howya doin'*. I recalled the report of American climber/writer David Roberts, who, paging through the guest register at the most popular hiker's hut in the Dolomites, had to go back 1,325 names to find his last compatriot. Vast hordes of Americans visit Venice, just 75 miles to the south, but apparently they all keep right on going. What are they, crazy?

Still, just now I am grateful for my countrymen's appalling geographical ignorance, for it sharpens the sense of the exotic one feels among these stirring peaks. A few hours ago, down below in the valley town of Selva/Wolkenstein, I had the feeling of being in the Swiss Alps: tidy chalet-style houses, red flowers in window boxes, steep green meadows, the far-off tinkle of cowbells. As my eye moved upward, the meadows gave way to pine trees, and I reflexively anticipated the rest of the usual Alpine scenario: the dark rubbly granite ridges, the snow-capped movie-logo pyramids looming massively past 14,000 feet.

But here in Val Gardena, this Alpine scenario goes wondrously awry at an elevation of roughly 6,000 feet. At around this level the sides of the valley, instead of continuing their upward slant, level off. Cresting the ridge above Selva/Wolkenstein, I was astonished to find before me an undulating high plateau of grass and wildflowers stretching away almost to the horizon—a world entirely invisible from the valley below. And rising thousands of feet out of this vast meadow, like tall craggy islands from a sea of green, were a series of reefs and spires of pink and white carbonate stone. These soaring ramparts grabbed my eyeballs, shook them, and fairly shouted, "You are not in Switzerland!"

Had I stood on this spot eighty years ago, however, I would have been in Austria. For centuries, the Dolomites and the surrounding region of South Tyrol were a part of the Austro-Hungarian Empire. The locals spoke German and wore leder-hosen. When World War I broke out in 1914, thousands of young men from Dolomite villages were shipped off to fight for Austria on the Russian front. But in 1915, Italy jumped into the war on the Allied side. Italian troops pushed north-ward into the mountains, and the outmanned Austrians took to the mountaintops and dug in for what turned out to be a bloody, pointless three-year standoff—a literal inversion of the futile slaughter unfolding in the trenches 600 miles to the north. The Dolomite campaign was perhaps the fullest expression ever of the art of mountain warfare.

As part of the postwar peace treaty, the Italo-Austrian border was moved northward about 50 miles to its present position at the Brenner Pass. Overnight the Dolomites became Italian, and Rome lost no time trying to wipe out the old Germanic culture. The name South Tyrol was outlawed, and carabinieri marched from house to house ripping down portraits of Emperor Franz Josef. Every village, river, and mountain peak was rechristened with an Italian name. Not even the dead were safe from Italianization; Tyrolean names on tombstones were obliterated by government decree and replaced with their Latin cognates. Thus the late Herr Karl Wald would be posthumously rechristened Signore Carlo Silva. World War II stirred this ethnic stew yet again, as thousands of Dolomite residents emigrated to Nazi Germany, then returned after its defeat.

By a stroke of great good fortune, it happens that both the Italians and Tyroleans have a long heritage of patience and accommodation with foreigners. Over the intervening years, ethnic tensions have eased, if not dissolved. Tyrolean culture has resurfaced, and towns, rivers, and mountains now have dual names. Tyrolean and Italian today coexist in a cordial apartheid, with generally separate schools and social groups but a common appreciation of their pastoral surroundings and the tourist dollar.

Oddly, the residents of the Dolomites have chosen not to erase the physical scars of their past conflicts. Eighty years later, the detritus of the Great War is still strewn about the landscape. A hiker may stumble across strands of barbed wire, spent bullets, ration cans, shell casings, even shreds of leather combat boots. Crumbling battlements, tunnels, precarious steel cables and ladders, and rubble from bomb blasts still dot the landscape north and west of Cortina, site of the fiercest fighting.

An oft-visited war relic is the grave of Sepp Innerkofler, a Tyrolean mountain climber and guide, widely considered the best Alpinist in the region in those days. In 1915 he was ordered by an ignorant Austrian commander to lead a five-man assault team up the steep northwest face of Mount Paterno, whose summit was held by the Italians. Innerkofler, fifty years old at the time, had been the first man to scale the northwest ridge, and he knew that such an attack was utter folly. But he stoically followed orders. (Innerkofler did, however, refuse his son's entreaties to accompany him, explaining, "Your mother must weep for only one of us.") Starting the climb in the dark, he soon outpaced his four companions, and as he neared the fortified summit, Innerkofler was alone in the light of early dawn.

It is not clear what happened next, only that Innerkofler subsequently fell to his death. At first it was believed that an Italian soldier, waiting above in ambush, had dropped a boulder on him, knocking him off a ledge. But after the war, Innerkofler's exhumed body was found to have what appeared to be machine-gun bullet wounds. The most accepted account today is that Innerkofler's fellow Austrian troops mistook him for an Italian and shot him off the wall from below. His gravestone, a grim reminder of the tragic futility of the Dolomite campaign, is there on the summit.

Realizing the hopelessness of such surface assaults, the two sides took to simply blowing each other off the summits. Below an Austrian-held peak called Piccolo Lagazuoi, the Italians spent six months digging a tunnel more than half a mile into the mountain, where they detonated 35 tons of blasting gelatin. But the Austrians, having felt the vibrations of the tunneling machinery, had already abandoned their position on the summit. In any case, the top of the mountain was virtually blown off, as were a number of others. The rubble is of course still there today.

Such puny efforts of man did nothing to diminish the landscape that attracted Europe's creative elite. Gustav Mahler spent his last summers near the Dolomite village of Toblach, just up the road from Cortina. In a rustic hut among the pine trees, surrounded by dramatic walls and spires, he composed

Das Lied von der Erde, as well as his Ninth Symphony and the adagio of his unfinished Tenth. Of the last, he told his wife, "The Dolomites are dancing this with one another." Perhaps Mahler should have spent more time talking to his wife and less time holed up in his "composing cabin"; while he toiled in isolation, she carried on in the main house with a young pianist who was their houseguest.

Is there something in the thrusting peaks of the Dolomites that encourages romantic longing? Franz Kafka, on sick leave with tuberculosis from his day job as an insurance clerk in Prague, wrote to his lady friend Milena that he had "breathed, although not quite in my right mind, pure, almost cold air in front of the first chain of the Dolomites. . . . What a country this is! Heavens, Milena, if only you were here. . . ."

And then there is the case of Henrik Ibsen. Visiting the village of Gossensass (a few kilometers up the road from the Dolomites proper) with his wife and son, the sixty-one-year-old Ibsen fell scandalously in love with an eighteen-year-old girl. The romance consisted mostly of stolen glances across the dining room, and the nearest it came to consummation was an intense conversation on a park bench, but the girl's diary describes Ibsen as a "volcano," and speaks of "true love" and "passion." The dour dramatist's Dolomite dalliance fizzled when the girl's family took her back home to Vienna, but he continued to write her passionate letters for years.

Mahler, Kafka, Ibsen—these were not the three most lighthearted, happy-go-lucky guys in the world. Yet each was drawn by a mountain range known for its bright, airy, almost playful landscape. In that paradox lurks the makings of a Ph.D. thesis.

American cultural celebrities, on the other hand, seem to be as Dolomite-shy as American hikers. The sole exception—unless you count Sylvester Stallone, who filmed *Cliffhanger* here—was the irascible expatriate poet Ezra Pound. Pound's daughter by his mistress was born in the Dolomite town of Brixen and sent off to be raised by a farm family in the nearby village of Gais. After the fall of Mussolini in 1943, Pound walked the 100-odd miles from Verona to Gais to visit his by-now-eighteen-year-old daughter. He arrived exhausted and footsore, and that night told her for the first time that he had another family.

It was not long thereafter that Pound's pro-Fascist radio broadcasts from Rome got him arrested for treason by the advancing U.S. forces. After being held three weeks in a metal cage in Pisa, he was sent back to the United States. A jury declared Pound unfit to stand trial due to an "unsound mind," and he was committed to a psychiatric hospital in Washington, D.C., where he remained imprisoned for twelve years.

Upon his release in 1958, Pound fled immediately back to northern Italy, to Brunnenberg, a castle on a hill just west of the Dolomites. There he lived with his daughter and grandchildren, did some gardening, wrote some poems, and watched the sun rise over spires and ramparts of rose-colored rock. Now, who's crazy?

OUTFITTERS

There is a surfeit of good outfitters offering hiking trips in the Dolomites. Here are the best of the bunch, in alphabetical order:

The *Above the Clouds* itinerary lies in the Brenta Range, a lesser-traveled outcropping to the west of the main Dolomite range. The trip starts and finishes in the resort village of Madonna di Campiglio and traces a six-day loop. You'll stay in *rifugios*, the fully equipped European-style huts scattered throughout the Dolomites. (*Rifugio* visitors carry overnight gear—pajamas, toothbrush, etc.—as well as the usual day-pack paraphernalia. Packs typically weigh 20–25 pounds.) The route includes the passes of Tre Sassi, Tuckett, and Forcolotta, and includes a bit of glacier walking and rock scrambling.

Alternative Travel specializes in culturally oriented hiking tours in Europe. (Their Dolomites itinerary, for example, includes tickets to the opera in Verona.) Alternative's hiking route is also in the Brenta; after a drive from Verona to the village of Madonna di Campiglio, hikers take a warm-up day hike to a nearby lake. The next morning you begin a five-day traverse across the Brenta Range, staying in *rifugios* each night. Hikers finish up in Molveno, a lakeside village in Val di Non. After a free day in Molveno, you'll drive back to Verona for two days of cultural touring, including a night at the opera.

Butterfield & Robinson, an upscale Canadian outfitter, starts its Dolomites trip in Bolzano, at the western end of the main range. After a ninety-minute drive to the village of Corvara, you'll do a warm-up day hike, overnighting in an old family-run hotel in Corvara. The following morning, you'll bus to Passo Gardena and hike back to Corvara, about 9 mostly downhill miles. The next day it's a 7-mile walk from Corvara to the village of San Cassanio, where you'll stay for two nights and make a 10-mile day hike to the Church of Santa Croce. Then it's on to the village of Cortina, with an overnight stop at Rifugio Fanes, one of the few *rifugios* with private rooms, which B&R of course reserves for its hikers. You'll finish up with a day hike out of Cortina.

Distant Journeys is a small company specializing in Europe. Co-owners Andrea Ellison and Julia Head are both former Outward Bound instructors. One or the other leads every Dolomites trip.

Two itineraries are available. (For both trips, hikers rendezvous in Innsbruck for the train ride to the start point at Welsberg.) The more challenging *rifugio* trip is a seven-day hut-to-hut trek that follows Alta Via 1 through the Pragser, Tofana, and Civetta mountain groups. A typical day is 7 or 8 miles; total distance is 49 miles.

The easier hotel-based trip covers the same general area, but hikers stay in full-service hotels each night and take daily walks of 5 or 6 miles. Total distance on foot is 27 miles over five days of walking.

Mountain Travel-Sobek starts its trip in Munich, Germany. From there you'll drive about three hours to Selva/Wolkenstein, where you'll stay three nights, making day hikes in the local area. These include a circumnavigation of Sassolungo and lunch excursions to Rifugios Puez and Re Alberto. (In all cases, you'll drive to and from the trailheads, in one case an hour each way.)

After a van ride to Cortina, there follow four days of day-hiking from bases in Cortina and Lago de Braies, including excursions to Lake Misurina, the Cadini Range, and Tre Cime Lavaredo. The trip concludes with a transfer back to the Munich airport.

Like Mountain Travel, *Sierra Club Outings* uses Selva/Wolkenstein as its initial base of operations, but you'll have to get yourself there. The group then moves on to Corvara for two days of day-hiking and one night in a *rifugio*. Final destination is Cortina, where you'll spend two more days day-hiking.

Wilderness Travel's quickie itinerary includes only four days of hiking. Overnights are spent in hotels in Cortina and Passo Giau, with one night in Rifugio Lagazuol. Staging city is Venice, and the trip includes a full day there for touring.

WHAT TO EXPECT

The hiking on these trips is generally moderate, averaging five to seven hours a day over typically smooth trails. (Some sections, however, can be quite steep.) Footpaths are generally very well maintained. Although terrain and daily mileage of these trips are generally comparable to those of Himalayan treks, the lower altitudes—typically 6,000 to 9,000 feet— make them easier.

On days concluding with overnights in *rifugios*, you'll carry personal overnight gear in addition to the standard day-pack load of rain jacket, water, snacks, and camera. Total pack weight may be 20–25 pounds.

Mountain Travel clients stay only in full-service village hotels with private baths. The other outfitters use some combination of village hotels and *rifugios*, the traditional Alpine mountain huts that typically offer dormitory-style beds with down comforters, excellent food (including beer and wine), hot water, and electric lights, as well as rustic gemütlichkeit and international camaraderie.

As hotels go, *rifugios* are fairly primitive, but considering their remote locations—miles from the nearest roads and often perched on precarious ledges—they seem like miracles of indulgence to American hikers unaccustomed to such wilderness amenities. All in all, it would be a shame not to spend at least one night in a *rifugio*.

None of these trips requires negotiating the notorious *via ferrata* ("iron way"), the steel cables and ladders that have been permanently fixed throughout the Dolomites to help hikers up and down steep terrain that would normally require mountaineering gear. Above the Clouds, however, does not recommend its trip for people with sensitivity to heights, and describes some routes as "airy."

The prime hiking season in the Dolomites is July through September. Try to avoid August, Europe's traditional holiday month, when trails and *rifugios* are packed.

RECOMMENDED READING

The Sunny Side of the Alps by Paul Hoffman. A fond reminiscence of the author's sojourn in the mountains of northern Italy, with a bit of history and lore thrown in.

IN BRIEF

Above the Clouds, 800-233-4499: 10 days, $1,575
Alternative Travel, 800-527-5997: 11 days, $2,620
Butterfield & Robinson, 800-678-1147: 7 days, $3,150;
    8 days, $3,375
Distant Journeys, 207-236-9788: 6 days, $1,350; 9 days,
    $1,495
Mountain Travel-Sobek, 800-227-2384: 10 days, $1,995
Sierra Club Outings, 415-923-5588: 8 days, $2,090
Wilderness Travel, 800-368-2794: 8 days, $1,995

Physical challenge, 2; Mental challenge, 2; Skills, 1.

NORWAY

ski touring

inn-to-inn

For nine hours now, you've been shuffling your skis through deep, wet snow the consistency of wet cement. The reputedly picturesque Norwegian peaks around you are invisible in the dense, unremitting fog. And here's the wind kicking up again, stinging your face with sleet. You're exhausted, soaking wet, shivering with cold, and the hut is still an hour away. And now—shit!—you feel a blister starting on your right heel. "Man, this sucks," you grumble to no one in particular. "This is really getting bad."

Shut up, you pathetic sniveling wussy. The ghost of Jan Baalsrud might hear you.

Half a century ago, Jan Baalsrud, a Norwegian World War II commando on the run from the occupying Nazis, skied and walked and swam and crawled 120 miles through these same frigid mountains. Over a period of two months he was starved, frostbitten, blinded, shot, and buried alive twice. You're complaining about a blister? Jan Baalsrud had to amputate his own gangrenous frostbitten toes with a pocketknife.

When the Nazis overwhelmed Norway in 1940, Baalsrud,

then a twenty-three-year-old soldier, fled to Sweden. He eventually found his way to England and the Linge Company, a British commando unit of Norwegian exiles. In March of 1943, after a year of training in the Scottish Highlands, Baalsrud and three compatriots set off from the Shetland Islands in a fishing boat loaded with explosives. Their mission: disable the Nazi air base at Bardufoss, on the distant north coast of Norway, long enough for an Allied convoy to sneak by undetected.

In their fishermen's guise, the saboteurs managed to bluff their way through the German coastal defenses and anchor near a small island along the coastline. But there was a betrayal, a sad failure of will by a frightened island resident. A German warship sped to the scene and opened fire on the fishing boat. The four men abandoned ship in a wooden dinghy, rowing frantically as machine-gun bullets whined around them. The dinghy was shot to pieces, and they swam the last 70 yards to shore in 35-degree water. As they tried to clamber up a rocky bank, three of the men were hit by shipboard gunners and fell motionless. But every bullet aimed at Jan Baalsrud missed.

As he fled up a snow-filled gully behind the bank, Jan was pursued by a shore patrol of four members of the Gestapo. Hiding behind a boulder, he aimed his automatic pistol at his pursuers from close range. Waterlogged and jammed with ice, it misfired, then misfired again. But the third and fourth shots punched into the chest of the first man in line, sending his body tumbling back down the gully toward the others. They retreated in panic.

Jan's only immediate escape was a snow-covered ridge several hundred feet above him. As he struggled to climb it, his dark form silhouetted against the whiteness, bullets and cannon shells from below churned the snow around him. Something tore at his big toe. He clawed frantically, slipping backward, sobbing in frustration and fear and pain as the flying snow sprayed his face. At last he reached the top and crawled over the ridge, out of sight, exhausted. The firing stopped. For the moment, he was safe.

Beyond the moment, however, all seemed hopeless. He was trapped on a small treeless island inhabited by perhaps fifty German soldiers who could easily follow his bloody tracks in the snow. He was alone in the Norwegian winter, soaking wet, numb with cold from his icy swim, shot in his big toe, missing one boot. To reach the mainland, he would have to cross two wide stretches of water and another much larger and more mountainous island, all patrolled by the Germans, who, upon his capture, would certainly execute him forthwith. If he ever did reach the mainland—also occupied by Germans—the nearest safe haven was the border with Sweden, 80 miles away across an icy wilderness.

Jan Baalsrud thought the matter over and decided he would go to Sweden. Hopping from rock to rock, laying false tracks in the snow, he walked down the back of the ridge to the beach on the far side of the small island. Ignoring a farmer's shed as too obvious a hiding place, he plunged once again into the icy ocean and swam to a small rock outcropping about 50 yards offshore. A few minutes later a search party of German soldiers appeared on the beach, milling, shouting, firing wild shots at imagined enemies. Jan, watching from the rock, felt a surge of elation: The soldiers, he realized, were afraid of him.

It was dusk. In his wet clothes, Jan knew that without shelter he would die of hypothermia by morning. It is said that a man's life expectancy in 35-degree water is three to five minutes, yet there was no other option but to swim again. Two hundred twenty yards away lay another small island, on which he could see one farmhouse. He remembered diving into the water in the darkness, the icy water hitting him like a hammer blow, but nothing else until he heard the voices of two little girls looking down at him as he lay on a rocky beach.

They led him to the farmhouse. The two women there, at first fearful, welcomed him instantly when he spoke to them in Norwegian. They had heard the shooting; they knew something was up, and that the Germans would be pounding on their door soon, certainly by morning. And they knew they would be executed on the spot if Jan were discovered in their house. Yet they hesitated not a moment. They warmed him, fed him, clothed him, massaged his numb limbs, dressed his wound, and gave him a rubber boot for his naked foot. They were the first of many Norwegian citizens who risked their lives to help him.

Before dawn the family's teenage son rowed Jan across 2 miles of ocean to the larger island. For four days he bushwhacked across its wild, rugged interior, marching up to twenty-eight hours at a stretch in his rubber fisherman's boots, battling snow squalls, testing all the outdoor survival skills he'd learned. At two farmhouses along the way he ate and slept while the farmers kept a watch out for Germans. From a fisherman, he learned the fate of his three comrades: one killed during the chase, the other two injured and, along with the eight British crewman of their fishing boat, brutally tortured, chained together, and shot.

In a fierce nighttime gale that hid them from the German patrol boats and shore-based searchlights, the fisherman rowed Jan 5 miles through heaving seas to the mainland. (Five miles was nothing to the old man; in his younger days he had often rowed 200 miles to go fishing.) Jan stepped ashore on the mainland carrying a treasure from the fisherman: a pair of cross-country skis and boots. Jan, like most red-blooded Norwegian men, was a demon on skis, and he set off down a snow-covered dirt road in the faint light of dawn with a feeling of exhilaration: He was on the mainland, on skis, finally finished with the ocean and the boats. Ahead of him lay a handful of villages, one range of mountains, and a desolate windswept high plateau. Beyond the plateau was Sweden.

He figured there would be Germans along the road, and he was right. Striding and hissing along at top speed, he came around a sharp curve to find a crowd of soldiers crossing the road just ahead—twenty, thirty, forty of them. There was no time to stop or turn around or hide, and so he kept going. In a few seconds he was literally among them, looking into their faces. They were sleepy-eyed, carrying mess tins and knives and forks, walking toward a house by the side of the road. They spread out to let the fellow pass and hardly gave him a second look.

Just beyond was a village and a roadblock manned by more German soldiers, armed and not so sleepy-eyed. They were checking papers. Twenty yards from the roadblock, Jan suddenly veered right, through a garden gate and behind a shed. There were shouts from the roadblock, and two or three rifle shots as he raced into the bushes. In a few minutes he was climbing strongly up the mountain under the cover of thick birch scrub. Confident of his speed on skis, he knew no German could catch him now, up in the high country, away from the road.

Climbing higher, he met the morning sunshine. In the clear air, Jan saw a fjord below him and the high plateau beyond. He could literally see his route to freedom stretched out before him across the wilderness—maybe 50 miles, two or three days skiing at most. His heart surged with joy, and he pressed on, arms and legs pumping.

He didn't think much of it when the snow began to fall about three P.M. But the storm intensified, and the visibility soon went to zero, a total whiteout. Trying to pick his way blindly down to the fjord, where there might be shelter, he skied across a steep slope of loose, soft snow. There was a cracking sound, a lurch, and suddenly the slope gave way. Jan tumbled over and over, straight down in a roaring cascade of snow. He couldn't breathe, he couldn't see. Then there was a blow to his head and all went dark.

He regained consciousness—an hour later? a day?—buried in soft snow, with his head miraculously poking out into the air. His pack and skis were gone. Dazed, he dug himself out and began to wander in the still-raging storm. All day and all night he wandered, and the next day, and the next—utterly lost, his mind numbed by cold and concussion, his feet nearly useless frozen clubs. The storm abated after three days, but by then Jan had become snow-blind; the glare from the snow had scorched his retinas. He began to hallucinate, to flounder aimlessly in the deep snow. All he knew was that if he stopped moving, he would die.

Near the end of the fourth day Jan bumped into something hard. He reached out and felt the rough, rounded bark in front of his face: another damn tree like all the others he'd run into. But then he realized the log was horizontal, not vertical, and that there was a wall of logs stacked on top of each other. Another hallucination? He felt his way along the wall and rounded a corner. There was a door, and a latch. It opened and he fell inside.

The owner of the cabin, in a village called Furuflaten, was a middle-aged bachelor farmer named Marius Grönvold. He dropped everything and, telling no one but his sisters, began nursing Jan back to health. Grönvold took Jan's hand and told him, "If I live, you will live, and if they kill you, I will have died to protect you."

Though Jan's vision gradually came back after a week, he was still unable to walk on his frostbitten feet, and Grönvold knew that he had to be moved soon. A German garrison in the village schoolhouse sent out regular patrols, and no secret of such magnitude could last for long in a village this small. (The storekeeper had already commented about the extra food Grönvold was buying.)

Grönvold knew of an abandoned log hut across the fjord, the only building on that side of the water. No one ever went there; it would be safe. On a starless night, with the help of a few trusted friends, he loaded Jan on a stretcher and carried him down the riverbed through town, right under the noses of the Germans in the schoolhouse, to a waiting boat. They sailed and rowed him across the fjord to the cabin—a windowless hovel 7 feet by 10—laid him on the crude bunk, set food and a kerosene lamp on the table, and promised to come back in a few days to check on him.

Jan lay there in the darkness, not knowing whether it was night or day. The pain in his frostbitten feet got suddenly worse, pulsing in waves up his legs and making him gasp in agony. Unwrapping his feet, he saw that his toes were black and swollen and oozed a putrescent fluid. For the first time, despair flashed through him; he knew that gangrene would eventually kill him if it were not treated. Day after day he lay there in the dark, unable to eat, in a stupor of pain and malnutrition. Where was Marius?

Delayed by a long storm, Grönvold didn't reappear until seven nights later. Jan's condition exceeded his worst fears; something had to be done, fast, or he would die in a few days. Grönvold returned home before dawn and, with help from the loose Norwegian underground network of Nazi resisters, hatched a plan so complex and audacious that its chances of success seemed virtually nil. But it was Jan's only chance.

In three days, the plan was ready. A carpenter working inside the Nazi garrison secretly fashioned a dozen intricate wooden pieces that, when smuggled out, were assembled into a sturdy sled proportioned to Jan's body. That night Grönvold and three other men sailed and rowed across the fjord once more, carrying the sled and a boatload of mountaineering gear. They shook Jan awake, wrapped him up in a blanket, strapped him to the sled, and began hauling and pushing and dragging him, foot by foot, up the steep rocky slope behind the hut. Jan, semiconscious, didn't really understand what was happening, but he trusted Grönvold.

Two thousand seven hundred feet above them lay the barren plateau, and a planned rendezvous with a group of men from Mandal, a village in the next fjord so tiny and poor and isolated that no Germans were stationed there. The fastest skier in Mandal was already racing out across the plateau to find and recruit the last and most critical link in the audacious plan: the Lapps, the native Arctic people who lived on the plateau, following their reindeer from camp to camp—people considered so primitive by the Nazis that they were beneath notice, not even worth subduing. The Lapps, if properly persuaded and paid, could haul Jan on the sled the last 30 miles to the Swedish frontier.

It is common for injured or sick people to be carried down steep mountains, but it is unlikely that, before or since, anyone has ever been hauled 2,700 feet *up* an ice-covered cliff, in the dark. Somehow, with ropes and ski poles and endless strength and patience, it was done. The four men dragged their semiconscious cargo toward the rendezvous point utterly spent yet glowing with triumph and hope. When they arrived, there was no one there. They searched and shouted at the top of their lungs, but the sound fell dead, muffled by the snow and the wind.

If Grönvold and the others were not home by evening, their absence would be noted by the Germans, and that, quite

simply, would be the end of them. There wasn't time to wrestle
Jan back down to the hut; there was no choice but to leave him
there, lashed to his sled, and hope the men from Mandal would
eventually arrive. And so, next to a large boulder, they dug a
hole in the snow to protect Jan from the wind and lowered him
down into it. They gave him the last of their food and a bottle
of brandy, and walked back down the mountain to their boat.
It was now up to the men from Mandal.

After so much extraordinary good fortune, it is perhaps no
surprise that when bad luck came Jan's way, it would be excruciating. At virtually the moment the party of skiers from Mandal was to set out for the rendezvous, a boat had unexpectedly
appeared offshore and pulled into the village dock. Six German
soldiers got off and began to walk around, checking house to
house. Were they on to the plot? By the time the skiers concluded that the search was only a coincidence, a blizzard had
moved in. Waiting out the storm, mad with frustration, the
men from Mandal didn't get to the rendezvous spot until four
days after the appointed time. They searched for hours, but
found nothing—only a thick, soft blanket of newly fallen snow
covering everything.

Three days later, word reached Grönvold of the failed search
mission. Distraught, he remembered his pledge to Jan. The
thought of Jan's decomposing body lying unattended, eventually exposed by the spring thaw, cut him like a knife. He decided to return to the plateau, at whatever cost to himself, to
give Jan's body a proper burial.

Once again he crossed the fjord by night, accompanied this
time by Agnethe Lanes, a young woman whose spunk and outdoor savvy he had long admired. The climb to the plateau was
easier without the sled, of course, though a vicious wind made
the last stretch difficult. He recognized the boulder where
they'd left Jan, and went down on his knees and began to dig in

the snow. He pawed down 3 feet, punching through into a small cavity, and there was Jan's ghastly waxen face staring up at him, eyes closed, covered with ice. "Don't look," he said to Agnethe. "He's dead."

Jan's eyes opened. "I'm not dead, damn you," he said. And he smiled.

When word of Jan's miraculous survival reached the men of Mandal, they realized they would have to haul him to Sweden themselves, for the plan to use the Lapps had fallen through. (The reindeer that the Lapps follow were still far to the south, and would not migrate that far north for weeks. And the Lapps themselves, who live very much in the present, are by nature reluctant to make promises for the future.) Though the men of Mandal rarely ventured onto the plateau, and knew nothing of the way to Sweden, their hopes were high as they lashed Jan into his sled. Their optimism was short-lived, however; pulling the heavy sled across the maze of hillocks on the plateau proved exhausting, and a storm began to move in. Six hours out onto the plateau, they turned back.

Jan decided it was best to remain on the plateau and wait— for better weather, for the Lapps, for the war to end, for whatever it would take to save him. To descend to Mandal would risk discovery and endanger the lives of all those who'd helped him. The men from Mandal laid him next to a rock and built him a snow wall to block the wind, and left him there once more, with promises to return with food. He lay there between the rock and the snow wall for three weeks, passing the time by counting the drops of melting snow and testing whether bread tasted better frozen or wet. He remembered with a sardonic smile the time in an Oslo restaurant when he had complained bitterly about a stain on the tablecloth. He worried about wolves. And he worried about his gangrenous, evil-smelling toes.

He decided to cut them all off. Fortifying himself with brandy, he carefully sawed at the black hard nubs with his pocketknife. Because he lacked the strength to throw the severed toes away, he set them on a small rock ledge beside him. After three days, there were nine toes lined up like pebbles in a child's collection. The little toe on his left foot didn't seem quite as bad as the others, so he decided to keep it.

The men from Mandal visited him every few days with food and rumors. A Lapp had supposedly promised to take him to Sweden, then changed his mind when he heard that the Germans were starting ski patrols on the plateau. A second, larger expedition of Mandal men attempted to haul him to Sweden a second time, but once again was turned back by weather after only a few hours. Jan's time on the plateau became an endless limbo of waiting . . . for what? Ten days after the second abortive attempt, Jan decided that it was no longer his duty to escape at whatever cost, but to die, and spare the good men of Mandal further risk.

Lying utterly alone in the vast winter wasteland, he reached for his revolver to cock it for the final shot. But his hands were feeble, and the cocking mechanism was rusty and stiff. He tried with all his might, but he couldn't cock the gun. He felt foolish, absurd. Were he not so ashamed, he would have laughed.

The rumors of a Lapp started up again. This time it would really happen, the men told him on their visits. Four men from another village who knew the Lapps and their language came up to serve as translators and go-betweens. They stood a vigil for four days, waiting. But word came that the Lapp had changed his mind again. It was the final blow. Jan's will to live, what little was left of it, disappeared altogether. As the men left him for the last time, he closed his eyes and felt the inner peace of one who has accepted death.

When he next opened his eyes, there was a man standing over him, very still. The man was small, with a swarthy face and narrow, slanted eyes. He wore a long embroidered tunic, leather leggings, and boots of reindeer fur with pointy toes. Jan dazedly mumbled "Good morning," but the man said nothing and continued to stand motionless over him for what seemed like hours. Jan closed his eyes again. Suddenly he was awakened by snorting and shuffling and the pungent smell of a large animal. Jan looked up to see that he was now surrounded by hundreds of reindeer—hot breath and hairy muzzles. After so many weeks of white nothingness, his eyes and brain hardly knew what to make of it. Was he hallucinating all this?

He was not. With a suddenness that bewildered him, two Lapps picked Jan up off his sled and laid him on a larger one. He felt blankets being wrapped around him, and then a sudden lurch, and the sled began to move. He raised his head, looked beyond his feet, and saw the hindquarters of a reindeer. One of the Lapps, skiing as naturally as other men walk, led it along. The herd fell in behind, and the vast antlered armada moved off. To where, Jan didn't know; neither of the Lapps had yet spoken a word to him.

Near the end of the second day across the great white plateau, Jan heard the first word he understood from the Lapps: Kilpisjarvi, the name of a long lake that straddled the Swedish border. Jan could see the hills on the other side of the lake, and hope and elation surged within him. But in a moment the elation died; the Lapps pointed to the frozen lake, squeezed handfuls of soggy snow, and shook their hands. The ice was too soft to cross.

Then came, from far off, the sharp report of a rifle. The reindeer jerked up their heads; the Lapps froze in confusion. Five men on skis stood on the crest of a hill a quarter mile away; a sixth knelt with a rifle pointed in their direction. There was another shot, and three of the far-off men began racing toward them.

Jan shouted, "Across the lake! Across the lake!" even though he knew the Lapps did not understand. The Lapps looked about in confusion. Desperate, Jan fumbled in his jacket and pulled out his useless revolver, brandished it, and screamed once more. The Lapps stared at him aghast, and then one of them jumped to the head of the reindeer pulling Jan's sled and shouted a command. The deer began to move, and in a few moments the herd poured down onto the slushy surface of the lake like a dark flood toward the Swedish shore. The men on skis, still firing from far behind, kept up their pursuit for a while. But finally they stopped and turned around and skied slowly back, occasionally glancing over their shoulders in wonderment.

OUTFITTERS

Above the Clouds starts its nine-day itinerary in the ski-touring center of Geilo, in the Hallingdal Mountains in western Norway. Skiers make a 75-mile out-and-back loop, overnighting at various mountain hotels and ski cabins along the way. Average distance per day is about 12 miles. Luggage is transported, so it's necessary only to carry a light day pack. Above the Clouds also offers an easier inn-based trip, also out of Geilo, from which skiers make day excursions.

Borton Overseas offers three challenging eight-day lodge-to-lodge itineraries in the Rondane, Hardangervidda, and Jotunheimen mountain ranges. Skiers carry full backpacks with all their gear. Total distances covered range from 50 to 80 miles.

Borton also offers a seven-day skiing/dogsled trip in far northern Arctic Norway, not far from where Jan Baalsrud made his epic escape. Starting in Lakselv, skiers shuffle and mush across the Finnmark plateau and back along the Karasjohka River. Skiers will visit encampments of Lapps (now called Samis), the nomadic reindeer herders who hauled Baalsrud to Sweden. Cost is $1,016.

WHAT TO EXPECT

The Above the Clouds trip, with day pack only, is the easiest of the lot. Daily runs average 12 miles over moderate terrain. Borton's 54-mile itinerary in the Rondane Mountains is generally flat and at moderate altitude, with a maximum run of 12 miles per day. These two would rate a 3 on our physical-challenge scale.

Borton's trip through the Hardangervidda range totals about 80 miles over steeper terrain (longest day: 14 miles), while the Jotunheimen circuit has a couple of 14-mile up-and-down days with significant elevation gains. On these two trips you'll often be breaking trail in soft snow. Call them a 4.

The huts and mountain hotels on these trips can range from serviceable to self-indulgent. Many have fireplaces and saunas. As long as you don't overmatch yourself physically, you should generally have a pleasant time along the trail. Cold is not the problem one might expect in the Norwegian mountains in winter; the exertion of skiing generates plenty of body heat. But of course a major blizzard out on the trail, always a possibility, can raise the mental challenge a bit.

Moderately experienced shufflers will do okay with the Above the Clouds trip and on Borton's dogsled outing. But Borton's three backpack tours demand more experience and technique. Borton's catalog warns that the Jotunheimen tour requires "several years experience cross-country skiing at high altitude . . . competence in long climbs and downhill runs in varying weather and snow."

Due to the extraordinarily brief midwinter days at this high latitude, the trips described here run in late winter and early spring, from February to May.

RECOMMENDED READING

We Die Alone by David Howarth. The full saga of Jan Baalsrud's incredible escape. Right up there with *Endurance*, among the great adventure tales of the age.

IN BRIEF

Above the Clouds, 800-233-4499: 9 days, $1,750
Borton Overseas, 800-843-0602: 7 days, $585; 8 days, $635

Physical challenge, 3–4; Mental challenge, 2; Skills 3–4.

OMAN

documenting traditional
arabian ships

It was an audacious plan for a young man whose father had not allowed him out of the house for six years, but it worked. In 1970, the twenty-nine-year-old son of Sultan Said bin Taimur, the absolute monarch of the Sultanate of Oman, overthrew his father in a superbly engineered palace coup, a coup that would have been bloodless had not the aging sultan accidentally shot himself in the foot with the Luger he kept next to his bed. The old man was hustled off to a waiting plane and shipped to a suite in London's Dorchester Hotel, from which he declined to emerge for the remainder of his life.

Nearly the size of Great Britain and home to perhaps half a million people, Oman before the coup was among the most backward and oppressed nations on earth. Malaria-ridden and mostly arid, it had 6 miles of paved roads, no hospitals, and just three schools, which taught only passages from the Koran. Outsiders were barred from the country entirely, except at the old sultan's personal invitation—and he didn't invite many. The gates of the walled capital city, Muscat, were locked at sundown, and people venturing from their homes after dark were required to carry lanterns. Bicycles, eyeglasses, radios, wrist-watches, and other trappings of Western decadence were banned. The old sultan would crouch at a palace window peephole with binoculars, scanning the crowds in the nearby marketplace for violators of his dictums. If he spotted one, palace guards were dispatched to arrest the perpetrator, who was whacked with long sticks and sent to jail.

Unaccountably, the Old Man permitted his teenage son to be sent off to England to be educated. After graduating from Sandhurst, the elite British military academy, the handsome, dashing young Prince Qabus, now something of an Anglo-phile, returned to Oman. He was immediately placed under house arrest by his father. The prince was allowed to read only the Koran, although it is said that his sympathetic mother managed occasionally to smuggle *The Times* to him.

In the late 1960s, as young Qabus chafed under his confine-ment, oil was discovered in Oman's remote Empty Quarter. More ominously, a Communist-supported guerrilla revolt was brewing among the mountain tribes of Dhofar, in southern Oman. It was clear that the country would soon be wrenched out of the fifteenth century one way or another, so Qabus, with the tacit approval of the old sultan's cadre of British military and economic advisers, made his move. The Omani people danced joyously in the streets for days.

It is unlikely that any person in the twentieth century has had such a vast and unbridled opportunity to mold a nation to his fancy as did the new Sultan of Oman. In 1970, the young Sultan Qabus (or "Super Q," as he came to be known among British expatriates) had before him a virtual blank canvas of a country, a primitive Islamic state still locked in the Middle Ages by the iron reign of his isolationist father. On his palette, as it were, he had billions of dollars in newfound oil money and the absolute authority to use it as he wished.

A quarter-century later, Sultan Qabus, now fifty-six years old, still rules. His likeness, with its piercing eyes and silver scimitar of a beard, adorns all denominations of Omani currency, as well as virtually every store and business in the country. During the recent twenty-fifth anniversary celebration of his reign, 100 million colored lightbulbs were gaily strung for miles along the country's major roads. (The effect on a newly arrived visitor, jet-lagged and bleary-eyed, can only be described as hallucinatory.) Qabus's Oman is today a peaceful, prosperous, and thoroughly modern state that still hews to its traditional Islamic culture but does not hesitate to embrace those Western trappings it finds a useful, such as the Boeing 747, of which the sultan has a pair. Among the jumbos' functions is flying in the London Symphony Orchestra to play Mozart at royal birthday parties.

Despite his absolute rule and occasional lapses into stereotypical oil-sheikh excess, Qabus has maintained the affection of most Omanis. He has, after all, brought them a prosperity unthinkable twenty-five years ago. Omanis can no longer complain that theirs is a remote, isolated government; Qabus has been known to round up his seventeen cabinet ministers and drop in on an encampment of Bedouin camel herders to listen to their grievances. He has decreed that the home phone numbers of the governing royal family be listed in a special section of the Muscat phone book. If you'd like to call, say, His Highness Sayyid Bin Shihab Thuwainy at home, dial 536213. If no one answers, try his three other homes, or two car phones, all listed in the book.

Although the sultan's personality is more loner than gladhander—he is unmarried, and has been described as "happy in the company of other soldiers and horses, happier with paintings and music"—Qabus occasionally drives around incognito in a Toyota Land Cruiser, stopping at random to chat with people along the road. (Such a practice can be dangerous; he was once injured when his stopped vehicle was rear-ended by another car.) There's a story that Qabus once picked up an elderly hitchhiker and asked the old man what he thought of the sultan. "He's okay, I guess," the man replied. "But he spends too much time in his palace. The sultan should get out more and talk to people." Qabus then invited the flabbergasted man to the palace for a visit.

Alas, Super Q did not screech to a halt to talk to our small group of Westerners, volunteers helping out an Australian marine archaeologist on a project to document traditional hand-built wooden Omani sailing ships. But as we searched for cave paintings of ancient ships, we met a man whose story pretty well sums up why Sultan Qabus has become the poster child for Benevolent Despotism.

Ali Ahmed is a mid-level government worker who lives in Salalah, Oman's second city. Born in the nearby mountains of Dhofar to a dirt-poor cowherding family, as a young man he supported the rebellion of his neighbors against the old sultan, although he himself was not a combatant. The insurgency continued even after the 1970 coup ("Back then, we figured, 'Like father, like son,'" he says today) and Ali Ahmed was arrested in 1973 by the new Qabus regime. He was convicted in a kangaroo court and sent to the infamous Jalali Prison, a grim four-hundred-year-old former Portuguese fort that overlooks the sultan's palace in Muscat. Two years later, the rebels were essentially defeated, but Ali Ahmed languished in Jalali until 1980.

Instead of harassing or blackballing its former political prisoner after his release, the Qabus government subsequently gave him a job and a salary that today supports a big new house in the suburbs and a double-cab Toyota pickup. Likewise, the incomprehensibly magnanimous Ali Ahmed displays in his living room a framed picture of the man who put him in Jalali. "The sultan is a good man," he told us. "Basically, he took care of all the problems that caused the rebellion. There was nothing left to fight about."

Ali Ahmed does have one gripe, however: He can't get his book published in Oman. A fanatical amateur archaeologist, he has written and photographed a beautiful coffee-table volume about Omani rock art, and has persuaded a wealthy sheikh in neighboring Dubai to underwrite its publication there. But any book published in Oman must be approved by the Omani Ministry of Information. Ali Ahmed's application to publish has been approved by two different committees, but, he says, has sat untouched on the Minister of Information's desk for more than a year.

Frustrated, Ali Ahmed sent a copy of the book to the sultan himself, asking him to speed the approval process. Qabus liked the book so much that he sent the former rebel sympathizer a personal check for 10,000 Omani rials (about $24,000). "He told me to buy a new car with it," says Ali Ahmed. "But the book has still not been approved."

Freedom of the press does not seem to be a matter of much interest to most Omani citizens, and certainly not to the government. All Omani magazines and newspapers are closely monitored, and may be shut down by the Ministry of Information for any reason. In 1993, the Omani owner of the English-language *Times of Oman* was thrown in jail for a week because the paper inadvertently published an ad that contained a vague likeness of Sultan Qabus riding a camel, which was deemed insulting.

A foreign journalist wishing to enter Oman is subject to a background check and thorough vetting of previously published writing. If there is reason to suspect a journalist may write controversial or unflattering words about Oman or the sultan, a visa may be denied. (Forewarned of this, I listed my occupation as "teacher" on my own visa application.)

One reporter who visited Oman for the London *Sunday Times* had the audacity to write about a longtime British military adviser and close associate to Sultan Qabus, the "powerful, reclusive" sixty-seven-year-old Air Marshall Sir Erik Bennett. The reporter noted, with impeccable innuendo, that Bennett, also unmarried, lives at the palace, and described him as "the most important person in the Sultan's life." According to a Ministry of Information official I spoke to, the reporter will almost certainly be banned from Oman in the future.

Having written the above paragraph, will I ever be permitted to return to Oman myself? Presumably not. Pity. It's a lovely place.

OUTFITTER

Earthwatch is a not-for-profit organization that sends lay volunteers to lend a helping hand on nature- and culture-related scientific research projects around the world. It currently offers some 160 projects.

On this particular trip, volunteers assist Tom Vosmer, a marine archaeology researcher with the Western Australian Maritime Museum. Vosmer's special interest is the Arab dhow, the traditional hand-built wooden ship that has sailed Middle Eastern waters for four thousand years. Oman has always been a commercial seafaring nation; the legendary Sinbad the Sailor reputedly lived in Sohar, on Oman's northern coast.

Sadly, with Oman's headlong modernization, the traditional sailing boats are becoming rapidly extinct. Vosmer's mission is to find the few remaining boats and document them in great detail, using tape measure, camera, sketchbook, and sophisticated optical surveying equipment to determine precise hull contours. Volunteers measure, snap photos, make sketches, run errands, and do whatever else is needed to support the project.

Itineraries change each year, but the trip I took focused on two boats, a 46-foot sewn craft called a *sambuk* at Raysut harbor in Salalah, on Oman's south coast; and a 110-foot *ghanjah* at Sur, the traditional ship-building center of Oman. We spent four or five days studying each boat, as well as looking for nautical graffiti—old paintings of ships in caves and forts—that might give hints about the design evolution of the craft.

Other itineraries have included visits to the remote Musandam Peninsula and underwater searches along the coast east of Sur. At this writing, itineraries for upcoming projects are still flexible.

WHAT TO EXPECT

This is not a physical trip. Volunteers spend most of their time sitting, standing, or walking around the boats. Reasonable agility is a help; you'll probably be clambering into small spaces with tape measure and camera.

Accommodations vary wildly. Ours ranged from a luxury seaside resort hotel to a flapping tent on a windy beach, to the living room floor of a local resident in Sur.

In general, you will not be as catered to as you might be on a regular commercial group trip. You are a volunteer helper, not a guest, and will be expected to do your share of cleaning up, loading supplies, and other menial tasks. On my trip, Vosmer kept us well diverted on off-days with side trips to markets and excursions into the desert. And I found the work itself mostly quite enjoyable. But Earthwatch volunteers in general cannot expect the level of clockwork planning and organization one would expect on a standard adventure trip. The "trip leader," after all, is a scientist, not a professional guide, and his primary focus is to do his research, not keep you amused.

Weather in Oman is generally excellent during the winter months. (Vosmer's trips typically run in December and January.) Daytime highs are 80 to 90 degrees, and cooler nights are the rule. Rain is unusual but not unheard of; our tents got briefly splattered one night.

No particular skill is required, but you should be a person of reasonable dexterity, resourcefulness, and common sense who is comfortable working with basic tools. A modest ability to take photos, sketch, and use a tape measure will make you much more useful on this project; the entirely unskilled may find themselves relegated to holding a plumb bob for hours on end.

RECOMMENDED READING

Arabian Sands by Wilfrid Thesiger. A classic first-person account of the intrepid British explorer's travels on camelback through Oman and Saudi Arabia in the late 1940s.

IN BRIEF

Earthwatch, 800-776-0188: 15 days, $1,695

Physical Challenge, 1; Mental challenge, 3; Skills, 1.

PORTUGAL

cycling in
wine country

There are not many things that a Portuguese is willing to die for. Certainly not democracy: The country lived placidly for eight hundred years under a succession of kings and dictators, and when it finally got around to a revolution in 1974, only five people were killed—two of them by accident. Nor empire: When ordered to fight to the death in defense of the colony of Goa, Portuguese soldiers laid down their arms at the first sign of the approaching Indian forces. Not even manly glory: In a Portuguese bullfight, the bull's horns are dulled and padded, and the animal is merely wrestled to the ground by a team of eight matadors. Nobody ever dies—not even the bull.

Ah, but wine, that is another matter. When the Marquis of Pombal decreed in 1756 that only one kind of wine would henceforth be supplied to local taverns, the Portuguese populace took to the streets in outrage. Five army regiments had to be summoned to quell the riots, and thirty ringleaders were subsequently hanged. The marquis announced that only the merciful generosity of the king had prevented a much larger number of executions.

Today, 15 percent of Portugal's population lives by making or selling wine. In the Minho region—the cool, damp, hilly grape-growing country along the northern border with Spain—the proportion may be half. Bicycle tourers have long been a common sight in wine-making areas such as the Napa and Loire Valleys, but it is only recently that bike outfitters have discovered the Minho, the little-touristed wine-making heart of the world's seventh-largest wine-producing nation.

For centuries, Portuguese wine has been held in low regard by connoisseurs, who disdain the traditional Portuguese prac-tice of blending grapes from many small vineyards. (The one exalted exception, of course, is port, the wine/brandy hybrid long favored in stuffy English drawing rooms, made from Douro Valley grapes and carefully aged in the town of Oporto.) Jonathan Swift once admitted, "I love white Portuguese wine more than claret. I have a sad vulgar appetite." This reputation for vulgarity was not enhanced by the export in the 1960s of Mateus and Lancer's, the heavily advertised fizzy pink Por-tuguese soda-pops favored by fraternity boys and upwardly mobile hairdressers. But since joining the European Common Market in 1986, Portugal has begun to get serious about its wine. Growers are ripping out old vines, planting new varieties, and producing more and more estate-bottled wines from single vineyards.

The specialty wine of the Minho region is *vinho verde*, or "green wine." The name refers not to the wine's color—it's usu-ally red, sometimes white—but the fact that the grapes are not quite ripe when picked. A brief fermentation results in a low al-cohol content, and, in the words of one wine critic, "a scintil-lating little bubbly . . . which is marvelously refreshing . . . it is all too easy to gulp it like beer on a hot day." (Cyclists are sternly advised against substituting *vinho verde* in their water bottles.) The *vinho verde* exported to the United States, how-ever, is sweetened and flat, nothing at all like the real thing, which is best sampled in the spirited little taverns of Minho towns like Monção, Barcelos, and Penafiel.

The Minho is the last stronghold of the small family vineyard, typically subdivided among offspring over many generations. Sixty thousand Minho farmers grow grapes on plots as small as a quarter acre, draping their vines across high trellises so that food crops like cabbage, corn, and beans may be grown underneath. (The Minho may be the only place on earth where grapes are harvested with ladders.) The small farmers haul their grapes, often by oxcart, to local wine cooperatives, which typically turn out less than two casks a year each, barely enough to supply the village taverns.

Scattered among these mom-and-pop operations, however, are a few dozen huge wine estates owned by wealthy families, some of whom have tended the same vines for centuries. The world's premiere *vinho verde* is made at Palacio da Brejoeria, a sprawling neoclassical manor house near the town of Monção. (The routes of several bicycle outfitters run right by the Palacio.) One particularly erudite wine critic describes the Brejoeria *vinho verde* as "a wine that has finesse . . . and great length."

Actually, the same could be said of the grandiose facade of the Palacio itself, which looks strangely familiar to those of us who consumed our share of Mateus in high school and college. The original promoters of Mateus, wishing to give their product a certain air of weightiness, approached the owner of the Palacio da Brejoeria for permission to put a likeness of the Palacio's facade on the Mateus label. In return, they offered a royalty on each bottle of Mateus sold. The owner of Brejoeria consented, but greedily demanded an immediate lump-sum payment instead of a royalty. The deal was done, and so was poetic justice: Mateus sales unexpectedly skyrocketed, and the chagrined owner lost out on royalties that would have exceeded his lump sum the first year and continued for a lifetime.

Palacio da Brejoeira does not open its doors to the public—

perhaps the embarrassment over the lost Mateus royalties is still too acute—but a few estates in the Minho have been persuaded to do so. Paço de Calheiros, a grand seventeenth-century mansion overlooking the Lima River valley, stands on rolling, wooded property owned by the same family since the land was granted to them by King Dom Dinis in 1336. Cyclists riding with Backroads or Progressive Travels, four-star outfitters known for opulent accommodations, stay two nights at Paço de Calheiros. One rider described the experience as fairy-talelike: After a rugged 59-mile ride through an ancient hard-scrabble landscape of oxcarts and dusty villages and peasant women stooping in the fields, you finally ascend a long hill and pedal through an iron gate and along a driveway lined with magnolia trees, past formal gardens to a fountain and the great stone staircase of a seventeenth-century mansion, and then— exhausted, sweaty, smelly—you are welcomed by the Count of Calheiros, a dashing, handsome man in his forties, wearing an ascot and blazer, with dark, slicked-back hair and piercing eyes, a man who, if you are a woman, will bow and kiss your hand in greeting, no matter how sweaty and smelly you are.

The count, in addition to being lord of this manor, is mayor of the nearby village that bears his name, president of the golf club down the road, and head of the local society of manor homes. He is quite accustomed to hobnobbing with celebrities; when Hollywood bigshot Jack Valenti landed a helicopter on his tennis court not long ago, the count was insufficiently impressed to remember his name a few weeks later. But if you are a cyclist, he will escort you through the massive front doorway, proudly show off his antiques, art, and tapestries, point out the first-floor shrine where his father is buried, ask you whether pheasant is satisfactory for dinner (the birds are raised by the count's gamekeeper), and invite you to sit by the pool with a glass of cool, white Pont de Lima *vinho verde*, made from grapes that were grown out beyond his stables. As you sit there, savoring the tart, bubbly wine and surveying your temporary realm, you have to agree: This is to die for.

OUTFITTERS

Backroads has both camping and inn-based itineraries. Both start in Spain, just north of the border, in the city of Santiago de Compostela. For inn-stayers, the cycling begins in Bayona, a three-hour van ride south of Santiago. From Bayona, the route leads south to the border and Vila Nova de Cerveira, then inland to Monção and Ponte de Lima, where you'll be greeted by the Count of Calheiros. After a day loop through the Lima Valley, it's on to Canicada, from where you'll make another day loop, this one through Peneda Geres National Park. The inn-based ride finishes in Guimarães; from here, cyclists are bused to Oporto for the trip home.

Campers follow the same general route, but stay in campgrounds in Bayona, Caminha, Calheiros, Geres, and Guimarães.

The standard route averages 32 miles per day, but long and short options can vary the daily average from 21 to 47 miles.

Easy Rider's itinerary covers the same general territory as that of Backroads, but in the reverse direction. From Oporto, riders transfer by van to Viana do Castelo, on the Portuguese coast just below the border with Spain. From there, you'll ride up the Lima River valley to Arcos de Valdevez, followed by a loop through Peneda Geres National Park. (Both nights you'll stay in a riverside manor house.) Then it's north to the wine-making center of Monção, and back east along the Minho River to the coastal town of Caminha. After a free day in Caminha, you'll cycle across the border and up the Spanish coast to Bayona, the end of the cycling itinerary. Return to Oporto is by van.

Average daily distance is 43 miles if you choose to ride the full route; shorter options reduce the average to 30 miles.

Easy Rider also offers three other trips in Portugal. One follows the coast below Lisbon, one covers the Alentejo region, and a third combines the Minho and Alentejo itineraries.

Euro Bike's itinerary includes equal time in Portugal and Spain. After a van transfer from Oporto to Ponte de Lima, cyclists ride to Ponte de Barca, Braga, Peneda Geres National Park, and Guimarães. Then it's a van transfer across the border, where you'll hit the road again in Corcubion and proceed to Cape Finisterre, Muxiz, Noya, and finally Santiago de Compostela. Daily distance is 30 to 35 miles, with longer and shorter options available.

Progressive Travel bills its itinerary as a pilgrimage to the relics of St. James in Santiago de Compostela, Spain. Although the trip begins in Oporto, you don't start cycling until the village of Braga. From there you'll work your way north across the border into Galicia, overnighting in Braga, Calheiros, Túy, and Pontevedra. Progressive's trip is short (only four days of riding), easy (average daily mileage is only about 35, and there is one rest day), and very luxurious (two nights with the Count of Calheiros). Progressive's trip may also be booked through Camino Tours (800-938-9311).

WHAT TO EXPECT

Mileage is not overwhelming on these trips, but the hilly terrain is not for the weak of quadricep. You should be an experienced long-distance cyclist in mid-season form. In all cases, however, there is a backup vehicle trailing along behind to pick up weary riders.

A highlight of these trips is the remarkable variety of charming and/or luxurious old castles, manor houses, and inns in which you'll stay. The sole mental challenge comes from grinding up long hills and, perhaps, the occasional rain shower. (Car traffic is generally very light; no problems there.) Backroads, whose company policy is to go all-out when it comes to lodging, puts its people up in particularly luxurious style.

Hardy folks who choose the Backroads camping trip will sleep in big tents at various European-style campgrounds, which are primarily designed for car-campers and have complete facilities. You'll have hordes of raucous neighbors, but it's a good way to get to know the European common folk.

This is not a ride for novice or tentative cyclists. You should be comfortable on narrow and/or rough roads, and possess good bike-handling skills to dodge wandering sheep and maneuver past oxcarts. Proper gear-shifting technique is essential on the numerous hills.

Trips run from July to October, but you may want to shoot for September—grape harvest season.

IN BRIEF

Backroads, 800-462-2848: 9 days, $2,498 inns or $1,198 camping
Easy Rider Tours, 800-488-8332: 9 days, $1,495
Euro Bike Tours, 800-321-6060: 14 days, $2,645
Progressive Travels, 800-245-2229: 7 days, $2,150

Physical challenge, 3; Mental challenge, 1; Skills, 2.

TURKEY

sailing the

turquoise coast

As our 747 began its final approach into Istanbul, I couldn't help thinking about the 1978 movie *Midnight Express*, a semi-true story of an American kid, busted for hashish at this very airport, who spends five nightmarish years in a Turkish prison. In the film, Turkey is depicted as a primitive, sadistic police state, and its people as leering, filthy brutes. I know it's only a movie, but the dark images linger.

It's not just the movies. There are certain disturbing historical facts. In 1821, at the Bridge of Alamana, Turks roasted alive, on a spit, the Greek deacon Althanasios, turning him into a human shish kebab. In 1824, Turkish soldiers herded 370 Christians, mostly women and children, into a cave in Crete and lit a bonfire at the entrance, suffocating everyone inside. The death of a million Armenians at the hands of Turks in 1915 is widely regarded as genocidal slaughter. Even as our plane touched down on the runway, there were reports of wholesale burning of Kurdish villages in eastern Turkey by government troops. What sort of people are these who commit such atrocities?

I am not the first to ponder the character of the Turks. In 1876, a British army officer, Capt. Frederick Burnaby, set off on a five-month journey through Asia Minor on horseback. His purpose, he wrote, was to answer the question "Are the Turks really such awful scoundrels? . . . Should I not behold Christians impaled and wriggling like worms on hooks in every high road of Armenia . . . ? This was not at all improbable . . . judging from the pamphlets which were continually being written about the inhuman nature of the Turks."

Sharing Burnaby's doubts, I was therefore astonished to have a number of undeniably human encounters with Turks in my first couple of days in the country. There was the fruit seller in Bodrum, eating a tangerine as I walked by his market stand, who reflexively handed me the remaining slices, as if incapable of passing up a chance for spontaneous generosity to a stranger. The young man who told a passing American woman, "My lady, you dropped something," and when she looked around in confusion, said with a gentle smile, "It was my heart." Or the cook on our 75-foot sailing yacht who, a few hours after meeting his American guests, was parading around the deck, gloriously drunk on raki and wearing only his underwear, arm in arm with a like-minded and like-attired newfound friend from Utah.

You make friends fast traveling by small boat. We were sailing on a traditional two-masted Turkish craft called a *gulet*, whose spacious decks and cozy private cabins make them ideal platforms for sybaritic voyages along one of the world's most alluring coastlines. The *gulets*, which have been sailing these waters in one form or another for centuries, were nearly extinct by the 1970s. But around that time the wealthy Istanbul crowd adopted it as a way to escape the madness of Turkish roads and explore the Aegean coastline, a rugged and inaccessible area festooned with ancient ruins. The idea of languidly sailing from cove to cove through warm turquoise seas, all the while swimming, snorkeling, and hiking to three-thousand-year-old cities, caught on quickly. The subsequent cruising boom has transformed the sleepy coastal towns of Bodrum, Marmaris, and Antalya into international resorts whose harbors teem with moored *gulets*, their wooden masts bobbing in vast thickets.

But the resurgent popularity of the *gulets* has come at a price: most are now frigates of illusion. The gleaming teak and mahogany hulls appear to be those of immaculately restored antiques, but most have been manufactured in the last decade. The masts and elaborate rigging are now mostly for show; diesel engines are the primary means of locomotion these days. Some *gulets* don't even carry sails. But the deception is harmless enough, and makes for a timely and comfortable, if not entirely authentic, voyage.

The sense of history one feels along Turkey's Aegean coast, however, is about as authentic as it gets. We were plying the same waters as the warships and galleons of Greece, Rome, Lycia, and Byzantium, whose empires ebbed and flowed along this coastline. Their civilizations left ruins on top of ruins, some of them accessible only from the sea. Alexander the Great passed this way, as did Antony and Cleopatra, Hannibal, Caesar, and the Virgin Mary. There has been enough war, love, worship, conquest, myth, betrayal, artistry, greed, genius, and death along these 300 miles of beach and cove to overwhelm even the most voracious student of history.

Three of the Seven Wonders of the Ancient World are right in the neighborhood. But ancient history is so tightly woven into the fabric of life here that they arouse little in the way of wonderment among the locals. Cows, goats, and turkeys graze the sacred marble slabs of the Temple of Artemis, now a vast foundation with a solitary column still standing from the original 110. We saw no other visitors there, only a nine-year-old girl rounding up the turkeys with a long stick, and a young boy, perhaps her brother, who tried to sell us picture postcards. Failing that, he conspiratorially pulled from his pocket two badly corroded coins emblazoned with the heads of Greek warriors. His asking price of only 250,000 lira (about $7) at first seemed a bargain for an ancient Greek coin, but we became suspicious when he quickly dropped the price to 50,000 lira, then 20,000. So happy was the young man to make a sale even at that low price that he threw in the second coin for free. The locals, of course, manufacture the bogus coins by the thousands, submerging them in the sea for six months to give them the patina of three thousand years.

The Turkish coastline has long been a flashpoint of enmity between Greeks and Turks, who have despised each other for centuries. Their proximity and mutual loathing result in some delicious ironies. For example, Ataturk, the heroic father of modern Turkey who founded the current nation-state in 1923, and whose picture adorns virtually every home and business in the country, was born in Greece. Ephesus, the superbly restored Roman seaport that is Turkey's top tourist attraction outside Istanbul, was originally built by Greeks—a fact Turkish tour guides concede only with prodding.

In the early twentieth century, this coastline belonged to Greece. But with the coming of Ataturk, more than a million Greeks were forced out of their villages in the new Turkey and exchanged for a like number of Turks then living in Greece. One of those instant Greek ghost towns, Kayakoy, still stands empty, a twentieth-century ruin only a two-hour walk from the beach through rugged, forested hills. A handful of Turkish families, braving the bad karma of the place, have moved in, using the two abandoned Greek Orthodox basilicas as stables for their farm animals. But, perhaps uneasy at the sacrilege, they hedge their bets: Windowsills are lined with tin cans full of basil and oregano to ward off any Greek spirits that may still haunt the town.

During our trip, Greece unilaterally declared an expansion of its territorial waters from 3 miles offshore to 12. This created an interesting situation, for any number of Greek islands lie less than 12 miles off the Turkish coast; the Greeks appeared to be claiming jurisdiction right up to Turkey's beaches. Indeed, the very waters in which we were sailing, a few hundred yards off the Turkish coast, were apparently being appropriated by Greece—a claim that of course elicited sneering derision from our crew. "The Greeks are filthy dogs," said our captain, spitting overboard for emphasis. "We will crush them like worms if they try to enforce their claims."

To make matters even more intriguing, at the time of our voyage, both countries were carrying out naval exercises in the same part of the Aegean, not far from us. Tensions were running high on both sides. Would Greek gunboats disrupt our snorkeling and on-board brunches with cannon fire? Would our *gulet*, along with its occupants, be pressed into battle against the infidels? Would we at last witness firsthand the reputed fierceness and cruelty of the Turks? Sadly, nothing came of the border spat, and our opportunity for a fine adventure was lost.

Instances of fierceness and cruelty, in fact, were entirely absent during our trip. On the contrary, friendliness and generosity seemed the order of the day everywhere we traveled in Turkey. By the end of our voyage, *Midnight Express* seemed an irrelevant cartoon that depicted a place and a people of which I saw no inkling. Brutish prisons and atrocities there may be. But as a citizen of a country that since 1978 has executed nearly three hundred prisoners, and which in 1945 incinerated 350,000 people—mostly women, children, and refugees—in Dresden, Tokyo, Hiroshima, and Nagasaki, I hesitate to judge the character of a people by the actions of its government and military.

Captain Burnaby, the English officer who rode his horse across Asia Minor, reached the same conclusion. After five months of firsthand observation, nowhere could he confirm the reports of impalings and other cruelties to foreigners then circulating in England. He found just the opposite, in fact. "Hospitality is rife . . . no matter where an Englishman may ask for shelter, he will never find a Mohammeden who will deny him admittance."

"Their generosity is equally great," he continued. "In fact, they carry this virtue to excess. People in [England] who abuse the Turkish nation, and accuse them of every vice under the sun would do well to leave off writing pamphlets and travel a little in Anatolia."

Even Burnaby's crusty manservant Radford, whose blunt observations of the Turks were a model of political incorrectness, came around in the end. After saying good-bye to their Turkish guide and helper, Radford conceded, "That Mohammed was not such a bad chap after all, sir. Them Turks have stomachs and like filling them, they do; but they have something in their hearts as well."

OUTFITTERS

Avenir Adventures starts its Turkey trip with five days of touring in Istanbul, Bursa, Troy, Kusadasi, and Ephesus. The *gulet* cruise, which begins in Marmaris, is a six-day out-and-back excursion to Fethiye. As with all the other outfitters listed here, the *gulet* cruise includes numerous shore excursions at towns, villages, and ruins along the route.

Far Horizons, which specializes in archaeological trips, has only one Turkey departure per year, in September. You'll spend twelve days cruising from Marmaris to Antalya. There are numerous stops at archaeological sites along the way, including a personal tour of Patara, the former Lycian capital, by the director of the site's ongoing excavation project. The trip also includes an "insider's" tour of ancient sites in Istanbul.

The itinerary of *Geographic Expeditions* includes twelve days of sailing, beginning in Antalya and working westward along the coast to Marmaris. There are, of course, daily stops for swimming and hiking to various ruins. On the way back to Istanbul, you'll stop at Ephesus. An extension to the rock spires and cave dwellings of Cappadocia is available.

The *Mountain Travel-Sobek* trip begins in Ankara, from which you'll drive to Cappadocia, before continuing to Antalya and Finike to board the *gulet*. Then it's six days on the water, cruising west from Finike to Marmaris. On the drive back to Istanbul, you'll stop at Ephesus. This trip includes virtually no time in Istanbul; you may wish to add a few days there on your own.

Overseas Adventure Travel, which includes airfare from New York in its trip price, takes you from Istanbul to Cappadocia for three days of touring, then to Finike to board the *gulet*. Seven days of cruising will take you to Marmaris, with the usual stop at Ephesus on the way back to Istanbul.

The *REI Adventures* itinerary includes an eight-day out-and-back sail along the coast from Marmaris, with stops at Caunos, Sarigerme, Batikhamam, Turuncpinar, Dislbilmez Cove, and Cenner Island. There are two days in Istanbul before boarding the *gulet*.

Starting in Istanbul, *Wilderness Travel* clients stop at Ephesus on the way to Marmaris, the starting point of the cruise. You'll spend eleven days on the water, making frequent stops along the way and finishing at Antalya. Then it's back to Istanbul for a day of touring.

WHAT TO EXPECT

This is about as soft as it gets—mostly lounging around on a *gulet* and walking around villages and ancient ruins. (Some trips also include several days touring by bus or van.) Optional day hikes to archaeological sites are typically one to three hours, over occasionally steep trails.

Aboard the *gulet*, you'll have all the comforts of home except space. Sleeping accommodations are very cozy indeed, suitable only for roommates with mutually amorous or erotic interests. Sleeping out on deck is a pleasant alternative that is preferred by some. Those with unbridled erotic interest might keep in mind that a hollow wooden ship has acoustic qualities not unlike those of a monstrously oversized cello. Few sounds will go unheard.

The idea of hanging out on a yacht may seem idyllic, but the reality can be a chore for some people. The languorous pace may make active, goal-oriented types restless. The tight quarters intensify group dynamics, and God forbid you should get a real jerk in the group, for there is simply no escape, other than the shore excursions. Also keep in mind that the sybaritic appeal of the trip may attract self-centered whiners who don't normally take an adventure trip, as well as the occasional party animal. If drunken revelry is not your idea of a good time, bring earplugs. Even if it is, bring them.

The weather is generally excellent, with warm, sunny days and cool nights. Rough seas are rare, but seasickness is a possibility for the susceptible.

You'll enjoy the trip more if you are an accomplished swimmer and snorkeler, comfortable in the water for long periods.

Trips run from May to October. July and August have the hottest weather and biggest crowds; expect some competition for choice mooring spots in the most picturesque coves.

RECOMMENDED READING

On Horseback Through Asia Minor by Capt. Frederick Burnaby. An 1898 account of the author's five-month 1,000-mile journey accompanied by his trusty servants Radford and Mohammed.

IN BRIEF

Avenir Adventures, 800-367-3230: 14 days, $1,995

Far Horizons, 800-552-4575: 6 days, $4,895 (includes airfare from New York)

Geographic Expeditions, 800-777-8183: 17 days, $2,690

Mountain Travel-Sobek, 800-227-2384: 12 days, $2,350 to $2,550

Overseas Adventure Travel, 800-221-0814: 17 days, $3,290 (includes airfare from New York)

REI Adventures, 800-622-2236: 13 days, $1,795

Wilderness Travel, 800-368-2794: 17 days, $2,495 to $2,745

Physical challenge, 1; Mental challenge, 2; Skills, 1.

ASIA
& THE
PACIFIC

H A W A I I

h i k i n g   t h e

o u t   i s l a n d s

The traveler to Hawaii who passes his days on the beach is a fool. Hawaiian beaches are not much different from thousands of others around the world: sand, water, waves, searing human flesh. The allure of Hawaii lies in its interior: waterfalls, lava deserts, jungles, rainbows, rivers of fire. We headed inland.

The Big Island

As we emerge onto the floor of the Kilauea caldera, our senses reel in confusion. Seconds ago my wife, Lisa, and I were hiking down a cool, dark jungle path, pushing aside umbrella-size ferns. Now we are staring out in befuddlement at a stark plain of black rubble, featureless but for columns of drifting steam. It is a 1950s comic-book artist's rendition of the surface of the moon.

Kilauea is generally considered the most active volcano on earth. At this moment, it is spewing red-hot lava into the sea from a rift a few miles south of here, churning up a column of steam and brown gas that drifts out to sea in a 30-mile-long plume. Kilauea periodically erupts in geysers of red-hot lava that shoot up ten times higher than Old Faithful's tepid burps. Walking across this landscape, tiptoeing past the steam vents, I am both thrilled and petrified at the prospect—slim but very real—that the ground beneath my feet could literally erupt in fire at any moment.

Following rock cairns for 2 miles across the caldera floor, we come to a crater within the crater. Halemaumau is a half mile wide and 430 feet deep. Its steep walls are frosted a sulfurous yellow, and more of the comic-book steam hisses from vents in the crater floor. Legend has it that here lives Pele, the Hawaiian goddess of fire, whose anger triggers volcanic eruptions. Near the crater rim I see what at first appears to be the leavings of a particularly thoughtless picnicker—a box of chocolates, five oranges and a grapefruit, a salami, and a bouquet of flowers, all spread out on a newspaper. Oddly, the food is untouched. This is not litter, but a traditional offering to Pele, tendered in the hope that she will stay quiet a little longer.

Like all gods, Pele works in mysterious ways. In 1824, at virtually the same spot on which we are now standing, a female Hawaiian tribal leader, recently turned Christian by determined missionaries, set out to demonstrate the futility of pagan worship. With the fervor of the newly converted, she marched into the Pele shrine that then stood on the rim of Halemaumau, shouldered aside a Pele priestess, and strode to the precipice, which in those days overlooked a cauldron of boiling red lava. Breaking a powerful taboo, she proceeded to eat sacred ohelo berries without first throwing an offering of them into the crater. After that sacrilege, she shouted, "Jehovah is my God! He kindled these fires. . . . I fear not Pele!" No retaliatory eruption ensued, and as word spread of the unpunished blasphemy, paganism in Hawaii began an abrupt decline.

A century later, the manager of the nearby Volcano House

hotel made another offering to Pele with rather different results. Kilauea had been dormant for years, and as a result the hotel's occupancy rate had declined to perilous levels. In desperation, the manager hiked down to Halemaumau and tossed into the lifeless pit a lei of ohelo berries and, for good measure, a bottle of gin. Reversing the usual procedure, he implored Pele to erupt. Within hours, smoke and steam began to billow forth, and red lava bubbled up the next day. The hotel was soon jammed with curious onlookers. Go figure.

We trek on over the rubble to Kilauea Iki, a smaller crater just east of the main caldera. Here the frozen lava floor is smoother, like an asphalt parking lot immediately after the nuclear holocaust, still warm to the touch. The steam, instead of merely wafting out of the earth, jets out here and there with an audible roar. Around the vents, plants grow like weeds in the crack of a sidewalk, nourished by the condensed steam. Curious, I casually thrust my hand into a crack, only to jerk it back out, nearly scalded.

Here, in 1959, occurred one of the most spectacular volcanic eruptions ever closely observed. In full view of hundreds of gaping tourists in their rental cars, a dozen lava geysers shot into the air simultaneously, one of them reaching 1,900 feet. As the spurting lava cooled, it fell in a smoking sleet of black stones that ranged in size from pea to piano. Thousands of birds, asphyxiated in midair by sulfurous gases, fell dead into the molten lake. By the time it subsided, the 1959 eruption raised the floor of the Kilauea Iki crater more than 300 feet.

Grateful to Pele for the boost in elevation, we wearily climb out of the crater into the jungle and make our way to the nearby Thurston Lava Tube. By now inured to the fantastic, we take it as a matter of course that a 20-foot-high tunnel would appear suddenly in the middle of a forest of ferns and blooming fuchsia flowers, and then proceed some 1,200 feet underground. A few million years ago, the tunnel was a subterranean conduit for molten lava. Today, by all appearances, it stands ready to accept a subway train, should the need ever arise for mass transportation in the Hawaiian rain forest.

Kauai

Having been disappointed a few years ago by the extravagantly named but modestly endowed "Grand Canyon of Pennsylvania," I have low expectations for the "Grand Canyon of the Pacific." But as we pull off Route 550 at a scenic viewpoint overlooking Waimea Canyon, I feel that surge of excitement that precedes a journey by foot into new and rugged territory. It may not be 7,000 feet deep like its Arizona namesake, but Waimea Canyon has the same reddish hue, and at a depth of 3,000 feet, it is still a crevice to reckon with. Up near its head I see something even the Grand Canyon cannot match: a pair of ribbonlike waterfalls cascading hundreds of feet down the canyon wall.

Hiking boots in place, we set off toward 800-foot Waipo'o Falls, the larger of the two cataracts we had seen from the viewpoint. The trail, at first gradually downhill through a forest fragrant with eucalyptus, soon dives steeply. As the vegetation thins out, vistas of the canyon open up below. Scrambling out along a vertiginous ridge to a viewpoint, we are forced to move on hands and knees over the loose, badly eroded red dirt, which is oddly free of vegetation.

The mystery of the bare dirt is soon revealed. On the next ridge we see a herd of goats, heads down and chewing. The goats, we learn later, were originally imported by European explorers and have roamed the canyon for centuries, wreaking environmental havoc wherever they go. Waimea Canyon goats are now fiercely protected from meddling environmentalists by hunters, who like to kill them for fun. It seems to me that shooting these goats would not be a particularly sporting proposition; from our current vantage point, one could easily pick off the nearby herd at will. Retrieving the bodies, however, would seem to require a rope, harness, and at least intermediate climbing skills. *That* would be fun.

The trail to the waterfall plunges into dense greenery again. Rain falls briefly, then the sky clears, then more showers. We eventually emerge from a grove of yellow ginger trees to a clear pool at the bottom of a modest waterfall, perhaps 20 or 30 feet high. We follow the stream a bit farther, and suddenly it disappears without a trace over a precipice, leading me to the sudden realization that we are not at the bottom of Waipo'o Falls, but its top. As Lisa grasps my ankles, I slither on my belly to the edge and peer down at the water accelerating silently away. I can just hear the faint thunder from far below.

We lie in the sun at the top of the falls, lulled by the gurgle of the creek, counting rainbows and the incessantly annoying tourist helicopters. By the time we doze off, the score is tied at four apiece.

Maui

It is four A.M., and the 10,023-foot summit of Haleakala looms somewhere above us in the darkness. We are following standard mountaineering procedure: depart for the summit in the middle of the night, so as to reach the top in the clear weather and ethereal light of dawn. We've been under way only a half hour, barely got our blood going, but already the Hertz Taurus is starting to feel the strain, downshifting repeatedly in the hairpins. As we climb, the air becomes steadily cooler, the trees smaller, and the road signs advise "Turn on Lights in Clouds."

At perhaps 9,000 feet we break out of the mist. One instant, white nothingness; the next, stars and the silhouette of the mountain against the faint eastern light. In the parking lot at the top are a dozen tour buses full of camera-toting pilgrims to the Haleakala sunrise ritual. As the sky reddens, motor-drives whine and flashbulbs pop. (Will someone please tell these morons that it is futile to use the flash on an object 93 million miles away?) We flee to a distant rock outcropping and watch the spectacle unencumbered by viewfinders. The sky turns a shade of red that I have previously seen only from the window of a jetliner.

As the redness fades and the sun clears the horizon, the pilgrim buses depart down the twisting road. We head in the opposite direction, hiking off down the Sliding Sands Trail into the Haleakala crater. Seven miles wide, it is not really a crater at all, but a valley of cinders scoured out of the summit by H_2O in all its forms: ice, water, and steam. While the young, active Kilauea was lunar in appearance, the older, long-dormant Haleakala more resembles the surface of Mars. From the red and brown sand of the crater floor rise a number of cinder cones, some as tall as 1,000 feet. When clouds envelop the crater, the cones poke up from the fog like islands from the sea—a miniature tableau of Hawaii itself. The crater floor is riddled with crevasses and caves. Into one of these deep pits, ancient Hawaiians would throw the severed umbilical cords of their newborns. This prevented the cords from being eaten by rats, which the Hawaiians believed would cause the babies to develop rodentlike facial features.

In a region so determinedly barren, we are astonished to discover at one point along the trail a cluster of large bushes with shiny spiked leaves. These are the famed silverswords, *Argyroxiphium sandwicense*, which exist nowhere in the world but the top of Haleakala. The silversword grows without flowering for anywhere from seven to thirty years until, with what biologist John L. Culliney calls "startling sexual exuberance," it thrusts a massive stalk 6 to 9 feet in the air and sprouts as many as five hundred red or yellow flowers. When the flowers fade, the plant soon dies and decomposes into what looks like a pile of ashes.

It strikes me as somehow fitting that the silversword has adopted the life cycle of the volcano itself: lingering dormancy, an unpredictable spurt into the air that is the color of fire, and a final return to dust—until the next eruption.

OUTFITTERS

Bill Crane of *Crane's Eco-Adventures* leads backpacking/camping trips on Kauai, Maui, and the Big Island. His itineraries vary from year to year, and he usually doesn't decide where to go until a few months before departure, so we can't list precise itineraries. He likes to stick to one island per trip, exploring it thoroughly rather than hopping around from island to island skimming the high spots. Destinations typically include the Na Pali Trail, Waimea Canyon, Haleakala, Hana, Kilauea, and the Waipio Valley. In each case, hikers camp out or stay in rustic cabins. Crane's trips usually include beach interludes to recover from the backpacking expeditions.

Eye of the Whale, owned by Kauai residents Mark and Beth Goodoni, offers a more upscale inn-based day-hiking trip that includes three days each on Kauai, Maui, and the Big Island. On Kauai, you'll take day hikes in Waimea Canyon, Kokee State Park, along the Na Pali Trail, and up Nonou Mountain. On Maui, hikers explore the West Maui Mountains, Haleakala crater, and climb to the viewpoint of Puu Olai. Then it's on to the Big Island and the crater of Kilauea Iki and the lush Waipio Valley. Beach and snorkeling sojourns are liberally sprinkled throughout the itinerary.

Accommodations are typically small inns, cabins, or B&Bs. Mark and Beth personally guide every trip.

WHAT TO EXPECT

Depends on which outfitter you choose. Crane's trippers will work hard physically, usually carrying full backpacks with food and camping gear, although on some days there may be pack-free day hikes. Daily walking distance ranges up to 10 miles. Eye of the Whale, on the other hand, offers a more gentle-manly hiking tour, with a pack-free daily walking distance averaging about 4 miles, with a maximum of 8. The going is occasionally steep—particularly on the Na Pali Trail and in Haleakala Crater—but should not present a serious problem for even the moderately fit. Daily elevation gains do not exceed 1,600 feet.

In terms of accommodations, there's a big difference between the two outfitters. Eye of the Whale employs a charming assortment of inns and B&Bs that provide all the comforts of home. About the only potential hardships we can think of are rain and mud. But you're tough. Suck it up.

Bill Crane demands true grit from his hikers. You'll stay in a combination of basic cabins and your own tent, which you'll be responsible for setting up and taking down yourself. You're also expected to pitch in with camp chores. The warm weather, however, makes the camping reasonably pleasant—unless serious rain sets in, in which case you'll suffer the usual miseries of bad-weather camping.

RECOMMENDED READING

Islands in a Far Sea by John L. Culliney. Musings on nature and man in Hawaii by a marine biology professor.

IN BRIEF

Crane's Eco-Adventures, 800-653-2545: 7 days, $700

Eye of the Whale, 800-659-3544: 10 days, $1,595. EOW also operates this same trip for four other outfitters, who in effect serve as booking agents. They are Above the Clouds (800-233-4499), American Wilderness Experience (800-444-0099), Journeys International (800-255-8735), and Road Less Traveled (800-488-8483).

Physical challenge, 2–3; Mental challenge, 1–3; Skills, 1.

MALAYSIA

into the heart
of borneo

The traveler to Borneo can gaze into the eyes of an orangutan, climb the highest mountain in Southeast Asia, watch at arm's length as a sea turtle lays its eggs in the sand, scuba dive along a 3,000-foot-deep sea wall, or sniff the stench of 2 million bats in a blimp hangar–size cave.

But to experience the heart and soul of Borneo, you must make a journey by riverboat. Roads are strictly a coastal phenomenon on this island of mountains and jungle; the mere motorist can only nibble around its edges. To the people of the interior, it is the rivers that are the lifelines of commerce and social intercourse. In the heart of Borneo, there is no north and south, no east and west, only upriver and downriver.

In the course of our travels from Mulu National Park, deep in the island's interior, to the coastal town of Miri, we traced virtually the entire length of the Baram River—and the evolution of Borneo river craft as well. On its upper reaches, where the Baram is no more than a precocious creek, we traveled in nimble motorized longboats only one evolutionary step above a hollowed-out log. Long as stretch limousines, they were only just wide enough to accept one set of fiftieth-percentile American buttocks. We sat on the floor like a six-man bobsled team as the water rushed by our elbows.

There was a crew of two. The bowman stood at the front with a bamboo pole to fend off obstacles in shallow water and to signal to the helmsman the bearing and distance of oncoming rocks and logs. The skipper stood in the stern, scanning the river ahead and jockeying the throttle of the outboard motor.

In shallow water, our helmsman employed a rather odd procedure: He continuously rammed the throttle of the 30 horsepower Yamaha from idle to full power and back to idle again, repeating the cycle every two or three seconds in a steady on-off rhythm. It made for a jerky, annoying ride and, it seemed to me, wasted a lot of fuel. Turns out, of course, there was a good reason for it. If we hit a rock, as often happens, there was a fifty-fifty chance that the propeller would be idling at the moment of impact, and would therefore not break off. Propeller repair costs—the major operating expense in these shallow waters—are thus cut by half.

In addition to their canny economic sense, the Borneo rivermen have reserves of resourcefulness unimaginable to modern-day Americans. We saw this firsthand one evening while lounging on the banks of the Baram in front of our lodge in the small river town of Mulu. Two young men, hooting and hollering, sped past in a longboat much like the one in which we'd arrived. Crossing another boat's wake, the driver made an exuberant swerve, which caused the insufficiently attached outboard motor to fly off the stern and disappear in a geyser of spray. Propelled only by its momentum, the engineless craft continued to glide down the river at high speed in utter silence, which was broken by the convulsive laughter of village onlookers even before the boat had come to a halt.

Nothing attracts a crowd like mishap, and within three

minutes, a half dozen longboats and twenty-five excited men and boys had converged on the spot where the motor had disappeared. They began diving overboard into the muddy 15-foot-deep water, each keen to be the first to find the sunken treasure. Within ten minutes, the motor had been located, hauled up with a rope, and taken ashore. Twenty minutes after that, the same two young men sped off in the same boat, its resuscitated motor humming smoothly at full throttle. As they disappeared around the bend, they were hooting and hollering still. A modern-day American would have just been ringing up his insurance agent by now and perhaps formulating plans to sue the outboard's manufacturer for the poor design of the motor mount.

As we proceeded downriver, the Baram became wider and the longboats larger and more elaborate. In Mulu, we stepped up to the next level of Borneo rivercraft: ten-passenger longboats equipped with raised seats wide enough for two people. Powered by twin 40-horsepower outboards, they required two helmsmen, who stood side-by-side in the stern and coordinated their throttle and steering movements to thread through the occasional logs and shallow spots in the widening river.

Once beyond the shallows, we transferred to a boxy forty-passenger diesel-powered enclosed craft that chugged along at perhaps 20 knots. It, too, was long and narrow, taking the log-canoe motif one more step up the technological ladder. The interior resembled that of a commuter airliner, with rows of seats four abreast, an aisle down the middle, and a window by each seat. Pleasant enough, but most of us preferred to lounge outside amid the luggage and cargo on the cabin roof, where the view of the passing rain forest was unobstructed. Reclining on a pillow of duffel bags, warmed by the sun and cooled by the modest slipstream, watching the walls of dense greenery pass by and the occasional heron scare up and flap away, I recall thinking that the citizens of Borneo seemed to have this business of river travel well in hand.

I was therefore entirely unprepared for what I saw as we pulled into the dock at Marudi, a throbbing market town where we would transfer once again for the final 100-mile run to Miri. There, nuzzling gunnel to gunnel into the dock like huge serpents at feeding time, floated what appeared to be two dozen jet airliners with their wings and tails excised. A closer look revealed that these were in fact not floating aircraft fuselages but rather the pinnacle of evolution in Borneo river travel, the express riverboat.

The aerodynamic sleekness of line of these craft was astonishing. One had almost the precise fuselage contours of the B-1 bomber, which is sinuously curved behind the cockpit to avoid a sudden buildup of shock waves during acceleration through the sound barrier, a velocity known to jet pilots as Mach 1. Since it was unlikely that the express boats could exceed even Mach 0.1, I could only conclude that the Coke-bottle fuselage shape was an aesthetic flourish, a boat designer's salute to his aeronautical brethren. Another express boat had a streamlined chine, a flat surface just above the waterline running from nose to tail, that gave it a startling resemblance to the SR-71 Blackbird, the sinister-looking Mach 3 spy plane.

A number of the boats had cockpit windows patterned precisely after those of popular airliners such as the Boeing 727 and McDonnell Douglas MD-80. (A private pilot and airplane buff, I am attuned to these delicate aesthetic distinctions.) There was even one boat with the familiar humplike cockpit of the 747. It was as if we had stumbled across a fleet of Borneo buses with '59 Chevy tailfins and Edsel grilles. As I rushed over for a closer look, however, the cockpit windows proved to be illusory, skillfully painted on to enhance the jet-airliner motif. I was later told by a guy in a bar in Kuching that a British TV documentary filmmaker fell for the trick, breathlessly reporting that those devilishly clever Borneo native chaps were actually salvaging surplus jet-airliner fuselages, installing diesel engines and underwater propellers, and turning them into passenger boats.

Of course, these craft have never taken wing in a previous life. They are designed and built in Sibu, a river town on Borneo's northern coast in the state of Sarawak. Operating primarily on the Baram and Rajang Rivers, they are the prime means of long-distance transport between the interior and the coastal towns. The express boats are designed specifically for local conditions—wide, smooth rivers; long distances between towns; no alternative means of travel—and are suitable for use nowhere else in the world. The express boats of Sarawak are a direct outgrowth of the cultural tradition and geography of this particular region, the ultimate high-tech refinement of the dugout canoes that have traveled Borneo's rivers for thousands of years.

According to the guy in the bar, the express boats are operated by highly competitive companies owned by ethnic Chinese families. Speed sells, and so they routinely flout the regulatory limit of 300 horsepower, souping up the engines and turbocharging them to 400 and more. The pilots are combinations of Chuck Yeager and Evel Knievel, an elite corp of dashing daredevils who are paid to push the envelope. A Malaysian insurance executive, whom I happened to sit next to on a plane to Kota Kinabalu, told me the express boats have a terrible safety record, with major accidents regularly hushed up. He said express-boat insurance is very expensive, and that consequently most companies do without.

Unaware of all this at the time, I could hardly wait to begin our journey to Miri in one of these sleek, shiny beasts. But one glance inside the cabin of our boat turned anticipation to fear.

The claustrophobic interior had all the appearance of a giant mailing tube, stretching nearly to the limit of vision, that had somehow been fitted with rows of miniature four-abreast seats. By the time I straggled aboard, all seats were full and the aisle was crammed with standees—or rather hunchees; the ceiling was no more than 5 feet high. It was a case of Concorde meets the Tokyo subway at rush hour.

I elected to ride outside. The smooth, curved surface of the fuselage made it awkward to sit on top, however, so I crouched on the narrow chine, which served as a walkway that ran the length of the fuselage. The paucity of fellow roof-riders aroused in me a sense of foreboding. On our previous boat, the majority of passengers rode outside. Why were all those idiots packed inside, rather than enjoying the sun and the breeze out here?

As the boat pulled away from the dock and began to accelerate, the answer all too quickly became clear. Within a few seconds, we had attained a speed I estimated at about 50 knots, slightly above the old U.S. national highway speed limit. The buffeting slipstream instantly tore off my hat, which disappeared in a maelstrom of spray. Hair whipped. Cheeks flapped. Fingers clenched the handholds in a deathgrip. Conversation with the few other roof-riders, carried on in windblown shouts, consisted primarily of guesses as to one's life expectancy after a fall overboard. My own estimate: perhaps two or three seconds.

The pilot, alarmingly young and wearing mirrored sunglasses, seemed to savor the speed and power at his command. Although provided with a sitdown cockpit and protective canopy at the very prow of the craft, he had removed the canopy and drove standing up, his upper body protruding into the wind like a golden retriever from a station wagon. A silk scarf would have been entirely appropriate under the circumstances.

At the first bend in the river, he cranked the boat into a

sharp right turn. I was appalled to feel the boat heeling over to the left, like a car. Something was seriously wrong. Properly designed planing boats—and aircraft, for that matter—are supposed to lean into turns, not away from them. Glancing toward the rear of the craft, I noticed yet another harbinger of doom. Lashed to the roof was a spare drive shaft and propeller, its blades glinting gold in the sun.

Squinting against the slipstream, I sighted an upriver boat in the distance bearing down on us at a closing speed of perhaps 100 miles per hour. We appeared to be on a collision course. Just as I began to coil my legs for the leap clear of the impending holocaust, the pilot cut the engine. The other driver did the same. The boats coasted directly at each other for several hundred yards before bobbing to a stop virtually nose to nose. One of our passengers hopped over to the other boat, and the pilots exchanged waves and roared off.

Up ahead, the sky turned black. The rain began slowly at first, the fat drops stinging my skin. The pilot ordered us few remaining roof-riders back inside, donned a motorcycle helmet and face shield, and resumed his standing position in the teeth of the gale. Our speed remained undiminished.

Crawling through the hatch, I assumed occupancy of the last few available cubic inches of interior space. Pressed by bodies on all sides, bent over at the waist, listening to the rain batter the roof an inch or two away from my ear and the occasional crash of thunder even above the sound of the engine, I hung on as the boat heeled from side to side in high-speed turns and skipped across occasional waves. There was a smell of sweat and diesel fuel. A yard from my face, a television monitor played a Japanese kung-fu movie at high volume, apparently to distract passengers from the fact that the boat had no emergency exits whatsoever. Some of the newest express boats, I'm told, are equipped with on-board karaoke machines. I imagine that Springsteen's "I'm Going Down" is a popular choice.

Upon our arrival in Miri and reintroduction to solid ground, a great wave of relief washed over me. I walked away feeling grateful to have survived. But then I stopped and turned around for a last look. God, is that thing cool, a dead ringer for the SR-71.

OUTFITTERS

Asia Transpacific Journeys's Borneo itinerary is a smorgasbord that includes diving paradise Sipadan Island, the Danum Valley, Sukau rain forest, Sepilok orangutan sanctuary, Mulu National Park, and Mount Kinabalu National Park. Activities include snorkeling, swimming, nature hikes, river trips, and cave exploration. Nontechnical climbs of 13,455-foot Mount Kinabalu and the Pinnacles—a rock formation in Mulu park—are optional.

The itinerary of British outfitter *Explore Worldwide* actually begins in Brunei, the tiny sultanate on Borneo's north coast. From there you'll fly to Mulu National Park for a jungle hike and visits to several caves and a village of the Penan tribe. Then it's down the river to Miri via longboat and express boat. There follows a nontechnical climb of Mount Kinabalu, a visit to a turtle-breeding island, and an orangutan sanctuary.

After arriving in Kuching with *Lost World Adventures,* you'll proceed upriver by longboat for a two-day stay in an Iban village that includes jungle trekking. There follow another river journey to Sukau jungle lodge, near Sandakan, and a visit to the Sepilok orangutan sanctuary. The trip finishes with a choice: two days of lounging around the luxurious oceanfront Tanjung Aru resort, or a two-day climb of Mount Kinabalu. (The climb is $275 extra.)

Outer Edge Expeditions's multisport adventure includes a climb of Kinabalu, a serious spelunking expedition into the caves of Gunung Mulu Park, a smoothwater kayak trip, a Class III whitewater rafting run, jungle hikes, and stays with Iban tribesmen. Group size is limited to six; price will be higher for small group size.

Overseas Adventure Travel's no-sweat itinerary includes visits to Mulu National Park, an Iban longhouse at Ulu Ai, Sepilok orangutan sanctuary, and Kinabalu National Park. There's also a one-day excursion to the sultanate of Brunei.

WHAT TO EXPECT

There are two main physical tests on most Borneo trips, both optional. The climb of 13,455-foot Mount Kinabalu is a challenging two-day affair. The first day is a five-hour hike that gains 5,400 feet; the second a three-hour 2,500-foot hike/scramble to the summit followed by a five-hour 7,900-foot descent.

The climb to the Pinnacles, the bizarre limestone formations in Mulu National Park, is a difficult and very steep two-hour climb up a rocky and tree-rooted trail. Low-altitude heat and humidity add to the challenge. The descent is also difficult, due to steepness and poor footing. (Be sure to wear stiff-soled shoes or boots; I stupidly wore running shoes up the Pinnacles and the soles of my feet hurt for several days afterward.) Both the Pinnacles and Kinabalu require a bit of scrambling with the aid of ladders and/or ropes.

Kinabalu and the Pinnacles aside, most of these trips demand only modest physical effort: leisurely day hikes, snorkeling, and walking through caves.

Accommodations are a very mixed bag. At times you may be lounging in the lap of luxury at fancy hotels, on other occasions sleeping in a jungle lean-to and picking off leeches. (Don't worry too much about the leeches. They're tiny and don't hurt a bit; the pesky little critters inject you with an anesthetic before they begin to suck your blood. Canvas "leech gaiters" designed to protect feet and calves are only partially effective. Unless you are seriously squeamish or a hemophobe, Borneo leeches are not a big deal.)

RECOMMENDED READING

Into the Heart of Borneo by Redmond O'Hanlon. The author, a fat lazy British literary critic, and his poet friend set out on a lunatic voyage to find a prehistoric rhinoceros. Simultaneously hilarious and horrifying.

IN BRIEF

Asia Transpacific Journeys, 800-642-2742: 16 days, $2,995
Explore Worldwide, 011-44-252-319-448: 14 days, $1,335.
   This trip can be booked in the United States by Adventure
   Center (800-227-8747).
Lost World Adventures, 800-999-0558: 15 days, $3,550 (including air fare from Los Angeles)
Outer Edge Expeditions, 800-322-5236: 16 days, $2,290
Overseas Adventure Travel, 800-221-0814: 17 days, $3,690
   (including air fare from Los Angeles)

Physical challenge, 2–3; Mental challenge, 2; Skills, 1.

MONGOLIA

horseback riding in
genghis khan country

Four P.M., June 25, 1994. On the windy steppes of southwest
Mongolia, it was a propitious moment indeed: the hour of the
horse, on the day of the horse, in the year of the horse. Atop
a hill on a rolling plain of grass, under an enormous sky, a
Buddhist lama and four monks chanted incantations before
a cairn of rocks. Leaving offerings of cheese and vodka, they descended the hill to a 150-acre paddock containing a herd of
small, shaggy horses with thick necks and bristly manes. The
lama tied a ceremonial blue scarf to a fence post and opened
the latch on the paddock gate. As it swung open, the horses—
a stallion named Patron, born and bred in a zoological park in
the Ukraine, and five mares raised in the Netherlands—edged
warily toward the opening.

When the six horses trotted out to freedom in their ancestral
homeland, it marked the first time in perhaps twenty-five years
that the world's only species of wild horse had run free. Known
locally as *takhi*, and in the West as Przewalski's (roughly, "sha-
VAL-ski's") horses, these wary, skittish creatures have never
been domesticated, not even by the Mongols, renowned as the

world's best horsemen. (There's a story that Genghis Khan, setting out on a campaign in 1226, encountered a herd of wild *takhi*, which so unnerved Genghis's own horse that it reared, throwing the ruler of half the known world to the ground.) The ancestors of the wild horse probably mingled with woolly mammoths and saber-toothed tigers; drawings of *takhi*-like animals appear in cave paintings in France that date back twenty thousand years. By 5,000 B.C., however, the horses had been exterminated by human hunters in Europe and had retreated to the remote steppes of inner Asia.

The *takhi* were apparently first seen by a European around 1720. John Bell, a Scotsman traveling to China in the service of Peter the Great, described them as "the most watchful creatures alive. One of them waits always on the heights, to give warning to the rest; and, upon the least approach of danger, runs to the herd . . . upon which all of them fly away, like so many deer." After Bell's brief and scientifically undocumented sighting, nothing was heard of the phantom wild horses for more than a century.

In 1878, however, Col. Nikolai Przewalski, a Russian explorer returning from Tibet, sighted two small herds of wild horses near what is now the border of Mongolia and the Chinese frontier province of Xinjiang. He tried vainly to shoot one, but the horses caught his scent from a 1,000 yards away and sprinted off "like a windstorm." From a local government bureaucrat, Przewalski received a gift of the skull and hide of one of the horses. Examined at the St. Petersburg Zoological Museum, they were pronounced a new species of horse, unlike any known domestic animal. In honor of the explorer, the new species was named *Equus caballus przewalskii*.

Private wild animal collections were all the rage among European nobility in those days, and word of Przewalski's horse spread rapidly. The first attempt to capture a P-horse (as they are now commonly referred to by aficionados) was commissioned by a Ukrainian land baron with the suitably self-important name of Friederich E. von Falz-Fein. The capture attempt was a dismal failure. The pursuers quickly discovered what Bell and Przewalski had already reported: that the horses were much too fast and skittish to be captured alive in the wide-open treeless terrain of the Mongolian steppe. Just getting close enough to shoot one required days of dogged pursuit.

The professional animal catchers hired by Falz-Fein, ever resourceful in the pursuit of their profession, finally figured out a way to capture a Przewalski's horse alive: go after newborn foals. The young horses could be run to exhaustion, then lassoed with a noose at the end of a long pole. (Mongolian nomads, persuaded by offers of winter boots and hard Russian currency, were enlisted to make the actual captures.) It was usually necessary to shoot the foal's mother, as well as protective stallions, but this was apparently considered just another cost of doing business.

The foals thus caught, however, died from lack of milk almost immediately. The resourceful animal catchers solved this problem by bringing in domestic mares to suckle the foals during the long journey back to Europe. (It was, of course, necessary to kill the domestic mare's own foal before she would accept the foster child.) Finally, in 1899, four young Przewalski's fillies arrived at von Falz-Fein's estate near the Black Sea.

But the big breakthrough occurred in 1901, when the renowned Hamburg animal catcher and dealer Carl Hagenbeck brought back a large shipment of Przewalski's horses for the Duke of Bedford. Hagenbeck, a man of no small ego, let it be known far and wide that his own crew of intrepid and ingenious animal catchers had chased down and captured the elusive horses. In fact, Hagenbeck simply bought them from a middleman in Asia who had already captured them for von

Falz-Fein. The wily baron, however, hoping to pressure the middleman into a lower price, had been holding up payment. Hagenbeck, with cash on the barrelhead, bought the horses right out from under von Falz-Fein's nose, to the baron's everlasting fury.

The capture and transport of Hagenbeck's horses to Hamburg was a massive undertaking. The hired horsenappers had seized a total of fifty-six foals—killing a number of stallions and mares in the process—and packed them into bags, which were slung onto the backs of camels, one on each side. The one-hundred camel caravan—ten were required just to carry the condensed milk for the hungry foals—took fifteen days to reach the Ob River in southern Russia. There the young horses were transferred to a riverboat, where the domestic mares awaited to suckle them for the remainder of their journey. The entourage eventually transferred to a train for the final 3,000-mile leg to Hamburg. Only twenty-eight horses survived the six-month journey.

The next year, a second hunt netted a batch of eleven, the survivors of a much larger catch. Meanwhile, the wild population of Przewalski's horses, already precarious, was shrinking rapidly. By the 1930s and 1940s, Mongolian nomads were infiltrating the horses' range with their own stock of cattle and sheep, driving the horses away from their grazing land and water. Chinese Kazakhs, having acquired repeater rifles, began to hunt them for food. By the 1960s, even the wandering nomads rarely saw wild horses anymore. The last confirmed sighting of a Przewalski's horse in the wild, by a Mongolian biologist, came in 1969. Soon thereafter, the species *E. przewalskii* become extinct in the wild.

After Hagenbeck's two big turn-of-the-century roundups, only a handful of P-horses were captured and returned to Europe, the last in 1947. The capture of these fifty-odd foals—

and the accompanying deaths of perhaps one hundred other foals, adult stallions, and mares—certainly hastened the breed's disappearance in the wild. Ironically, though, in the end the brutish business was all that saved *E. przewalskii* from complete extinction.

At first, the captured horses fared poorly. A number died behind bars, and captive breeding proved difficult in the early days. Only thirteen animals reproduced. World War II was particularly hard on the P-horse population; Allied firebomb attacks killed a number of them in the Hamburg zoo and the Schorfheide nature preserve near Berlin, which Hermann Goering had established as a refuge for all the historical species of the Reich. By 1946, only thirty-one Przewalski's horses remained alive in captivity.

In the late 1950s, however, zoos began to cooperate in their breeding efforts, exchanging animals and selecting mates to minimize inbreeding. A detailed studbook was created, with genetic information on every Przewalski's horse ever captured or bred in captivity. By 1970, the captive population had grown to two hundred, and today it stands at well over a thousand—enough to support the current program of reintroduction into the wild. As of 1996, eighteen Przewalski's horses had been released in Mongolia's Hustain Nuru reserve, and twelve more were nearing the end of their two-year acclimatization periods inside the paddock at the reserve headquarters. So far, it has been among the most successful reintroductions ever of an almost extinct species to the wild.

Even after a dozen generations in captivity, the Przewalski's horses have maintained their stubborn independence. Only two are known to have been ridden, briefly and with great trepidation on the part of both horse and rider. A picture from the 1920s shows a fur-hatted Russian man sitting astride a P-horse with studied calmness and a very tight rein. (If you look closely, you can see a rope tied around the animal's right rear ankle.) "I assume the guy in the picture was bucked off three seconds after it was taken," says Lee Boyd, a biologist who did her Ph.D. dissertation on the behavior of Przewalski's horses and has spent thousands of hours observing them, almost always from a distance.

"You could stand in a corral for five years with a Przewalski's horse and never get close to it," agrees Linda Svendsen, who's tried. A P-horse fancier, she is codirector of Boojum Expeditions, which operates horseback treks in the Darhat Valley of Mongolia, just north of the Hustain Nuru reserve.

The Mongolian horses ridden on Svendsen's treks are close cousins of the Przewalski clan, and share some of their traits: small, sturdy, tough, and independent. "There was a rodeo every morning when we tried to saddle them up," reports Boojum rider Tim Cahill. The normal gait of the Mongolian ponies—a short, jarring trot—is perfectly suited for the rough, tussocky terrain of the steppe, but entirely unsuited to human anatomy, or at least American human anatomy. Boojum riders, who tend to walk funny by the end of their trips, call it the Mongolian Death Trot.

But even the tough little Mongolian pony, like a dog among wolves, is no match for his wild relatives. Some years ago, a feral herd of escaped Mongolian domestic horses encountered a Przewalski's stallion in the wild. The P-horse attacked the rival stallion, killed it, and ran off with his band of mares. A nomad who later found the dying feral stallion reported that "His legs were broken, his ears torn off, and his skin was torn to shreds. His internal injuries appeared to be just as severe."

Boojum's horse trips in Mongolia conclude with a visit to the Hustain Nuru reserve to see the Przewalski's horses. Those animals doing their transition time in the paddock are easily viewed. As for catching a glimpse of the P-horses that have already been released into the wild, "It's anybody's guess," admits Svendsen.

OUTFITTERS

Boojum Expeditions pioneered horseback trips into central Asia in 1985. Its Mongolian itinerary begins in Beijing, whence trip members fly to Ulaan Baatar, the capital of Mongolia. After a day of sightseeing, including a visit to a herdsmen's festival, you'll fly to Moron. From there, trip members pile into a converted Russian troop transport and drive for two days ("Sometimes on what you might call a road," adds Boojum director Linda Svendsen reassuringly) to the village of Renchinlhumbe in the Darhat Valley. There you'll meet your Mongolian horses and wranglers, and take a short shakedown ride. Then it's eight days of riding, across vast meadows, through forests, and over high mountain passes. The precise riding itinerary will unfold according to circumstance, but will almost certainly include a visit with a band of Psaatan "reindeer people." Accommodations are in two-man tents. There is no vehicle support; supplies and equipment are carried on packhorses.

Return trip from Renchinlhumbe to Beijing will retrace the route in reverse, with a detour to the Hustain Nuru reserve to see the Przewalski's horses.

Boojum offers another trip in the same general area that includes four days of riding along the eastern shore of nearby Lake Hovsgol, with vehicle support. Travelers then abandon their saddles and pick up paddles for a five-day self-supported sea-kayak trip (no boat or vehicle accompanies the kayaks) down the western shore of the lake. Trip length is sixteen days; cost in $3,650.

A newcomer to the Mongolian horse-trekking scene, *First Contacts* offers an itinerary generally similar to Boojum's but with twelve days in the saddle instead of eight. The riding begins and ends in Tsagaan Nur. The company, despite its name, does not visit the reindeer people because it feels contact with Westerners changes their culture. Group size is limited to six.

WHAT TO EXPECT

This is a trip into a very remote area, rarely visited by outsiders. Vehicle breakdowns, lost luggage, uncertain fuel supplies, bad weather, and many other factors can alter the course of the trip.

Daily riding time averages about six hours per day, but because of the uncertain itinerary, there may be days when you'll spend up to nine hours in the saddle. Even though the horse does all the work, "everybody's pretty pooped at the end of those days," reports Svendsen. Altitude, which ranges from 5,000 to 9,000 feet, may be a factor for some people.

The Mongolian wranglers do most of the camp chores and take care of the horses. You may saddle and unsaddle your own mount if you wish. Your only responsibility around camp is to set up and take down your own tent.

A high tolerance of pain will make this trip more enjoyable. Even regular horseback riders may find the jarring gait of the Mongolian ponies to be a literal pain in the butt for the first few days, although the Russian calvary saddles are quite comfortable. And God help you if you haven't been on a horse in a long time. To get your butt in shape, schedule at least three one-hour riding lessons the week before departure. And don't forget the ibuprofen.

Horses are inherently unpredictable. As with any horse trip, there is the potential for injury due to falls, even for expert riders.

Novice riders are not allowed on these trips. At the very minimum, riders should be able to trot and canter a bit—the level of technical expertise one might expect after a half-dozen lessons. More important than raw riding ability, however, is your comfort level around horses. If you have basic riding skills, are not afraid of horses, and have good "horse sense," you'll do fine.

RECOMMENDED READING

In Search of Genghis Khan by Tim Severin. A modern-day horseman's account of his ride across Mongolia in the footsteps of the great Mongol emperor.

IN BRIEF

Boojum Expeditions, 406-587-0125: 19 days, $3,950
First Contacts, 520-779-1966: 26 days, $5,500

Physical challenge, 2; Mental challenge, 3; Skills, 3.

NEPAL / TIBET
climbing mount everest

As Bob Hempstead, arms and legs flailing helplessly, slid on his back headfirst down a 45-degree ice slope toward the 10,000-foot drop-off of Mount Everest's North Face, it seemed increasingly unlikely that he would achieve his goal of becoming the first person in history to twirl a lariat on top of the world's highest mountain.

He'd been so close. Hempstead and several fellow climbers had been trudging single-file up a steep, wind-scoured ridge at nearly 29,000 feet, only a few hundred feet from the summit. Passing a slower climber in front of him, Hempstead had briefly stepped off the trail of boot tracks on the icy, hard-packed snow. His crampon had slipped and his feet had gone out from under him quick as lightning—just at the moment he was debating which rope trick to perform on the summit: the Butterfly, in which the lariat is spun in a vertical plane while oscillating from the left to right side of the body; or the Little Flat Spin, a more basic maneuver in which the rope is spun in front of the body in a horizontal plane.

The thirty-eight-year-old Hempstead had been doing rope

tricks and competing in rodeo roping events since he was a ranch kid in the Sand Hills of Nebraska. From a standing start on a good cow pony, he could burst from the chute, chase down a skittery, ornery steer, lasso him around the horns, and jerk him off his feet, all in about six seconds. Even after Hempstead had moved to Alaska and got a computer job with Arco in the Prudhoe Bay oilfields, he would practice rope tricks to alleviate the boredom of the long Arctic winter nights. "My trick rope goes with me everywhere," he says. Butterflies, Little Flat Spins, Wedding Rings—Hempstead could make a rope dance and sing.

During the weekly flights from Anchorage up to Prudhoe Bay in the Arco 727, he'd look out the window and see 20,320-foot Mount McKinley, the highest mountain in North America. One thing led to another, and, after two failed attempts, in 1992 he stood on McKinley's summit, unfurled a lariat from his backpack, and did a Wedding Ring, a trick in which the rope is spun in a horizontal circle at knee level while the roper stands inside the loop. He liked the feeling of being the highest roper in North America. A year later, Hempstead became South America's highest roper with a Little Flat Spin on the summit of Argentina's 22,834-foot Aconcagua.

When you start hanging out with mountaineers, the talk inevitably turns to the Big One: Everest, the Mother Goddess of the World, highest peak on the planet, the mountain that has killed, at last count, 150 climbers. Hempstead heard the talk, of course, and he learned that Everest was no longer the sole province of professional climbers on million-dollar expeditions. It was now possible for amateurs to climb Everest as paying clients under the tutelage of expert guides. Many "real" mountaineers snorted in contempt at these paying clients, calling them wealthy dilettantes with more money than brains, whiners who expected to be babied to the top, ego-driven fools who endangered their own lives and the lives of others. But a surprising number of these wealthy dilettantes and ego-driven fools were making the summit and returning safely, which annoyed the "real" mountaineers even more.

Hempstead certainly wasn't wealthy, but the house he'd bought in Anchorage in 1990 had unexpectedly appreciated in a sudden real estate boom. So he sold the house in 1993 and moved into a rented cabin. With the proceeds, he wrote a check for $25,000 to a British mountaineering guide company called OTT Expeditions, packed up his lariat and $9,000 worth of mountaineering gear, and flew off to Tibet.

In the main market square of Lhasa, the Tibetan capital, Hempstead figured he needed a little roping practice. So he pulled out his lariat and started doing some tricks. In a matter of seconds, several hundred astonished Tibetans had gathered to watch. The crowd went wild when he did the Wedding Ring, clapping and shouting as he leaped in and out of the spinning circle of rope. Just for fun, he lassoed a tall young man in the audience. "The people around him laughed a lot more than he did," recalls Hempstead, genuinely perplexed that anyone would fail to be delighted by such circumstances.

Also notably undelighted were the local Chinese police, who keep a vigilant eye out for any public assembly of more than three Tibetans. (Their fear of revolutionary plotting is not entirely unfounded; the Tibetans universally despise their Chinese occupiers.) Three cops showed up within minutes, dispersed the crowd, and ordered Hempstead to put away his rope. One can only imagine the grisly scene if they'd tried to confiscate it.

The drive from Lhasa to Everest base camp, a broad expanse of jumbled rock and gravel at 17,000 feet, took three days. Two trucks and thirty-five Land Cruisers carried the OTT expedition, which consisted of three guides, sixteen clients, and twelve Nepalese Sherpa porters, plus two tons of equipment and supplies. When they arrived at base camp, they found 140 climbers from more than a dozen other expeditions already there. After a week or so of unpacking and sorting—and acclimatizing to the thin air at this altitude—Hempstead and his companions set off along the East Rongbuk Glacier, accompanied by forty-two yaks loaded with their gear, to Advance Base Camp, a vast slum of mountaineer's tents in a rocky ravine at 21,000 feet that is the main staging point for the assault on Everest.

At that point, the group divided up into three-man climbing teams, each of which would attack the summit while the other teams rested or recovered. Hempstead joined the Farm Guys team, which included Mick and Kelly, an Australian and a New Zealander who had both grown up on farms. The three country boys shared a patient, slow-but-steady approach to mountaineering that might be called the Old-Bull Attitude, after a well-known farmer's joke: An old bull and a young bull are surveying a field of cows. The young bull says, "Man, look at all the cows. Let's run over and fuck one." To which the old bull replies, "No, son, let's walk over and fuck 'em all."

For the next three weeks, Hempstead and his companions and their staff of workhorse Sherpas patiently shuttled up and down the mountain, carrying equipment, food, and bottled oxygen to a series of higher and higher camps, laying the logistical groundwork for the final assault on the summit. It was exhausting toil, for the air at that altitude had barely a third of the oxygen at sea level. (They were conserving the precious bottled oxygen for the final summit attempt from the last camp at 27,000 feet.) Bundled up against bitterly cold winds and blowing snow, carrying 20 or 30 pounds of gear on their backs, the climbers walked in tiny measured steps, pausing every few seconds to gasp for breath. Everything seemed to happen in slow motion. After five or six days of this brutal toil, they would have to retreat all the way down to base camp at 17,000 feet to rest and recover from the killing lack of oxygen on the upper reaches of the mountain.

Each load-carrying foray from base camp took Hempstead and his teammates farther up the mountain—first to Camp I at 23,000 feet on the North Col, then to Camps II and III at 24,000 and 25,000 feet. When the Farm Guys left base camp for the third time, they were aiming for the summit. Mick, however, had come down with bronchitis in the dry, cold air, and Kelly had hurt his knee in a fall a week earlier. Neither could go above Camp I this time. So Hempstead set off from the North Col alone. He spent the night by himself at Camp III, then pushed on the next morning toward High Camp at 27,000 feet, the final jumping-off spot for the summit. Blessed with good weather, he arrived at High Camp just as the sun was setting over the extraordinary panorama of the Himalayas. There he found Patrick, a Frenchman from another team, and two Sherpas, Babu and Lama. They decided to form an impromptu summit team.

Hempstead took a brief nap. Then, wearing an oxygen mask at last, and with his electrically heated socks turned up to high, he departed for the summit with his three new companions at around ten P.M. The foursome struggled through the frigid darkness in their Frankenstein boots and bug-eyed masks, their way lit by faint headlamps. The weather once again was perfect—clear, calm, about zero degrees—but they now faced the technically trickiest part of the climb, a series of crumbling cliffs called the Yellow Band, the First Step, and the Second Step. They pulled themselves up the steep sections hand-over-hand along previously fixed ropes, securing themselves with safety harnesses and lines. Even in the darkness, Hempstead could see that some of the ropes were badly frayed.

When the dawn began at four A.M., they were just below the Second Step, the most technically difficult part of the route. The brightening sky revealed, just off to their right, the North Face, the nearly vertical 10,000-foot dropoff to the glacier from which they'd started so long ago (what was it now—three weeks? four? five?). If you squinted in the faint light, you could just make out something pink about 500 feet down—the body of a fifty-four-year-old Australian who, after six failed attempts, finally made the summit in 1994, only to plunge to his death during the descent.

An aluminum ladder, installed by a Chinese expedition in 1975, led through the trickiest part of the Second Step. It was in this general area that legendary British climber George Mallory and his partner Andrew Irvine were last seen during their valiant 1924 Everest attempt. Did they succeed in scaling the Second Step and reaching the summit before they perished, thereby beating Edmund Hillary and Tenzing Norgay to mountaineering's greatest prize by twenty-nine years? No one knows.

Helped along by the valiant Sherpas, who carried their extra oxygen bottles, Hempstead and the Frenchman clawed their way up the Second Step without mishap. ("I was so scared that I peed my pants," Hempstead now admits.) From the top of the Step, it appeared to be clear sailing to the summit, no more than a quarter mile away along a smooth edge. "I thought I had it made," recalls Hempstead. He began to think about Butterflies and Little Flat Spins.

A climber from another group, Greg Childs, was right behind Hempstead when he slipped. "He's a croaker for sure," Childs recalls thinking as he watched Hempstead rocket down the ice slope and disappear over the precipice. "Then I heard his weak-lunged cry for help. . . . I still don't understand what kept him from taking the big dive. When I got to him he was lying on a steeply tilted coffee-table-size slab of rock, on his back, head pointed down the mountain," Childs later wrote in *Climbing* magazine. "Seeing his legs and arms waving about reminded me of the character from Franz Kafka's story 'The Metamorphosis,' the guy who turns into a beetle and who, when he tries to walk like a man, falls over and lies on his back wriggling around pathetically."

Hempstead clung desperately to the rock with both hands, using what Childs described as "a batlike kind of technique." Hempstead's head was literally hanging out in space. "I could look back over my shoulder and see the whole North Face down there," he recalls, chuckling now at the absurdity of it all.

In a miracle of serendipity, Childs happened to notice an old hank of climber's rope lying partly buried in the snow at his feet. As Childs lowered the rope to him, Hempstead realized he would have to let go of the rock with one hand to grab it. "That took a lot of willpower," he recalls. "Then Babu showed up and dug another rope out of the snow and lowered it down. And now I had to let go of that rock completely." Hempstead took a deep breath and said a prayer to the same god that had positioned the rock directly in his path and deposited the ropes in the snow at Childs's feet. Then he let go of the rock and grabbed the second rope. It held.

As Childs and Babu hauled him up to safety, Hempstead suddenly realized that his tailbone hurt—a lot. When he tried to stand up, his left leg collapsed (damage to a spinal nerve, it was later discovered). But there was the highest point on earth 150 yards away, and no way in hell was he going to give up now. Walking and falling, walking and falling, Hempstead at last crawled onto the summit, too exhausted and gimpy-legged to even stand up. Somebody took his lariat out of his backpack, and sitting on his knees Hempstead flicked the rope into a lethargic wobbly Little Flat Spin. The folks back home in

Nebraska would probably laugh at this raggedy-ass excuse for a rope trick, but it would have to do.

OUTFITTERS

Before choosing an outfitter, decide which route up the mountain you prefer. Commercial guided ascents of Everest are made on both the north (Tibet) and south (Nepal) sides of the mountain. (The summit lies on the border between the two countries.) The South Col route through Nepal has been considered the "standard" route up Everest ever since Hillary and Tenzing used it to make the first ascent in 1953. But as Tibet has opened up to outsiders in recent years, and as the Nepalese government has jacked up Everest expedition fees to exorbitant levels, the North Ridge route through Tibet has become more popular. Each route has its pros and cons.

The South Col route is easier technically. The only difficult spot is the famed Hillary Step, a 40-foot ledge just below the summit. There is usually fixed rope at this point, however, and climbers typically "jumar" up it, a relatively straightforward procedure. The south side is also more protected from prevailing winds, and has better odds for good weather.

On the downside, there is the Khumbu Icefall, a dangerous stretch of jumbled glacier just above base camp that must be traversed with precarious ladders and fixed ropes, and is prone to sudden avalanches. Many people have died in avalanches in the Khumbu Icefall over the years. The best strategy for getting through it safely is to move quickly and pray to the proper mountain gods.

The other major bummer of the South Col route is the expense—typically around $65,000 for a guided climb. This is partly due to the $10,000 expedition fee that Nepal assesses each climber (you have to pay your guide's fee as well, of course), and partly due to the fact that all expedition supplies must be carried in by porter about 75 miles to the base camp.

To climb Everest from Tibet via the North Ridge, on the other hand, typically costs "only" about $25,000. Logistics are far simpler because one can drive right to base camp and use yaks all the way to 21,000 feet. Tibet still charges modest fees, and sets no limit on the size of each expedition, which allows for larger groups and greater economies of scale.

The bad news is that the north side is more difficult to climb. Although the lower part of the mountain is technically easy, the approach to the summit is steep and exposed, and the fixed ropes that lead through a series of rocky cliffs may be buried by snow. Stumble on the summit ridge, as Bob Hempstead did, and you'll more than likely fall 10,000 feet down the mountain's North Face. All this is complicated by the northern side's legendarily bad weather and fierce winds.

Until recently, the vast majority of Everest summiteers, both commercial clients and independent climbers, used the South Col route. But in 1995, due to freakish good weather on the north side, sixty-seven people summited from Tibet, only two from Nepal.

Among those outfitters using the South Col route is *Adventure Consultants*. After the tragic 1996 death on Everest of proprietor and head guide Rob Hall, the New Zealand–based company is carrying on under the leadership of Guy Cotter. (Ed Viesturs, the prominent American climber, now serves as assistant head guide.) Learning from the 1996 disaster, Adventure Consultants now uses a more conservative approach for Everest climbs, with a maximum of five clients under the tutelage of two guides. More emphasis is placed on self-sufficiency, and clients must perform well on the lower slopes before being allowed to attempt the summit. "They'll have to earn their way to the top," says Viesturs.

Alpine Ascents International is one of the pioneers of guided Everest climbs, and has put thirty-two commercial clients on the summit since 1992. Its primary Everest guides are Todd Burleson, Peter Athans, and Wally Berg, who among them have summited Everest six times. AAI uses the South Col route.

Another New Zealander, Russell Brice, runs *Himalayan Experience 8000*, which is based in Chamonix, France. Brice prefers the north side, where he has led commercial groups four times and put six clients on the summit. Group size is twelve with two guides.

International Mountain Guides is a three-man consortium of Rainier stalwarts Eric Simonson, Phil Ershler, and George Dunn. Simonson will lead a spring 1998 north-side expedition limited to six clients. Each client will have his own personal guide and Sherpa porter, an ultra-conservative strategy Simonson has used successfully on other 8,000-meter peaks. Unfortunately, the strategy is also ultra-expensive—more than double the cost of other north-side expeditions, although still less than a south-side commercial trip.

OTT Expeditions was the first outfitter to put a commercial client on the summit from the Tibetan side, in 1994. (Bob Hempstead was one of nine OTT clients to reach the top in 1995.) The British company uses both the North Ridge and South Col routes; the present schedule calls for the South Col in 1997 and the North Ridge in 1998. Head guide is John Tinker.

WHAT TO EXPECT

If you have to ask, you almost certainly can't hack it. Just for the record, you'll spend a month or so hauling heavy loads up steep slopes, often through deep snow, at altitudes above

20,000 feet, where there is perhaps one third of normal sea-level oxygen available. (You will use bottled oxygen the last few thousand feet.)

As the grisly events of 1996 illustrate, this is one trip where death is a real possibility. Nearly 150 people have been killed while attempting to climb Mount Everest over the years. Roughly 600 have reached the top; if you're into risk/reward management, that works out to a summit/death ratio of 4 to 1.

Within that harsh context, however, commercially guided clients have a surprisingly good safety record on Everest, even considering the 1996 deaths of two guided clients in a sudden storm. (Three other victims—Rob Hall, Andy Harris, and Scott Fischer—were guides on commercial expeditions.) The deaths rekindled the debate about whether "amateur" climbers belong on Everest, but in fact six expert "professionals" also died on the mountain that day, and several guided clients from the same expeditions summited and returned safely. In the end, it seems, timing and fate played a larger role than climbing experience. In any case, Everest climbers, particularly those with an obsession about reaching the summit, are strongly urged to have their affairs in order before leaving home.

Even if you don't die, the misery will be extreme: exhaustion, bitter cold, hellacious winds, altitude sickness, hunger, and dehydration—not to mention the unrelenting fear of avalanche, storm, or slip. Under extreme altitude and weather conditions, even routine camp chores become exhausting drudgery. Your guides are there only to lead, advise, and rescue if possible. As Bob Hempstead says, "The secret to success on Everest is that, in the end, you've got to look out for yourself."

Although relative novice mountaineers have managed to reach the summit of Everest—Peggy Gudgell became the second American woman to reach the top in 1988 despite never having climbed above 14,500 feet before—you should be a skilled, experienced mountaineer with, at the very minimum, a peak like Denali or Aconcagua already under your belt. Advanced technical climbing technique is not necessary, but you should have a foolproof self-arrest, since climbers don't rope together on the icy upper slopes. (Just ask Bob Hempstead.)

RECOMMENDED READING

Into Thin Air by John Krakauer. The gripping account of the 1996 Everest tragedy by one who survived it.

Mother Goddess of the World by Kim Stanley Robinson. A historically and technically authentic screwball comedy about an impromptu expedition up Everest to find the bodies of long-lost climbers Mallory and Irvine.

Cowboy Roping and Rope Tricks by Chester Byers. Written in 1928 by the revered master who inspired Will Rogers, this is still the Bible of the sport.

IN BRIEF

Adventure Consultants, 011-643-443-8711: 70 days, $65,000

Alpine Ascents International, 206-378-1927: 66 days, $64,000

Himalayan Experience 8000, 011-33-450-53-73-87: 71 days, $30,000

International Mountain Guides, 360-569-2604: 65 days, $56,000

OTT Expeditions, 011-44-1142-588-508: 60–70 days, $25,000–$65,000

Physical challenge, 5+; Mental challenge, 5+; Skills, 4.

NEW ZEALAND

tramping the

south island

Consider the paradox of the Milford Track. The three-day trek from lake to sea, renowned for its scenic glories, is billed as "the most beautiful walk in the world." But the Milford is also a popular tourist destination and strictly regulated by the authorities. On a typical day in season, two or three hundred people tread its mossy rocks, and "trampers" (local argot for hikers) must have advance reservations and stay in huge motel-like lodges along the way. Not my style.

Nor was it any longer my style to simply arrive at the airport with a backpack and wing it, as I might have twenty years ago. Fortunately, in the middle ground between tourist and vagabond stands the lanky figure of Alan Riegelman, a sixty-three-year-old Vermonter-turned-Kiwi who runs backpacking trips along lesser-known trails on New Zealand's South Island. Alan's operation is small, to say the least; the CEO and chief stockholder is also the fellow who plans the routes, writes the brochures, leads the hikes, and washes the dishes on the trail. Traveling with Alan, his brochure brags, is "like having an old friend give you a personal tour of his country." Sounded good to me.

The Riegelman personal touch surfaced early. The predeparture info pack included a questionnaire about food and wine preferences and an impassioned lecture on the evils of running shoes, which are banned from his trips. Having happily hiked for years in running shoes, and worn them to 16,700 feet on Mount Kenya. I responded with an equally impassioned screed to the contrary. Alan promptly rebutted by phone from New Zealand. We at last agreed that I would bring along both running shoes and hiking boots, but that when I suffered the inevitable compound spiral fracture of the ankle while wearing the runners, I would not come crying to him.

Alan was there to greet me at the Christchurch airport, along with his assistant guide, Chris, an Australian woman who grew up on an Outback ranch and had worked for years as a forest ranger. We drove back to a local motel, where I met the other half of what turned out to be a two-man group: Bruce, a friendly young fellow who was taking a break from college to see the world.

"You may have noticed that I like to talk a lot," Alan told us over dinner. We'd noticed. Alan views silence with horror and revulsion, as dead air to be filled with sound bites about the local flora, fauna, culture, geology, and folkways, along with appropriate citations of poetry. "If I get on your nerves, just tell me to shut up." Once or twice, politely, we did.

The next morning, preparations began for the first of the trip's three backpacking excursions: a five-day trek along the little-known St. James Walkway, which loops 42 miles through the Lewis Pass Scenic Reserve. Alan laid out a vast array of foodstuffs, and Bruce and I began to greedily cram fruit, bread, cheese, granola, and candy bars into our backpacks. It quickly dawned on us, however, that we'd be carrying that food on our backs for several days. I restrained my gluttonous urges and managed to keep my pack down to a fairly modest 35 pounds.

The drive to the trailhead of the St. James Walkway took a couple of hours. The trail started off in rolling forest, but quickly plunged into the steep, narrow Cannibal Gorge, where we were introduced to a fixture of New Zealand hiking trails: the swinging bridge. Four cables stretched across the chasm, the bottom two supporting a wire mesh walkway while the upper pair served as handrails. Top-heavy with our packs, we wobbled and bounced precariously across, keeping a wary eye on the waters of the Ada River rushing below.

After five hours of shadowing the river along steep wooded cliffs, we reached Ada Pass Hut, one of four along the St. James, all relatively new and surprisingly livable. A two-tiered sleeping platform accommodated about twenty people, and the kitchen/dining room had big tables and a picture window view of the Spenser Mountains. A woodstove stood ready to dry out wet clothes, although we didn't need that—yet.

Only one other hiker appeared at the hut that night, a wiry Kiwi dairy farmer named Graham. A veteran of the Milford Track, he was already pronouncing the St. James Walkway scenically superior to the Milford, as well as vastly less crowded. (We were to see only four other people the rest of the way.) He watched with envy as Alan and Chris prepared a dinner of chicken breasts sautéed in papaya sauce, curried rice with raisins, and fresh coleslaw, topped off with fruit compote doused in Cointreau.

Graham tagged along with us the next day. The beech forests soon gave way to open meadows dotted with herds of cows and semi-wild horses. Still following the Ada River, we skirted a snow-dappled peak called Faerie Queen (named by an eccentric Irish explorer who gave the nearby landscape literary and classical names) and strolled through wind-billowed meadows to Christopher Hut, which had a splendid view of the broad, sweeping valley below.

When it came time to sleep, I moved outside and unrolled my sleeping bag under the stars, behind a fence that had been erected "for campers wishing to avoid the attention of curious cattle," according to a local guidebook. The night sky was strange indeed at this latitude; the Big Dipper was nowhere to be seen, Orion was upside down, and there were two hazy star clouds floating near the zenith. Gazing up into the void, I had an astronomical epiphany that explained the vague sense of unease I'd felt since my arrival in New Zealand: down here, the sun moves across the sky "backward," from right to left.

We walked for two more days through the rolling meadows of two large cattle stations in the Ann and Boyle River valleys. ("Station" is Downunderese for "ranch.") Alan had warned us about possible encounters with bulls, which are aggressive toward humans and are said to have trampled a few hikers along the St. James. Sure enough, on day four Bruce and I rounded a clump of trees to see athwart the path a menacing 2,000-pound cut of sirloin with large, sharp horns.

We made feeble threatening noises and gestures, which were of course ignored, before retreating to wait for Graham the dairy farmer, who we hoped could defuse the standoff. He coolly assessed the situation, set down his backpack, and with slow, purposeful steps walked directly toward the animal, like a matador without a cape. Bruce and I, in awe of this quiet 120-pound man's raw courage, watched from the rear. As he approached to within 5 yards of the bull, it bolted and loped away.

Bruce and I rushed up to Graham and clapped him on the back, exclaiming over his bravado. He solemnly accepted our accolades, then burst out laughing. "It wasn't a bull, mate. Just a steer. You didn't notice he'd had his balls cut off?"

We soaked off five days worth of sweat and grime in a hot sulfur bath at the trail's end, and then drove three hours to Nelson, on the north coast. Alan's home there, a cottage called

Tealcot, is perched so close to a small brook that we were able to feed trout from his deck. Bruce stayed at Alan's place, while I bunked with neighbors of Alan's just down the creek.

After a rest in Nelson, we set off for Abel Tasman National Park, a semitropical seacoast an hour's drive to the north. There we boarded a passenger launch and steamed 9 miles up the rugged coastline. After a stir-fry dinner around a campfire, we camped on the beach at Bark Bay, listening to the possums rustle around our packs in search of midnight snacks. The next day's hike took us through ferns and forests back down the coastline, with stops along the way for ocean swims in the chilly blue water. We made sure to pay careful attention to the tides, which periodically flood low sections of the trail for several hours at a time, and made it back to Nelson on schedule, in time for pizza on the deck at Tealcot.

Bruce didn't eat much pizza, and the next morning, as we drove through the outskirts of Nelson on the way to our next stop at Franz Joseph Glacier, he complained of a stomachache. A few minutes later, he was kneeling on a sidewalk, retching blood. His appendix had burst.

The trip was clearly over for Bruce, so Chris stayed in Nelson to attend him in the hospital while Alan and I continued the trip. As we headed out of town, Alan muttered darkly, "If this had happened four days ago, Bruce could be dead now."

The view of the Southern Alps at Franz Josef was obscured by low clouds, but the day nevertheless revealed the stunning contrasts that make New Zealand such a natural wonder. In the morning I donned spiked boots for a walk on the glacier; in the afternoon it was a hike through a semitropical rain forest. At one point I looked out through cool mist from a mantle of ferns and hanging moss to see the 200-foot-thick, 5-mile-long river of ice directly below. Can any other place in the world offer such a gamut of splendor in one glance?

Ominous clouds once again hung low as we drove the 40

miles of dirt road and dry creekbeds to the start of our third and final trek, a three-day walk up the Matukituki River valley to Mount Aspiring. After a side trip up a cascading stream to Rob Roy Glacier, a massive crown of ice atop a high ridge that continually sent ice chunks thundering down toward us, we trudged into Aspiring Hut just as the drizzle began. The rain came in torrents all night, and showed no signs of letting up the next morning. The river was already ugly and swollen, and Alan feared that our route back might be impassable for days if the rain continued. He decided to head back to the trailhead and get out while we could. For five hours we slogged through meadows and freshets that had been dry the day before. Fording the last creek, within sight of the car, I was nearly swept off my feet by the fast-running knee-deep water.

Soaked and weary, we drove through half a dozen rapidly rising creeks that had sprung up across the muddy road. As we forded the last one, the bumper-deep water surged over the hood and the motor died just as we coasted out of it. Alan, ever prepared, pulled out a can of WD-40 and sprayed the ignition wires. The car sputtered back to life, and we straggled to a motor camp in Queenstown by nightfall, thankful to once again have a waterproof roof over our heads.

After a rest day in Queenstown, we drove north to Mount Cook, a snow-covered peak that at 12,349 feet is the highest point in New Zealand. I was just as glad that our Mount Aspiring trek had been cut short, for it gave us an extra day at Mount Cook before we finished up at Christchurch. Our quarters at Mount Cook were a small guest house at a high-country sheep station on the shores of Lake Pukaki, a brilliant blue lake fed by glaciers.

Clouds often obscure Mount Cook—we'd talked to one poor fellow who'd left after five days without ever having seen the summit—but the next morning dawned clear and calm.

While Alan stayed behind to catch up on paperwork, I happily shed my backpack and ventured off on a rather arduous 12-mile solo day hike up a rubble-strewn valley to Hooker Hut, directly below the face of the mountain.

After dinner back at the sheep station, I strolled to the top of a hill behind the guest house to watch the sun go down. Amid silence so total that my ears roared, the western sky reddened and Mount Cook began to glow golden in the distance. Hordes of rabbits took to thumping the ground, and I heard the faint bleating of sheep a mile away. Lake Pukaki's glacial waters were so resolutely blue that they did not reflect the fire that soon enveloped the entire sky. I sat without moving for an hour, until the fire faded and I could pick out Orion. It was still upside down.

OUTFITTERS

Country Walkers runs a semiluxurious inn-based trip to the best-known South Island destinations: Christchurch, the West Coast (Franz Josef and Fox Glacier), Queenstown, Mount Cook, Lake Wanaka, and Milford Sound, plus the Lake Moeraki Wilderness Lodge. Easy day hikes only.

Nature Expeditions International's South and North Island itinerary includes the Milford Track, Mount Cook, Urewera National Park, and Rotorua, as well as Auckland, Queenstown, and Christchurch. Easy day hikes only. Accommodation in inns and lodges.

New Zealand Travelers, owned by Alan Riegelman, operated the trip described above. The current itinerary includes eight days on the trail (five days on the St. James Walkway and three in Mount Aspiring Park) plus visits to Christchurch, Nelson, Franz Josef, Wanaka, Queenstown, and Mount Cook. The two-day trek in Abel Tasman National Park has been eliminated for 1997. The NZT trip differs from the others listed here because trekkers stay in remote huts and carry their own gear in backpacks. Typical loads are 30–35 pounds.

NZT also offers a "day-hike option" for travelers who don't want to carry heavy packs or sleep in huts. This trip is comparable in difficulty to the other trips listed here. While the backpackers are out doing their thing, day hikers stay in lodges and take day walks and outings to nearby attractions—fishing villages, wineries, whale watching, and so on. Between backpacker treks, the two groups travel together, a nice arrangement for a couple mismatched in physical vigor. The day-hike option is $2,795.

For those short of time, NZT also offers a twelve-day option at $2,200. Hikers skip the St. James Walkway and join the group in Nelson on day eight of the regular itinerary.

Wilderness Travel's eighteen-day itinerary includes a three-day tramp of the Routeburn Track, one of New Zealand's classics, plus day hikes at Mount Cook, Mount Aspiring, and Fox Glacier. There's also a day of sea kayaking in Milford Sound, plus visits to Lake Wanaka, Queenstown, Kaikoura, and Christchurch.

WHAT TO EXPECT

Moderate-to-strenuous day hikes are the order of the day on most of these New Zealand tramping trips. Daily walking distance is typically less than 10 miles, and the terrain is not overwhelming, although the Routebourne Track has its moments.

The New Zealand Travelers' trip is tougher; although the trails are at low altitude and not particularly steep or difficult, the 35-pound pack makes it a bit more of a physical challenge. The St. James Walkway, which follows river valleys, is flat, with the exception of the slog up over the Ann Saddle. The Mount

Aspiring trail is also generally flat, although optional side trips to Rob Roy Glacier and Cascade Saddle are steep in places. You can shed your heavy pack for these side trips, however.

In terms of mental challenge, NZT's backpacking trip, described in the narrative, rates a 2. The huts along the St. James Walkway and in Mount Aspiring are quite livable, although there are no hot showers, NZT's inn-based day-hike option would rate only a one in terms of mental challenge, as would the inn-based trips offered by the other outfitters.

The major potential misery in New Zealand is the weather. Clouds can obscure views for days at a time, and it is bound to rain at some point during the trip.

Prime time is November through February, the austral summer season. Try to avoid January, the traditional vacation month down under, when the trails will be mobbed.

IN BRIEF

Country Walkers, 800-464-9255: 12 days, $2,550
Nature Expeditions International, 800-869-0693: 21 days, $3,490
New Zealand Travelers, 800-362-2718: 18 days, $2,595
Wilderness Travel, 800-368-2794: 18 days, $2,455

Physical challenge, 2–3; Mental challenge, 1–2; Skills, 1.

PAKISTAN
trekking to
snow lake

Which is the most beautiful alpine vista in the world?

Mountain fanciers are typically reluctant to answer such a question. They'll hedge and haw and say something like, well, who's the most beautiful woman in the world? To argue the relative aesthetic merits of the Grand Tetons, Ama Dablam, and Fitzroy is as fruitless as trying to rate those of, say, Kim Alexis, Catherine Deneuve, and Evonne Goolagong.

But there's one place, in remote Pakistan, that is so overwhelming in its visual power and drama and texture that a number of people who've been there have been willing to put aside the dithering and declare that this is The Place. The Most Beautiful Place in the World.

The Place is improbably remote, a week's walk from the nearest human habitation, which is itself the last outpost in the hardscrabble frontier region of Baltistan. Probably no more than a hundred Westerners have ever been to The Place, fewer than have stood atop Mount Everest. Perhaps the difficulty and satisfaction of just getting there have colored their aesthetic judgment. Perhaps not.

The Place is called Snow Lake. It is a vast glacial basin ringed by high peaks of the Karakoram Range. Hidden at an elevation of about 16,000 feet, it lies at the source of the Biafo and His-par Glaciers, which spread down from it like two long, bony fingers.

The first Westerner to see Snow Lake was the British explorer Sir Martin Conway, who journeyed there in 1892. A veteran mountaineer, he had spent his life exploring the Alps and Himalayas, and it is unlikely that anyone then alive had seen more of the earth's mountain scenery. Here is how he described his first sight of Snow Lake as his party crested the pass at the top of the Hispar Glacier:

"We expected to look down a long valley such as we had come up, but there was no valley in sight. Before us lay a basin or lake of snow. It was beyond all comparison the finest view of mountains it has ever been my lot to behold, nor do I believe the world can hold a finer.

"This lake was bounded on the north and east by white ridges, and to the south by a splendid row of needle peaks. . . . From the midst of the snowy lake rose a series of mountain islands. . . . I forgot headache, food, everything, in the overwhelming impression this majestic scene impressed upon me, and the hour and a quarter we were privileged to gaze upon it passed like the dream of a moment."

The needle peaks lining the Biafo Glacier nearby were like nothing Conway had ever seen. "We discovered new developments of mountain grandeur for which we were not prepared. . . . The auguilles of Chamonix are wonderful, and possess a grace and outline all their own, but these needles outjut them in steepness, outnumber them in multitude, and outreach them in size. The highest of them flings its summit more than 23,000 feet in the air, and looks abroad over a field of mountains that finds no superior in the world."

To reach Snow Lake, Conway's expedition had climbed up the Hispar Glacier and across the 16,900-foot Hispar Pass. It then proceeded down the Biafo Glacier to the village of Askole. It was the first documented human traverse ever between the kingdoms of Nagar and Baltistan, which, although next-door neighbors, had no contact whatsoever because of the intervening high terrain. In Conway's time, not even the hardiest local people ever made the journey—although local legend had it that, fifty years previously, a horde of eight hundred Nagar men had traversed the route to loot Balti villages, making off with not only cows, sheep, and goats but a number of women as well.

Interestingly enough, Conway did not share the Nagar men's fascination with the charms of Balti women. Quite the contrary, in fact. Once again proving that he was no faintheart when it came to aesthetic calibration, Conway described the women of Askole as "a most ill-looking lot." Indeed, when he and his men sang their favorite bawdy song around the campfire—a ditty that went, "We love you all, petite and tall, whate'er your beauty or grade is. . . . Coy or coquette, blondes or brunettes, we love you all, bewitching ladies"—Conway cautioned that "a mental reservation had certainly to be made for the hags of Askole."

Nor did later expeditions to Snow Lake have much good to say about the locals. Another British explorer, Eric Shipton, characterized the people of Askole as "a depressingly weedy crowd." The husband-and-wife geographer team of William and Fanny Bullock Workman, who followed in some of Conway's footsteps in 1908, complained mightily of the "stupid and inexcusable conduct" of their Nagar porters, whom they referred to, in their impeccable Victorian style, as coolies.

In the Bullocks' book, under the chapter heading "Difference in Coolie Standard for Wood Load When Bringing It and

Using It," they reported with weary resignation and careful documentation that the coolies' wood bundles ranged from only 16 to 35 pounds when they had to carry the wood to camp. But when it came time to take wood for their own campfires, "it was amusing to note that their conception of the amount of wood in a load had increased in six- to ten-fold proportion. . . . The policy of the Nagar people, in this as in all else, was to render as meager service as possible and secure all they could for themselves." The Workmans neglected to note how much wood they themselves had carried.

The flint-hearted couple, although not as effusive as Conway in their description of the view of Snow Lake, did grudgingly concede that it "disclosed a remarkable scene of snow-beauty."

Shipton, in his account of his 1937 journey to Snow Lake, made one particularly startling observation: "While contouring around the foot of the ridge, we saw in the snow the tracks of an Abominable Snowman. They were eight inches in diameter, eighteen inches apart, almost circular, without sign of toe or heel. . . . However many-legged it was, the beast was heavy, the tracks being nearly a foot deep. We followed them for a mile, when they disappeared on some rock. The tracks came from a glacier pool, where the animal had evidently drunk, and the next day we picked up the same spoor on the north side of Snow Lake."

Shipton's narrative continues: "The Sherpas judged them to belong to the smaller type of Snowman, or Yeti, as they call them, of which there were apparently two varieties: the smaller, whose spoor we were following, which feeds on men, while his larger brother confines himself to a diet of yaks. My remark that no one had been here for thirty years and that he must be devilishly hungry did not amuse the Sherpas as much as I expected! The jest was considered ill-timed, as perhaps it was, the three of us standing alone and forlorn in a great expanse of snow, looking at the strange tracks like so many Robinson Crusoes."

Shipton, a serious explorer and surveyor, was not known for flights of fancy or wild imagination. Perhaps he simply fell under the spell of Snow Lake and was driven temporarily mad by overwhelming physical beauty. It's been known to happen.

OUTFITTERS

The four companies who run Snow Lake treks—*Concordia Expeditions, Geographic Expeditions, KE Adventure Travel,* and *Wilderness Travel*—all offer the same basic itinerary, which essentially retraces Conway's route in reverse.

After flying or driving from Islamabad to Skardu, you'll travel by jeep through Braldu Gorge to Askole, where the trek begins. (It's often necessary to hike the last stretch to Askole due to washed-out roads.) The trek route proceeds briefly up the Baltoro Glacier, then turns northwest up the 37-mile-long Biafo Glacier for about a week to Snow Lake. From there, trekkers cross the pass at Hispar La and make the five- to six-day, 38-mile descent of the Hispar Glacier to the Hunza Valley. Return is via jeep to Karimabad and Gilgit, then by plane or jeep (depends on the weather) to Islamabad.

Variations in trip length are due to different time allotments by outfitters for traveling to and from Islamabad, sightseeing in Islamabad and Gilgit, and "cushion" days in case bad weather delays or cancels flights to Skardu and from Gilgit, or washes out the road to Askole.

WHAT TO EXPECT

In some ways, the Snow Lake trip is physically easier than the typical Himalayan trek, in other ways more difficult. The ascent, along a literal river of ice, is very gradual—about 1,000 feet per day—with no significant ups and downs along the way. On the other hand, the footing is often quite difficult as you pick your way along the rubble-strewn glacier, hopping from one rock to another over sometimes slippery ice. In many places, there is no trail as such. Agility and surefootedness are nearly as important as stamina.

Maximum altitude is an energy-sapping 16,900 feet, and you'll spend about a week above 13,000. The gradual ascent, however, allows good acclimatization.

The difficult footing, isolation, crevasses, snowstorms, and an eerily desolate landscape make this a tougher mental challenge than most Himalayan treks. "This trip is very hard on your mind," says Geographic Expeditions guide Vassi Koutsaftiz. "It is not a pleasant environment. There's nothing but rock. You're completely isolated from people."

Moreover, the trip is not without danger. Trekkers must sometimes leap across crevasses on the glacier, and it may be occasionally necessary for the group to "rope up"—link themselves together with stout climbing ropes so that if one member slips into a crevasse, the others can pull him out.

In terms of altitude sickness, the long gradual ascent is a double-edged sword: It allows for good acclimatization, but if a trekker is stricken, the usual remedy—a quick descent of several thousand feet—simply isn't possible. Helicopter evacuation may be a possibility on the Biafo Glacier but is unlikely on the Hispar. There are no villages or people whatsoever along the route.

The weather can be unpredictable, with blizzards and total whiteout conditions possible at any time. Heavy snow can be a serious problem because it covers up the crevasses. In at least one case, this has forced trekking groups to turn back and retreat down the Biafo before reaching Snow Lake. Weather may prevent flights from Islamabad to Skardu, and the return flight from Gilgit. In that case, grueling, dusty two-day jeep rides will be necessary.

Gilgit, the town where the trek finishes, has been the scene of Suni vs. Shiite religious strife in recent years. (In the late 1980s, 3,500 people were reportedly killed in clashes set off by a disagreement over the precise time of first sighting of the new moon, which signifies the end of a major Muslim holiday.) A few trekking groups have been delayed by such clashes, or required military escorts to depart.

Because of the unpredictable weather, Snow Lake treks are feasible only in July and August.

RECOMMENDED READING

Where Men and Mountains Meet and *The Gilgit Game* by John Keay. Adventure-book maven Tom Cole calls these "the finest history of exploration, diplomatic wrangling, high-altitude spying, and general good fun in the western Himalaya and Karakoram."

IN BRIEF

Concordia Expeditions, 719-395-9191: 28 days, $3,800
Geographic Expeditions, 800-777-8183: 30 days, $4,190
KE Adventure Travel, 800-497-9675: 22 days, $2,995
Wilderness Travel, 800-368-2794: 27 days, $3,295

Physical challenge, 3; Mental challenge, 4; Skills, 2.

SIKKIM
trekking to
kanchenjunga

To gaze at the highest point on earth has a certain appeal, of course. But thousands of tourist trekkers now swarm the Everest region of Nepal, and the unique local culture has come under full assault from Western values. Sherpa teenagers wearing Patagonia, Nike, and Vuarnet now outnumber the Buddhist monks at Thyangboche and Thame.

"Go to Sikkim," a well-traveled acquaintance advised. "Only a few dozen Americans a year trek there. It's like Nepal was twenty-five years ago." And, he assured me, my lust for visual peak-bagging would not go entirely unfulfilled, for Sikkim has the third-highest mountain in the world, 28,208-foot Kanchenjunga. Okay, so it's not Everest, but a sacrifice of two slots in the tall-mountain pecking order seemed a small price for a quarter-century hiatus in the encroachment of Western civilization.

Americans typically know Sikkim, if they know it at all, as the tiny Himalayan Shangri-la whose king married a young American woman, Hope Cooke, in 1963. Strategically bordering Nepal, Tibet, and Bhutan, it was forcibly annexed by India in 1974. Sikkim has maintained its traditional Himalayan Buddhist culture, however, and most of its citizens, taking the long view, consider the Indian presence merely a temporary bureaucratic annoyance.

The security-conscious Indian government forbids individual trekking by foreigners in Sikkim, and limits commercial groups to a handful of routes. The most popular of these leads to Goecha La, a 16,400-foot pass 3 miles south of Kanchenjunga with an in-your-face view of the mountain.

Our trip to Goecha La did not begin auspiciously. Due to botched plane reservations in Delhi, most of the trekking group arrived at Bagdogra, the nearest airport to Sikkim, two days late. There we discovered that the trip leader, who was supposed to have met our flight, had apparently been advised of our arrival date by the same incompetent who had made the plane reservations. Leaderless, we ended up hitching a ride from Bagdogra to Darjeeling, our jumping-off spot for Sikkim, with a busload of German tourists. Aboard this ramshackle machine our adventures began, as they so often do in the third world, rather sooner than we had anticipated.

The wretched road to Darjeeling twists 60 miles and climbs 6,000 feet into the Himalayan foothills. For the most part, the road is too narrow for large vehicles to pass. Thus, whenever our bus met an oncoming truck, one or the other had to stop and backtrack, sometimes several hundred yards, to a spot wide enough to squeeze by. Astonishingly, there was no argument about who would give way; the drivers all seemed to know the wide spots by heart and dutifully proceeded—forward or backward, as required—to the nearest one. Of course, all following traffic had to back up as well, and the result was maddening gridlock.

Trucks and buses typically carried a crew of two: one to drive, the other to serve as a rear lookout for the intricate backing-up maneuvers. Our lookout would slap the side of the bus in code to let the driver know how much clearance he had: bop-BOP-bop-BOP meant "plenty of room," bop-BOP meant "enough room," and a succinct BOP meant "barely enough room." No bops meant "stop."

At one particularly sharp curve along a 1,500-foot drop-off, we met a large truck coming the other way. The overly optimistic drivers tried to squeeze by but miscalculated the clearance. The truck jammed against the rock wall on the inside of the curve, while its fenders scraped ours as we teetered literally inches from the edge. (Guard rails? Surely you jest.) It was a stymie; neither vehicle could move forward or back.

There followed a long series of excruciating inches-at-a-time back-and-forth maneuvers, punctuated by a drumbeat of bop-BOPs and wild gesticulation among the drivers and lookouts. We passengers had no choice but to watch the drama from the inside, since our only exit door opened directly into the abyss. As I sat there—deprived of sleep for seventy-eight hours, abandoned by my outfitter, inhaling diesel fumes from the truck's exhaust pipe just outside my window, feeling the bus periodically lurch toward the edge as the truck nudged against it—I wondered whether our impending deaths would be chronicled in one of those insidious little one-sentence *New York Times* "bus-plunge" filler stories.

It all worked out in the end, of course. After thirty minutes of painstaking maneuvers, the truck finally got by. We eventually made it to Darjeeling and found our hotel, a gloriously seedy hilltop relic of bygone British colonial elegance called the Windamere. I collapsed into bed within seconds.

Our trip leader, Daku Tenzing Norgay—a smiling, vivacious Nepali woman of a certain age and the widow of famed Everest summiteer Tenzing Norgay—eventually appeared, full of apology and good cheer. She took us to her home for tea and sweet cakes, and told an elaborate joke about yak butter that I didn't quite get. Tall for a Nepalese woman, with a stately bearing and long black hair pulled back tightly into a braid, she had smooth skin, perfect teeth, and a raucous, deep-bellied laugh. I adored her at once.

It is virtually mandatory for tourists in Darjeeling to make the half-hour pilgrimage by taxi to Tiger Hill, a scenic outpost from which to watch the sun come up over the Himalayas. But, hoping to avoid the predawn traffic jam—and get some extra sleep—a few of us instead walked to a nearby overlook five minutes from the hotel that I cannot imagine inferior to Tiger Hill in any way. Mist in the east obscured the sunrise on this morning, but through a break in the clouds to the north, we suddenly glimpsed the summit of Kanchenjunga, some 50 miles away. I gasped in astonishment. To one whose scale of reference is the Rockies and Alps, it seemed preposterous that rock and ice could float so far above the horizon.

The trip by Land Rover from Darjeeling to Gangtok, the capital of Sikkim, traversed another narrow, twisting, tortuous road. From Gangtok we continued through steep green valleys to Pemyangtse, site of Sikkim's most revered Buddhist monastery. We arrived after dark, and the next morning, as I rolled over in my hotel bed, I could see out the window the entire five-summited Kanchenjunga massif, much closer now, glowing eerily in the first light of dawn. But the mountain soon disappeared behind the ridgetops as we endured one last hair-raising drive, to the remote village of Yoksum. It was the literal end of the road.

The party that embarked on foot the next morning consisted of fourteen trekkers, three Sherpa guides, nineteen porters and cooks, and four lumbering dzos, surefooted yak/cow hybrids whose great arcing horns belied their docile manners. The porters astounded us with their load-carrying abilities and choice of apparel. One fellow, apparently planning to drop by a disco immediately upon his return, wore polyester slacks, a sport coat, and the Sikkimese equivalent of penny loafers. Other favored footwear ranged from shower thongs to rubber galoshes to nothing at all.

The first two days of walking took us rather steeply up a lush valley of oak, spruce, magnolia, and rhododendrons. Kanchenjunga still lay frustratingly out of sight behind the steep ridges. To avoid gaining too much altitude too quickly—which can cause headaches, nausea, and general malaise in those not acclimated to high elevation—we pitched camp after lunch on the second day at Phedang, a meadow at 12,000 feet. There we were entertained by the dzo handlers' futile attempts to deal with one particularly recalcitrant animal, whom Daku christened the Naughty Dzo after it fomented a dzo stampede that nearly flattened my tent, with me inside it. This beast was to become a treklong source of amusement.

On the morning of the third day, we crested a knoll to see once again the Big One, as we'd come to call it. Still some 20 miles and a four-day walk away, it was flanked by a gracefully sculpted 22,000-foot peak called Pandim and a gang of anonymous 20,000-footers. (Only in the Himalayas are 20,000-foot mountains anonymous.) After a lengthy sojourn of gazing and photo-snapping atop the knoll, we trekked on to Dzongri, a lovely campsite set in a rolling meadow just below the tree line.

Dzongri was a special place for Daku, for it was here, as a fourteen-year-old porter on a climbing expedition, that she first caught the eye of her husband-to-be, Tenzing, then the training director of the Himalayan Mountain Institute. Born at 15,000 feet, the unschooled daughter of a Nepalese yak farmer, Daku had run away from home at thirteen to escape an arranged marriage. Taking with her funds totaling 60 rupees

($1.20) and four young friends in similar premarital straits, she walked through the mountains for eighteen days to Darjeeling.

She married Tenzing in 1959, when she was seventeen and he forty-five. Because of his mountaineering renown, they traveled the world together and knew many famous people. But her life was not an easy one with the hard-drinking Tenzing, and she longed for the high places. "I always feel better out in the mountains," she told me. "At home there are many problems. The lower you go, the more you have to think about." She started her own trekking company in 1969, and when Tenzing died in 1986, she devoted her efforts to it full time. She had no interest in remarrying. "Once is enough. I don't like to be squeezed in my life."

Her boisterous personality delighted us all. At one point, using a titanium ice screw she had bartered from some Russian trekkers, she began goosing members of the group at random. Donning one of the Russian's military-style camouflage hats, she crouched behind a log and sprayed the group with imaginary machine-gun fire, complete with sound effects. About one obnoxious female member of our group, she muttered conspiratorially to the rest of us, "Maybe we can marry her off to a yak herder and get rid of her."

At Dzongri, our tents lay just below a steep grassy knob that jutted up 1,000 feet and promised superb views of the Big One. Having been enthralled by my two previous early-morning views of the peak from afar, I organized a predawn mission to climb the knob and watch the first rays of the morning sun light the summit. My three bleary-eyed recruits and I started in the darkness at 4:30 A.M. and arrived at the top in the first faint glow of dawn to find a row of Buddhist prayer flags waving gently in the breeze. We sat mute among the whispering flags, the snowcapped peaks towering around us, as the sky brightened. None of us was particularly religious, but when the summit of Kanchenjunga suddenly turned golden, we all agreed that if there were a God or Buddha or whatever, he (or she) was probably not far from this time and place.

From Dzongri, we hiked through expanses of rhododendrons (what a spectacle it must be in May!) and along the Prek River, a broad gash of white boulders. We followed the river valley, past yak herders and piles of prayer-inscribed *mani* stones, around which Buddhists must walk only clockwise. Five days out from Yoksum, we finally pitched our tents at Jemathang, next to a holy lake at 15,750 feet. It was the jumping-off spot to our final goal: Goecha La, the 16,400-foot pass in the shadow of Kanchenjunga.

Once again we rose before dawn, this time in hopes of reaching the pass before midday clouds obscured the view of the summit. The altitude and rough, rocky terrain turned back three of the group, but eleven of us pressed on through the barren landscape. Daku kept our spirits up by, among other devices, assuming a primatelike posture and leaping from boulder to boulder while shouting "I am the yeti! The Kanchenjunga yeti!" (Indeed, the very first reported sighting of a yeti, or Abominable Snowman, occurred in Sikkim in 1889.) Traversing one last tricky snow-covered slope, we arrived at the pass just as the first wisps of cloud began to stream from the summit looming above us.

As prayer flags whipped in the bitter wind, Daku picked up a stone and added it to a ceremonial pile. She then burned an offering of incense branches, sprinkling rice, nuts, and seeds into the fragrant flames. We had conquered a mere pass, not a summit, but we felt thankful to the mountain gods just the same.

OUTFITTERS

Geographic Expeditions's itinerary includes the ten-day trek described in the narrative, from Yoksum to Goecha La and back, plus visits to Gangtok, Darjeeling, and Kalimpong. The company also offers a thirteen-day, $1,680 version of the trip called the Rhododendron Trek, in the spring only. Walkers start at Yoksum, but proceed only as far as Dzongri, where they'll stay for three days, making day hikes among the forests of blooming rhododendron nearby.

The itinerary of *Journeys International* is a bit less challenging than the others listed here. It stops one day short of Goecha La, but adds two days of low-altitude walking from Pemyangtse Monastery to Yoksum, the usual starting point. This is not all bad; the lower populated valleys are extraordinarily beautiful. If the weather is perfect, as it sometimes is in November, it may be possible to talk the trip leader into a dash to Goecha La, but don't count on it. The trip also includes two days each in Gangtok, Darjeeling, and Delhi.

The climbing-oriented company *KE Adventure Travel* offers a more challenging version of the Goecha La trek. Proceeding from Yoksum along the usual route, you'll establish a base camp just below the pass at about 16,000 feet and spend four days exploring the area, including some basic climbing instruction on surrounding mountains. There is less emphasis on the local culture; you'll zoom through Gangtok and spend only one full day in Darjeeling.

KE also offers a variation that includes, in addition to the standard Geocha La trek, a five-day walk along the Singalila Ridge, which follows the Nepal-Sikkim border and offers stunning views of Everest, as well as Kanchenjunga. Length is twenty-three days, price, $2,595.

Mountain Travel-Sobek, which ran the trip I describe above, no longer offers a Sikkim itinerary because of the sad death of Daku Tenzing Norgay, its regular trip leader. On a Buddhist pilgrimage to Nagaland in eastern India in 1994, Daku came down with a mysterious gastrointestinal ailment and died en route home to Darjeeling. She was fifty-two.

WHAT TO EXPECT

This is a typical Himalayan trek, with six to eight hours per day of hiking along trails that can be quite steep, at altitudes from 6,000 to 16,000 feet. The push to Goecha La is the most challenging day, but since it is an out-and-back hike, the weary or footsore may elect to stay in camp at Jemathang.

You'll carry only a light day pack with snacks, camera, and rain jacket. Porters or pack animals carry the rest of your gear and all the camping equipment. The trek staff sets up and takes down your tent, cooks all the meals, and does the washing up. There are trekkers' huts along the way, but most are not particularly inviting, and may be crowded in peak season. Expect to stay in your tents and eat meals out in the open. Temperatures may fall well below freezing at night at higher altitudes. As with any trip at this elevation, altitude sickness is always a possibility.

Himalayan trekking is not without its luxuries, however; the kitchen staff typically wakes trekkers each morning with a cheery greeting and a cup of steaming hot tea handed in through the tent flap.

No particular skills are required. There is an occasional scramble across rocky sections of trail, and two precarious swinging bridge crossings. Participants in the KE Adventure Travel trip will learn some basic mountaineering skills, but none are required beforehand.

Prime times for Himalayan treks are March to May and October to November. Fall months have better weather and clearer air. In the spring, the flowers are out, but so are the leeches at lower altitudes.

RECOMMENDED READING

Time Change by Hope Cooke. Not a literary masterpiece, but an intriguing insider's look at the last years of Sikkim's royal family by the young American woman who married the king in 1963 and reigned as queen until its conquest by India in 1974.

IN BRIEF

Geographic Expeditions, 800-777-8183: 18 days, $2,745
Journeys International, 800-255-8735: 24 days, $1,795
KE Adventure Travel, 800-497-9675: 23 days, $2,695

Physical challenge, 3; Mental challenge, 3; Skills, 1.

VIETNAM
bicycling from hanoi
to saigon

In his continuing nightmare, Wilson Hubbell floats in the sky and looks down in helpless agony as his comrades are engulfed in flames. He watches them try to claw through a fence that blocks their escape, or fall to the ground and curl up against the onrushing wall of fire. Usually, he awakes in a cold sweat, moaning softly.

Hubbell isn't your typical talk-show Vietnam veteran. He isn't paralyzed. He didn't do drugs, didn't commit any massacres, didn't father any Vietnamese children. He did his three years, came home, went to college, married, got a good job, resumed his lifelong passion for long-distance bicycling, and lived a pretty normal life.

"I expected Vietnam to disappear with time," recalls Hubbell, now a fifty-year-old city planner in Santa Barbara, California. "But it was creeping back into my life, and I didn't understand why."

Hubbell didn't understand a lot of things about war when he enlisted in the army in 1966. He'd grown up watching fifties war movies where the line between good and evil was clearly drawn, and where the good guys always won. He thought being a waist gunner on a B-17 would be about the coolest thing in the world. In the army recruiter's office, checking out his options as the draft closed in, he saw a poster of a door gunner crouched behind an M-60 machine gun in the belly of a CH-47 Chinook helicopter. "Could I sign up to be one of those guys?" he asked.

"Yes, we have openings," said the recruiter with a straight face.

Hubbell spent eighteen months in the central highlands of Vietnam as a crew chief and door gunner on a Chinook. "It was a pretty hairy time to be in the helicopter business," he recalls. The sixteen choppers in his unit were regularly hit by ground fire. Three were shot down in one six-month period. "After those crashes, we'd get sent out to gather up guys' remains to send home to their families. There usually was nothing left to send home but a watch and a wedding ring. It was not a pretty way to die."

In early 1968, Hubbell was eating lunch under the rotors of a Chinook parked at LZ Uplift, a landing zone and artillery base in Binh Dinh province. Without warning, a North Vietnamese mortar round hit the LZ's ammo dump, and shells began exploding in a fiery chain reaction. While the pilot frantically raced through the complex engine startup procedure, Hubbell crouched beside the helicopter and monitored the engines and rotors, his job as crew chief. The ground shook with the concussions of the exploding shells, and fiery shrapnel whistled around his head. After forty-five terrifying seconds, the Chinook's rotor blades had gathered enough speed to lift the machine into the air. Hubbell clambered into the Chinook's rear door as it whup-whupped away. They stayed low, dodging trees at an altitude of 15 feet, "so we wouldn't have far to fall in case we got hit by the flying debris."

Once at a safe distance, the chopper circled back and hovered overhead as the ammo dump was consumed by the explosions and fire. The helicopter crew could do nothing but watch as a dozen American soldiers died, some of them trapped between the advancing inferno and the base's perimeter of razor-edged concertina wire. A few minutes later, Hubbell's chopper was ordered by radio to leave the scene. They followed orders.

Back home, immersed in school, job, family, and his beloved racing bicycles, Hubbell tried to put his Vietnam experience behind him. "Vietnam veterans had a stigma, so I kept my mouth shut," he recalls. But the nightmare wouldn't go away. It didn't happen very often, usually when he was overstressed at work, or too busy to get in his regular mileage on the bicycle. But still he saw the flames.

Hubbell joined a discussion group of Vietnam vets, and that seemed to help. He realized he wasn't as bad off as some of the other guys. He learned about survivor guilt. After three years with the group, he believed he'd finally come to grips with Vietnam.

When Hubble saw the ad in a bicycle magazine for a three-week 1,200-mile bike tour from Hanoi to Saigon (Ho Chi Minh City, they called it now), he was intrigued. The tour was the kind of high-mileage cross-country trip he liked. The route ran through Binh Dinh province, only a few klicks from his old base camp with the First Aviation Brigade. He could have a badly needed vacation, get in some good mileage, and have a nostalgic look at his old haunts. Hubbell signed up for the trip.

As his airliner made its final approach into Hanoi, he looked out at the familiar red dirt and the sun glinting off the rice paddies. The first person he saw on the ground was a customs agent, dressed in the uniform of the former North Vietnamese Army. "The hair stood up on the back of my neck," he recalls. "Twenty-five years ago the guy would have tried to kill me, and now I'm standing there like nothing had happened."

His apprehension grew as he rode the bus to the hotel. The

cheery lilt of Vietnamese voices triggered a strange feeling of dread. "I'd spent a year and a half being suspicious of every Vietnamese person I'd ever seen. We were told again and again that the local people could get you killed."

While the rest of the group spent the first two days sight-seeing in Hanoi, Hubbell hardly left the hotel. "In my mind, the hotel was our LZ. I was safe as long as I stayed inside the perimeter." He began to get physically ill, and had terrible nightmares those first two nights. Buddies who'd been killed in action came to him in the dream and jeered at him. "We died fighting this war, and now you're coming back here for fun? Just to ride your fucking bike?"

He woke up from the nightmare and looked out the window. This time he wasn't in Santa Barbara. Frightened by the inner demons he thought he'd exorcized, Hubbell decided he couldn't go through with the trip. The next day, as the rest of the group pedaled off for Saigon, yipping in giddy excitement, he was slumped in a taxi, exhausted and depressed, heading back to the airport and home.

A month later the organizer of the bike trip called and offered a second chance on the next year's trip, at no cost. Hubbell's friends in the veteran's group urged him to try again. They assured him he would not be dishonoring the dead, that riding a bicycle through Vietnam wasn't just a lark, that it was his vehicle back to those places where he needed to make his peace. They gave him the locations of their old base camps, and asked him to stop by and take a picture for them, or say a prayer for an old pal, or nail a unit patch to a nearby tree.

"I knew I had to start confronting those problems that were still in my head," Hubbell says. He made a list of his buddies' old base camps, learned a bit of Vietnamese, and headed back to Hanoi with his bicycle and a renewed sense of mission.

Hubbell greeted the customs officer in halting Vietnamese

and got a surprised smile in return. In the hotel, the old feelings of dread came back, but he stifled them. "I was determined to stay. They'd have had to carry me out of there."

Venturing out of the hotel, he was astonished at the overwhelming friendliness of the local people. He visited a memorial to civilians killed when B-52s hit Bach May Hospital during Nixon's 1972 Christmas bombings. Standing there in front of the memorial—a statue of a woman carrying an injured child, shaking her fist at the sky—Hubbell was greeted warmly by passersby. Teenagers smiled and tried out their English. Old women invited him to their homes for lunch. "The North Vietnamese were friendlier to me in Hanoi in 1995 than the Americans were in California in 1970," he says in wonderment.

Hubbell and the others pedaled off down National Highway One, the paved road that runs the length of the country. Among the rice paddies and palm trees and thickly wooded hills he saw few visible reminders of the war. Some fish ponds made of bomb craters, a few U.S. Army trucks that had somehow been salvaged and kept running all these years, an old Vietnamese man who'd worked at an American base in the south and still spoke English with an Alabama drawl. And everywhere people traveled by bicycle. "Why aren't you driving a car?" they would ask the Americans. "You are wealthy. Why are you riding a bicycle?"

On the fourth day, the group rode through the former DMZ, the demilitarized zone that had separated North from South. On day nine they reached Qui Nonh, 6 miles from Hubbell's old base camp. Leaving the other riders, he turned off Highway One and headed west on a dirt road. In the distance he saw the lush green hills and instantly recognized their profile, the way a mother remembers her child's face. Two curious teenage boys on bikes stopped to gawk at him, and he asked directions in Vietnamese. They understood and led him to his old base camp, which to Hubbell's surprise was now a small Vietnamese army outpost. The buildings were new, but through the fence he recognized his old helipad, a grid of corrugated metal planking still visible in the grass.

The young soldiers at the gate stared at him uncomprehending. "I might as well have been from Mars," Hubbell recalls. Seven or eight more soldiers came out of the guardhouse to stare at him. Although cordial, they did not allow him inside to look around.

He asked the kids to lead him around to the back side of the camp and the small village that had been just outside the wire from his "hootch," or sleeping hut. The village was still there, and through the fence Hubbell recognized several buildings from his old compound. He snapped some photos through the wire and turned back toward the village. There, watching him grimly with hands on hips, were three Vietnamese soldiers.

Hubbell tried to explain. *"Toi du lich. Toi hoa ky."* I am a tourist. I am American. The soldiers didn't smile. As the villagers gathered around, expressionless, Hubbell started handing out the baseball caps he'd brought along as goodwill gifts. The soldiers still looked grim. Then he pulled out his bag of patches and gave each soldier a green and black First Aviation Brigade emblem. He explained as best he could the history of the unit. And then he pulled his heels together, stood erect, and gave them a snappy salute.

As he turned back to his bicycle, Hubbell felt a great calm wash over him. "It's okay, now," he thought to himself. "It's over. I've ended this war in my mind. I can go home now."

He felt a tap on his shoulder. One of the soldiers was holding out a cigarette. Hubbell doesn't smoke, but this was no time for the surgeon general's warning. A villager, wearing a baseball cap, invited Hubbell and the soldiers into his living room for tea. They talked about the military life. "Their army and my army weren't that much different," says Hubbell. "Once upon a time, I'd been in their shoes." They shook hands all around and drank a toast to *hoa binh,* to peace.

The two kids were still hanging around, and one of them said, "Follow me," and pedaled off to a house in a nearby village. A slender man about Hubbell's age came out of the house and squinted at Hubbell with intense eyes. *"Hoa ky?"* the man asked. American? Hubbell nodded. The man pointed at himself and said, "VC." Talking and gesturing, they discovered that during the war the man had attacked Hubbell's old base camp while Hubbell was stationed there. It is likely that the two had exchanged gunfire.

The VC invited the door gunner into his house for cigarettes and rice wine. He pulled out a picture of himself in his old guerrilla uniform and gave it to Hubbell. On the back, he wrote a brief Vietnamese poem that, roughly translated, reads, "The engraving on a tombstone wears away in a hundred years, but friendship lasts forever. Your friend, Than."

OUTFITTER

Cycle Vietnam runs its Hanoi-to-Saigon trip each January. Cyclists follow National Highway One, the country's primary north-south road, for 1,200 miles, visiting such landmarks as the "Hanoi Hilton," the notorious prison for captured U.S. pilots; the guerrilla tunnels of Vinh Moc; the Citadel at Hue, Da Nang, and China Beach; My Lai, Dalat, and the former U.S. embassy and presidential palace in Saigon. This tour is unusual because of the large group size, up to forty people.

Riders have the option of a seven-day detour along the Ho Chi Minh Trail, the secret jungle route by which supplies were smuggled south to support the guerrilla war. This route, which is mostly dirt, requires a mountain bike or rugged cross-bike, and costs $200 additional.

WHAT TO EXPECT

This is almost certainly the most physically demanding commercial bicycle tour in the world. Average daily distance is 83 miles, with three days above 100 miles and one 117-mile day. Only one of the fourteen riding days is less than 66 miles. (There are two rests days.) Some sections of the road are rough, which adds to the physical challenge. Moreover, these rough roads demand a sturdier, fatter-tire bike that is less efficient than the skinny-tire lightweight racers typically used on high-mileage road tours. As a result, riding effort will be noticeably increased. Riding 117 miles on a 30-pound bicycle with semi-fat tires is a challenge that should not be underestimated.

You don't have to ride every mile, however. An air-conditioned bus serves as a "sag wagon," trailing along behind, ready to pick up the weary and the saddle sore. Typically, less than half the riders cover the full 1,200 miles. A few cycle only 40 or 50 miles a day, treating the trip as a bike 'n' bus combo. That's just fine with the outfitter.

This is not a camping trip; you'll typically stay in modest hotels and guest houses, usually with air-conditioning and bath. A variety of other factors, however, combine to boost the mental-challenge rating to a 3. The weather will often be hot and muggy, with the possibility of continual rain. For the unprepared, there lurks the chance of a wretched case of saddle sores. In case of an accident, medical care may be primitive and far away.

The road, although paved, can be rough. There are no shoulders as such. Although traffic is not heavy by American standards, trucks and buses are plentiful—this is, after all, the country's main highway. Prepare to suck diesel fumes on a regular basis. In addition, you may occasionally find yourself forced to yield the right of way to a water buffalo.

Finally, even if you are not a Vietnam vet, seeing places like My Lai and Bach Mai hospital can be depressing for many Americans. Not everyone can get past the memories and the stigma of the war. As the Bicycle Vietnam brochure admits, "It is not an easy tour physically or mentally, and is not for everyone."

On the bright side, however, the Vietnamese people are extraordinarily friendly toward Americans. Everywhere you go, you'll be mobbed by curious locals. And the countryside has recovered well from the war; there are few visible in-your-face reminders of it.

RECOMMENDED READING

Dispatches by Michael Herr. A spare and sobering war correspondent's account of the Vietnam conflict that perfectly captures its horror and futility.

IN BRIEF

Cycle Vietnam, 503-282-8499: 21 days, $2,750

Physical challenge, 4; Mental challenge, 3; Skills, 2.

AFRICA

BOTSWANA
exploring the
okavango delta
by elephant-back

In a fit of editorial whimsy some years ago, *Road & Track* magazine published a "road test" of a full-size mechanical elephant. With merciless objectivity, the test driver, who allegedly rode mahout-style on the vehicle's back, criticized its limited top speed, sluggish acceleration, and difficult driver access. On the other hand, from his unobstructed perch 13 feet above the ground, driver visibility was superb, better than that of any vehicle ever tested by the magazine.

This was no surprise to Randall Jay Moore, a swashbuckling mustachioed forty-five-year-old American who is perhaps the world's premiere trainer of African elephants. Moore has spent thousands of hours riding the huge beasts—the real ones—and it occurred to him in 1989 that, despite the technical shortcomings uncovered by *Road & Track,* an elephant would make an ideal game-viewing safari vehicle. Visibility, the sine qua non of any game-viewing conveyance, would of course be unsurpassed. Traction in swampy areas would exceed that of even a Toyota Land Cruiser. And the admittedly excessive exhaust emissions, although perhaps offensive to humans, would not spook game in the wild, as diesel fumes sometimes do.

Moore has made his notion real. Today, from a base camp on the banks of the Xhenega River in the southwestern Okavango Delta of Botswana, awestruck animal lovers make game-viewing forays into the surrounding marshland and savannah on the backs of four adult elephants—Abu, Benny, Cathy, and Bibi—accompanied by a rambunctious "brat pack" of youngsters too small to be ridden. During their weeklong stays, riders see the vast panoply of African wildlife—zebra, buffalo, giraffe, impala, lion, and leopard, as well as wild elephants—from close range, for the wild animals see Moore's lumbering safari vehicles more as comrades than intruders.

But for most visitors, the lions and giraffes are almost beside the point. What lingers in the memory are the elephants themselves. Intense day-to-day interaction with enormous, intelligent, well-socialized, and highly individual animals is a mind-boggling experience for the uninitiated. "You gaze up into their tiny, long-lashed brown eyes, you feel the flick of their fly-swatting tails, you hear the sound of their snorting trunks, like someone blowing the cobwebs out of an old garden hose," rhapsodized one visitor. To live for a week with Abu, Benny, Cathy, and Bibi is to make dear, unforgettable friends.

The elephants' life sagas, like Randall Moore's, are marked by improbable turns of fate. Moore, an aimless, rebellious, cynical young man in the early 1970s, by chance happened to visit the private Oregon wildlife farm of an eccentric couple named Morgan Berry and Eloise Berchtold. There Moore was astonished to find, among hundreds of other exotic animals, a herd of elephants roaming the forest. He had an epiphany of sorts, and begged Berry to give him a job. A few days later, Moore was shoveling elephant manure, happier than he'd ever been in his life. He went on to help Berry and Bechtold train a trio of African elephants for circus performances.

Tragically, a few years later, Berry and Bechtold were killed by two of their elephants in grisly accidents. Moore, by then a

wildlife biologist, inherited the African trio, and became obsessed with the idea of returning them to their homeland and
releasing them into the wild, a feat never before accomplished.
With the sponsorship of ABC Television, whom he persuaded
to make a documentary film, Moore eventually returned the
elephants to Kenya, and finally to South Africa, where they now
roam wild with an adopted clan in a protected game reserve.

Buoyed by his success and looking for a scheme to return
more zoo and circus elephants to their homeland, Moore contracted with a South African movie producer to find and train
three more elephants for a film entitled *Circles in the Forest,* a
colonial frontier tale of man vs. nature. The main character was
a wise and benevolent bull elephant named Old Foot.

The part of Old Foot called for a large male with impressive
tusks and an even-tempered intelligence. Moore recalled seeing
just such an animal at the Dallas Zoo some years before, a big
bull named Abu. Born in 1965 in South Africa's Kruger National Park, Abu had been orphaned when park rangers shot
his parents in a culling operation, and was subsequently sold to
an American zoo.

When Moore arrived in Dallas to take a look, he found Abu
locked in a tiny barn, apparently unwashed for months. The
miserable creature had been sleeping on a concrete floor in his
own feces, which had become embedded in folds of his skin
and triggered festering infections. Zoo employees told Moore
that Abu had tried to run away from his daily chore of carrying
children in small circles, and was now considered unreliable.
He was a rebel, an elephant with a reputation.

Despite the stories, Moore sensed in Abu a good disposition,
and decided to buy him.

Just down the road, at the Fort Worth Zoo, lived another
huge bull, even larger than Abu. Also a Kruger orphan, Benny
appeared forlorn and was afflicted with "floppy ear syndrome,"
a condition caused by poor nutrition in which one ear flaps

forward instead of back. Benny had spent fifteen years in a
small cage, alone, and was in the habit of incessantly rubbing
his tusks on the cement wall of his cell. One formerly magnificent tusk was worn down to nothing, and the other was a nub
oozing fluid when Moore came upon him.

Moore felt so sorry for the enormous beast that he offered to
buy him on the spot. The zoo readily agreed, and in fact gave
him Benny for nothing.

Cathy, a medium-size female, had been captured in Uganda
in the sixties and subsequently sent to a safari park near
Toronto, where she was now up for sale. Moore, captivated by
her elephantine eyelashes—eyelashes to die for, eyelashes long
enough to sweep leaves from trees—closed the deal. The movie
team was complete.

The elephants' disparate personalities emerged almost immediately. Like an aging prison lifer set in his ways and fearful
of the outside world, the hulking Benny proved reluctant to
leave his Forth Worth cell. It took four winches to get him into
the truck. When Cathy's turn came to be loaded, Benny planted
his backside in the doorway and refused all human entreaties to
the contrary. Cathy, after waiting patiently in the rain for an
hour, eventually took matters into her own tusks, with which
she gave Benny two sharp jabs in his humongous butt. Benny
yelped, jumped, and expeditiously stepped aside to admit his
new companion. That set the tone for their relationship, which
remains much the same today: the huge, lumbering male henpecked and dominated by the petite, sassy younger female.

Abu, meanwhile, seemed to love the drama of change. He
practically ran from his barn into the trailer, and quickly took
to his new surroundings. On the transatlantic journey by ship,
Abu sauntered about the deck as if born to seafaring, trumpet-
ing occasionally to passing whales. Benny, on the other hand,
only rarely consented to move, and had to be winched in and
out of the trailer for his on-deck sojourns. Cathy contentedly

took her place in the middle of the pecking order. During their monthlong homecoming journey, the unlikely 33,000-pound trio endured boredom, confinement, below-zero temperatures, and Cape rollers, huge waves that had them skidding perilously across the deck, railing to railing, before Moore and a deckhand could lead them back into the safety of their trailer.

The trio flourished in their new environment on the movie set in South Africa's Knysna Forest. Abu turned out to be a natural star, a veritable Warren Beatty of pachyderms who lived for the adulation of the camera. On command, he chased crowds of villagers through the forest. He saved the movie's human hero from drowning by lifting him gently from the water with his tusks. He demolished a movie-set general store, knocking down walls and spearing a bag of flour in a dramatic explosion of white dust, a scene that prompted Moore to accuse him of overacting.

Cathy appeared in a few scenes in *Circles in the Forest* as well, at one point chasing an actor up a tree. But the dull-witted, floppy-eared Benny, despite his Schwarzeneggeresque stature, did not have the stuff for drama, and remained on the sidelines.

The film, although a huge success in South Africa, was never released in the United States. But Abu has since performed in a number of American movies, generally living up to the hype of his promotional brochure, which describes him as a cross between Rambo and Captain Kirk. Abu's biggest U.S. film credit is *White Hunter, Black Heart,* the stunningly bad Clint Eastwood vehicle in which Abu performs a fearsome charge and "kills" a native tracker, in the process displaying more acting talent and charisma than Eastwood or anyone else in that execrable film.

Even in his less glamorous job hauling safari-goers through the Okavango, Abu is still the star. "He's the head honcho and he knows it," says one camp visitor. He toys with humans; when handed a can of beer to deliver to his rider, he will playfully insert it in his mouth before passing it up, drenched in elephant saliva.

Benny is still the timid, reluctant, henpecked hulk. On safari outings, Cathy bosses him around. Moore calls him a meatball. Even the brat pack picks on the gentle giant, spooking him with mock charges that fool no one else. The mahouts must prod and cajole him to perform even the simplest task. One gets the feeling that Benny would really rather be left alone to spend the rest of his life dozing under an acacia tree.

Cathy is a favorite of guests, partly because of her cracker-jack personality, and partly because Cathy-riders are more likely to have a close encounter with a wild elephant. On several occasions young bulls from nearby herds have approached to make her acquaintance. Fortunately, the relationship did not proceed beyond mutual sniffing. Otherwise, in Moore's words, "It would have been a unique experience for the people riding Cathy at the time."

Bibi, a fifty-year-old female who had been languishing in a Sri Lankan zoo, joined the group in 1993, as did two young males, Mthando Bomvu (a Swahili name that means "piece of shit") and Nyanka Nyanka ("painted penis").

Among the brat packers, Miss B and Mafunyane are notorious. The former, who has adopted Bibi as her surrogate mother, is described by one recent guest as a spoiled brat. "She makes a big show of independence and wanders off from the herd. But when she loses sight of Bibi, she stops in her tracks, starts wailing, and expects the entire caravan to come to a screeching halt for her benefit. She's quite marvelous."

Mafunyane, seven years old, is a master of trunk-related chicanery. A favorite trick is hosing down unsuspecting guests with his drinking water. One client describes trying to take an afternoon nap under a tree, but being repeatedly nudged awake by Mafunyane's hairy snuffing proboscis.

This herd of misfits—orphans, refugees, rebels, rejects, neurotics, prima donnas, spoiled brats—has a powerful, almost spiritual effect on people who get to know them. One guest reflected that, after his week with the elephants, he'd sooner wear his grandmother's teeth around his neck than buy an ivory ornament. Furthermore, he declared, "It would be easier for me to kill another human being than to shoot an elephant."

He continued, "My most enduring memory was leaning forward on Benny's back with my hands resting on his shoulder blades, feeling those massive bones moving beneath his warm skin. It was a bit like hugging a stranger and being surprised at the sensation of another life. Then Benny swung his trunk up and touched me on the hand. It was just a brief communication between me and an African elephant, but there is only one word to describe the feeling: love."

OUTFITTER

Esplanade Tours is the American agent for Randall Moore's elephant-back safaris. Guests stay at Abu's Camp, a permanent base along the Xhenega River in the Southwestern Okavango Delta, and make daily forays into the surrounding region by elephant, canoe, jeep, or foot, in terrain ranging from marsh to plains. Each guest is guaranteed a minimum of seven elephant-back rides during the six-day stay, which runs Wednesday through Monday. Animals typically seen include zebra, giraffe, buffalo, impala, lion, leopard, and other elephants. Fishing and bird-watching outings are also available.

Physically, this may be the softest trip in the book. Your biggest challenge will be stepping up onto the kneeling elephant's back. Once aloft, you'll merely sit and observe the passing wildlife. (Neck muscles, however, may get sore from constant swiveling.) Game-viewing outings by jeep and canoe are similarly sedentary. Optional foot safaris are available for those wishing to occasionally push their heart rates above 90.

Abu's Camp has five twin-bedded stand-up safari tents with private bucket shower and "long-drop" loo. Gourmet bush cuisine features fresh-baked bread, linen tablecloth, fine silverware, and all the booze you can drink ("in reasonable quantities," according to the brochure). The only skill that might prove helpful on this trip is the ability to pour wine with the proper twist of the wrist.

But not everything is sweetness and light. Sprawling for hours across the broad, bony back of an elephant can be uncomfortable, despite the well-padded saddles with guard rails, called howdahs. Although outings are typically scheduled for the cooler morning and evening hours, midday heat and dust are an inevitable part of the African experience. And, of course, there's always the possibility that an inattentive safari-goer will accidentally tread in elephant dung. (Hey, we never promised you a rose garden.)

Abu's Camp is open to visitors March through November. The staging city is Maun, Botswana, where you'll be picked up in a small plane and flown to the camp at no charge.

RECOMMENDED READING

Back to Africa by Randall Moore. The full story of Moore's life with African elephants and his efforts to reintroduce them to the wild.

IN BRIEF

Esplanade Tours, 800-628-4893: 6 days, $5,000

Physical challenge, 1; Mental challenge, 1; Skills, 1.

ETHIOPIA

rafting the omo

The Omo River, which snakes down from the Ethiopian highlands to Lake Turkana, offers the whitewater rafter a gamut of attractions unmatched by any river in the world: frothing rapids, 1,000-foot-deep gorges, large and exotic wildlife, and remote tribal villages rarely visited by outsiders.

The hazards of the Omo, however, are equally stunning in their variety: the frothing rapids may drown you, some of the wildlife would like to eat you, and, until recently, the occasional unfriendly native, given the opportunity, might hurl the occasional spear at you. But the most serious threats to life along this remote, wild river are invisible. A vast array of disease-causing parasites, bacteria, and viruses make up a panoply of pathology perhaps unsurpassed on our planet. "In Ethiopia you can catch every disease known to Africa, except for *loa-loa*," exults Dr. George Fuller, a tropical disease specialist who's floated down the Omo seven times. "It's a great place to study."

Among the maladies one may contract along the Omo are (in alphabetical order) blackwater fever, cholera, dengue fever, dysentery, echinococcus, elephantiasis, filariasis, guinea worm disease, hepatitis, kala-azar, Lassa fever, leishmaniasis, leptospirosis, malaria, river blindness, schistosomiasis, sleeping sickness, typhoid fever, typhus, and yellow fever. The current superstar of tropical disease, the Ebola virus, has not yet been documented along the Omo, but one of the major Ebola outbreaks occurred in Sudan, right next door.

Some diseases on this grisly roster are quite rare, or easily preventable. But four in particular deserve special attention from the Omo traveler.

Schistosomiasis

Also known as bilharzia, "schisto" is caused not by a virus or bacteria but by a tiny parasite. Its life cycle begins in what biologists primly refer to as the "fecal bolus"—you and I would say turd—of an infected human, or perhaps a monkey or baboon. The egg eventually finds its way into water, where it hatches into a microscopic larva that seeks out the nearest water snail. Boring into the snail, the larva multiplies and mutates through several generations into fork-tailed creatures called cercariae, which consume the snail's reproductive organs, essentially castrating it. The cercariae then erupt, *Alien*-like, through the snail's skin, and continue erupting every twenty-four hours, for the remainder of the snail's life.

Back in the water again, the cercariae turn their attention to passing humans—whitewater rafters, say, whose raft has capsized, or who are just taking a quick dip to wash off three days of dust and stink. The wriggling cercaria burrows into its host, literally digesting its way in through the skin in a couple of minutes. The victim at this point may feel a minor itch.

Once inside the host, the cercariae ride the bloodstream to the liver, which serves as a giant schisto singles bar. Males and females pair off and, nestled together, wriggle their way upstream like tiny salmon through the veins to the area around the intestines. There, nestled in the capillaries, they grow into worms about three quarters of an inch long, taking up a life of what George Fuller calls "hedonistic overindulgence. . . . They spend their lives making love . . . the long, slender female worm entwined in the folds of the broader, stouter male. . . . They remain secure, nestled together, bathing in food and warmth, copulating for life, which can be as long as thirty years. . . ."

This is not a bad fate for an organism whose life literally began in shit. But it is a bad fate indeed for its human host. The one hundred or so eggs that each female lays every day—and there may be one hundred females in each host—begin to pile up in the liver. A few weeks after infection, about the time the rafter is settling back into his job and family routine back home, he will begin to feel various vague flulike symptoms—upset stomach, diarrhea, mild fever. If left untreated, stomach pain will become more serious as fluids build up in the abdomen and cause severe bloating. Eventually, the liver fails. On one Omo raft trip, in the low-water year of 1988, a half dozen rafters came down with schisto, including one who was paralyzed when a worm unaccountably ended up in his spinal cord.

Prevention: Stay out of still water, which is preferred by the snails that harbor the parasite. If submerging is unavoidable, towel off briskly immediately afterward.

Treatment: One dose of a drug called praziquantel will kill the worms, although it cannot relieve symptoms of accumulated liver damage.

River Blindness

As a child growing up in a remote village in Mali, Yiriba Bissan had one job: Each morning he would grasp the small end of his blind uncle's walking stick and lead the old man to a big tree outside the village, where the two would sit all day in the shade. It is a scene played out thousands of times a day all over Africa in certain villages where sightlessness is as much a sign of old age as gray hair. These villages of the blind are all located near swift-running rivers. The elders are victims of onchocerciasis, or river blindness, a disease carried by tiny black flies that can breed only in rapidly moving water.

The upper Omo, of course, is one of Africa's swiftest rivers, roaring and burbling and providing a constant stream of nutrients and oxygen to the larval flies that cling to rocks just below its surface. When an adult black fly bites a human, it may pass on a tiny larval parasite called *Onchocerca volvulus,* which takes root in the skin of its human hosts. After a year or so, each larva has developed into an acorn-size nodule containing a yard-long female adult worm and several smaller males, all cozily coiled around one another in their nuptial cocoon. The adult worms do no real harm, but their prodigious offspring of tiny filamentlike baby worms, called microfilariae, swarm through the skin of the host. A single victim may harbor as many as 200 million microfilariae. Random bits of skin viewed through a microscope will show dozens of the wriggling threads.

The swarming microworms trigger such skin conditions as "leopard skin" (spotting due to depigmentation), "elephant skin" (a thickening and toughening), and "hanging groin," an elephantiasislike condition in which the scrotum and folds of loose skin from the groin hang down as far as the knees. Eventually, the microworms reach the eyes, and blindness results.

But, hey, there's a bright side: It takes years of repeated infection to cause blindness. And nobody ever dies—though some victims might wish for such a fate. A strain of river blindness in Yemen causes itching so intractable that a number of its sufferers have been driven to suicide.

Prevention: Avoid the bites of black flies. This is not so easy if you are busy negotiating a Class IV rapid, hanging on for dear life with both hands, hoping madly to avoid capsizing into crocodile-infested waters. Long-sleeve shirts and long pants will help ward off the flies, but who wants to bundle up when the temperature is 105 degrees in the noonday sun?

Treatment: Fortunately, there is a very effective drug, ivermectin, which kills the microfilariae with one or two doses. Medical references differ, however, about its effectiveness against the adult worms, which are also sometimes surgically removed, or treated with suramin, a very toxic drug.

Sleeping Sickness

Some years back *Ripley's Believe It or Not!* claimed that the African tsetse fly could attain a speed of 800 miles per hour. Not! But, having evolved to chase down sprinting antelopes, the fly routinely cruises at 60 miles per hour and may well be able to hit 100 in short bursts. In any case, no Omo paddler should plan on outrunning the swarms of tsetse flies that infest this part of Ethiopia. Nor do insect repellents seem to have any effect on them. "You can slather yourself with DEET and the damn things bore right in," says Don Heyneman, a parasitologist who went down the Omo with George Fuller in 1988. "You go down that river, you're going to get bitten by a lot of tsetse flies, that's for sure."

Tsetse flies, of course, carry trypanosomiasis, or African sleeping sickness, a very sobering disease with a fatality rate of 50 to 90 percent and no truly effective treatment. Early symptoms include painful swelling of the lymph nodes in the armpits, groin, and, especially, the back of the neck. Centuries ago, canny slave traders would inspect their merchandise by feeling the back of the slave's neck. Those with lumps would be rejected.

Open sores develop as the swollen lymph nodes begin to drain through the skin. When the *Trypanosoma* parasites eventually work their way across the blood-brain barrier, the central nervous system begins to shut down, leading to drowsiness, headaches, tremors, and convulsions. Usually, coma and death follow.

There is, however, some good news for Omo rafters. Of the two varieties of African sleeping sickness, the one most often found in the Omo region is the Gambian strain, which is somewhat less deadly than the Rhodesian, or East African genus. So y'all relax and have fun now, hear?

Prevention: Avoid being bitten by tsetse flies. (Yeah, right.)

Treatment: Intravenous eflornithine or melarsoprol. The latter, while more effective, is an arsenic compound that has, according to a standard medical reference, "all the usual arsenical effects on GI, neurological, and renal systems."

Blackwater Fever

Not quite malaria, blackwater fever is a mysterious "complication" of the most virulent and deadly form of malaria, the one caused by the microscopic parasite *Plasmodium falciparum*. Once injected into the bloodstream by the female anopheline mosquito—a species in great abundance along the Omo—the *P. falciparum* parasites invade the liver. There they multiply and, like a perfectly synchronized army of tiny Pac-men, fan out into the bloodstream to attack the host's red blood cells. Once inside a blood cell, each parasite multiplies rapidly into dozens of tiny spores. Then, with exquisite choreography, the spores burst simultaneously from their respective ravaged red cells and immediately begin seeking out new blood cells to destroy.

Untreated, this cascading chain reaction of red-cell destruction continues every forty-eight hours until the host—racked by chills and fever, with dead blood cells accumulating in his brain—either develops an immunity or dies. Death can occur with frightening speed, sometimes within hours after the initial symptoms. Though *P. falciparum* has probably killed more humans than any other disease, most people who catch it these days do in fact survive.

Still, survivors cannot breathe easy. A very unlucky minority of people who live through *P. falciparum* subsequently develop the devastating blackwater fever, in which the body's remaining red blood cells—those that escaped the malaria parasite—for some reason begin to rupture and die. The broken-up red cells collect in the urine and oxidize, turning the urine dark. "Essentially what happens with blackwater fever is that you piss out your bloodstream," explains Don Heyneman.

Oddly enough, white people seem to be the primary victims of blackwater fever. And the risk seems to be higher for those who have regularly consumed small amounts of the traditional malaria curative, quinine—the amount you'd find, say, in a gin and tonic. Thus it is no surprise that British colonists in East Africa suffered terribly from blackwater fever.

Beryl Markham, who grew up in Kenya in the early 1900s, wrote in *West with the Night,* "people with blackwater always die if they are moved, and nearly always die if they are left alone. . . . A man can be riddled with malaria for years on end, with its chills and its fevers and its nightmares, but if one day he sees that the water from his kidneys is black, he knows that he will not leave that place again, wherever he is. . . ."

Prevention: Avoid mosquito bites, as well as gin and tonics. Take prophylactic mefloquine, a synthetic analog of quinine.

Treatment: Quinine, intravenously if the patient is in a coma.

OUTFITTER

Sobek Expeditions made the first descent of the Omo in 1973. Today, merged with Mountain Travel to form *Mountain Travel-Sobek,* it is still the only outfitter with the guts to run this river. From Addis Ababa, rafters drive north and overnight at a hot-springs resort in Wollisso. The put-in is at the nearby Gibe Bridge. The upper section of the river, which takes about two weeks to negotiate, is extremely isolated and cuts through a deep canyon. There is abundant Class III whitewater and wildlife, but few local people. The lower section of the river, after it emerges from the canyon, has less wildlife and no serious rapids, but numerous tribal groups live along its banks. The Bodi, Mursi, Chara, and other tribes had not seen white men at all until the first Sobek pioneers came down the river in '73. They now welcome the annual influx of riverborne visitors

A bridge about halfway down the river allows for resupply and the option of doing either half of the trip. The Upper Half option takes seventeen days overall and costs $3,290; the lower half is nineteen days and $3,490.

WHAT TO EXPECT

Sobek uses only oar boats because paddlers leaning out over the side make too tempting a target for the Omo crocs. The guides do the rowing; essentially, all you do is sit. On land, however, customers are expected to help load and unload the rafts each day. There are optional daily hikes up tributaries, usually short, sometimes moderately strenuous. If you crave physical exertion, the guides are more than happy to let you row the long stretches of flat water on the lower section of the river.

This is an expedition-style trip in which you'll be expected to set up your own tent, wash your own dishes, and help out with camp chores, including loading the rafts. As mentioned above, there are numerous hazards: rapids, crocodiles, hippos, and of course a forbidding gauntlet of disease-carrying bugs and parasites. The river is extremely isolated, and outside medical help may be many days away. The weather can be beastly hot in the lower section.

RECOMMENDED READING

Rivergods by Richard Bangs and Christian Kallen. A first-person narrative of ten exploratory trips down wild rivers around the world, including the 1973 first descent of the Omo. Coauthor Bangs is a founder of Sobek Expeditions.

Manon's Tropical Diseases edited by Gordon Cook. The standard medical reference text.

IN BRIEF

Mountain Travel-Sobek, 800-227-2384: 28 days, $4,290

Physical challenge, 1; Mental challenge, 4; Skills, 1.

MALI

bicycling to
dogon country

It is not easy to fall in love with a country that is the third poor-est in the world, that has an illiteracy rate of 90 percent, where lepers wander city streets, and where the average citizen is dead by the age of forty-four. And what is the charm of an African country without rain forest or snowcapped peaks, without lions, elephants, or gorillas?

Nevertheless, Leslye Abbey fell in love with Mali. "I had a mad love affair with this country," she says. "Mali enveloped me. It was magical."

You could call Leslye Abbey a Long Island shaman. A fifty-two-year-old social worker and psychotherapist from North Bellmore, New York, she is a psychic healer of the modern age who discovered in Mali that she would really rather live in an-other era. Sitting in an ancient cliff dwelling at the foot of the Bandiagara Escarpment, near the Dogon village of Teli, she suddenly realized that she wanted to spend the rest of her life gazing out over that village, waiting for her vision. "I felt as if I had connected with my past life," she says quietly.

Abbey found her inner peace on an eighteen-speed Shogun

mountain bike. She was part of a cycling tour organized by Bicycle Africa, a one-man company whose one man is forty-three-year-old Seattle resident David Mozer. A Peace Corps volunteer in Liberia in the 1970s who later worked in village development for the U.S. embassy there, Mozer may properly be described as an old West Africa hand. He personally leads every Bicycle Africa trip. His philosophy of travel is basic and nitty-gritty: no support vehicle, no support staff—no support whatsoever, in fact. Cyclists are entirely dependent upon the local economy for their existence. They eat the local food and stay in village hotels or private homes. "I don't like the idea of camping out in tents and cooking our own food," says Mozer. "It isolates us from the local people. The whole idea of my trips is to submerge ourselves in local life as much as possible."

This philosophy seems custom-made for Abbey, who simply can't bear to pass up the possibility of meeting an interesting person. Constantly trailing behind the other riders, she stopped and detoured at the slightest provocation. She talked to shopkeepers, taxi drivers, herdsmen, kids. She bought them food and gave away her clothes. She dropped into local bars, where she was invariably the only white person, and the only woman. She was always greeted warmly. The fact that Abbey knew not a word of the local language did not deter her in the slightest. "The other people in the cycling group were yelling at me because I was never with them. But they rode so fast, and once they got to where we were going, they were so tired they went to sleep. What did they see?"

Abbey saw a lot. In the town of Sofara, she hung out with the well man, whose job was to tend the well and supervise the distribution of water among the children sent to fetch it. Surrounded by squealing kids, the well man performed magic tricks, orchestrated games, settled quarrels, and passed on the stories and legends that were the heart of his cultural tradition.

In a country where schools are a rarity, he was a very important man.

Looking for professional and spiritual brotherhood, Abbey sought out Sofara's marabout, the traditional healer of mind and spirit—in effect, the local shrink. His office was the dusty courtyard of his adobe hut. He wore a blue satiny robe embroidered with great gold flowers, but the cuffs of plaid pants peeked out from under his robe. His rate was 5,000 francs per session, about $10.

Sitting cross-legged on the floor, Abbey told him that she, too, worked with people who were in spiritual pain, who were out of harmony with the universe. The marabout agreed to use his spiritual powers to protect her during her travels, and to grant her the power to do good work with her patients back home. It was a special moment of communication between two psychic healers. Then, laughs Abbey, "Like a schmuck, I asked him if he could find me a husband." The marabout smiled, and replied that he would have to sleep on that one. He told her to come back at six the next morning.

When Abbey returned, the marabout agreed to use his spiritual powers to send her a husband. Then he gave her three gris-gris—Muslim prayers inscribed on paper intricately folded to the size of a thumbnail. She now wears the gris-gris around her neck in a tiny silver Tibetan prayer locket. "Since I got back to Long Island, I've met a lot of husbands," she says. "Unfortunately, they're all other peoples' husbands. I guess I wasn't specific enough with him."

It was not until she pedaled into Dogon country, however, that Abbey found her true spiritual soul mates. Despite the poverty and grinding toil of their lives—or perhaps because of it—the Dogon are an intensely spiritual people. For five hundred years, they have lived in isolation along the desert cliffs of the Bandiagara Escarpment in central Mali, scratching out an existence growing millet in the dry sand, much like the prehistoric cliff-dwelling Anasazi Indians of the American Southwest.

The Dogon's animist religion infuses every aspect of their lives. Diviners predict the future by analyzing the tracks of foxes in the dust. Sorcerers decorate their houses with skulls, animal horns, millet porridge, and blood. Villages are laid out in the shape of the human body. Each grass-roofed house is laid out in human form as well—a circular kitchen at the head, the living area in the torso, and bedrooms stretching from the shoulders. The main entrance is the genitals.

Sex is the basis of the Dogon's creation myth and many of its rituals. The details of the Dogon religion were revealed to a French anthropologist in 1946 by a blind Dogon elder, Ogotommeli. In thirty-three days of intense conversation, Ogotommeli laid bare the details of the Dogon spiritual world as perhaps no indigenous culture ever has revealed itself to an outsider. The Dogon creation myth he recounted is a grand cosmic soap opera that goes something like this:

The God Amma created from clay a female earth, with an anthill for a vagina and a termite mound for a clitoris. When Amma tried to make love to the earth, the termite mound rose up, blocking his way. But Amma cut down the termite mound and ravished the excised earth. From this troubled union was born not a human being but a jackal, who subsequently defiled its mother earth. Amma made love to the earth a second time, without resistance. The progeny were twin gods called Nummo, who were the essence of water, the source of all life.

Amma decided to make the first two humans another way; this time creating them directly from clay. Each was endowed with two sexual identities. The man's femaleness resided in his foreskin, the woman's maleness in her clitoris. Nummo immediately circumcised the man, and his foreskin turned into a serpent. The man made love to the woman, and when she gave birth, her clitoris detached itself and turned into a scorpion. Thus Dogons by tradition can achieve their sexual identity only after circumcision or clitorectomy.

Female clitorectomy is performed privately, without ceremony. But male circumcision is a dramatic rite of passage for Dogon boys. The visitor to Dogon country who is very lucky in his timing might notice mysterious fires burning at night along the Bandiagara cliffs. These are the fires of the circumcision ceremony, held every three years. The young boys of the village are led to special grottos along the cliffs, where no woman can see. In the cave, an elder produces a snake that represents Lebe, the First Ancestor. A live chicken is fed to the snake, and the boys are told that if they cry out in pain during the circumcision, they, too, will be eaten by the snake. Each boy is then cut while sitting on a smooth stone that is black with centuries of bloodstains. For the next month, the boys remain in the grotto, healing and listening as the elders impart their ancient wisdom and traditions.

It's perhaps no surprise that a professional psychotherapist might take a special interest in a culture whose creation myth involves rape, incest, mutilation, and ambiguous sexuality. But, says Abbey, "mostly it was the warmth and spirituality that I saw in these people, despite all their physical hardships. The shadow of death is always with them, but they go about their lives with a calmness of spirit that I have been seeking my whole life. When I met the Dogon, I felt like I had connected with the other side of the universe."

OUTFITTER

The *Bicycle Africa* itinerary begins in Bamako, Mali's capital. From there you'll fly with your bike to the dusty desert city of Timbuktu. (Yes, that mythical place is in Mali, a rare bit of knowledge that might win you some bar bets.) After a day of two-wheel sightseeing in Timbuktu—no bus tours—you'll board a riverboat for a two-day trip up the Niger River to Mopti. From Mopti, the group proceeds by bicycle to Sofara, Djénné, Somadougou, and Bandiagara, averaging about 45 miles each day over roads that are sometimes paved, sometimes not. From Bandiagara, gateway to Dogon country, you'll ride 12 miles to Djiguibombo, which perches at the top of the cliffs. From there, it's a 6-mile hike down to an overnight stay in the Dogon village of Teli. You'll walk back up the next morning, then ride the 58 miles back to Mopti, with an overnight stop along the way in Songo. From Mopti, you'll take an overnight bus back to Bamako.

WHAT TO EXPECT

Daily mileage is moderate by bicycle touring standards—37, 55, 37, 12, 21, and 37 miles—but a number of factors make this a tough trip. First of all, unlike most bike tours, there is no sag wagon to fall back on. (In a pinch, you could always flag down a bush taxi.) Second, you'll be carrying 20–25 pounds of your own gear in panniers, which slows the pace considerably. Third, you'll be riding mountain bikes or cross-terrain hybrids, which are less efficient than road bikes. And finally, it's damned hot most of the time.

This is not a trip for beginners. You should be in good riding shape, easily able to knock off 50 miles on a road bike without a second thought.

Although this is not a camping trip, it gets the same mental-challenge rating—a 3—as a typical camping trip. Far off the tourist trail, you'll stay in hotels, guest houses, and private homes that are sometimes primitive by Western standards. There may or may not be electricity, hot water, or indoor toilets. There will certainly be mosquitoes. You'll sleep one night out on the deck on a riverboat, another sitting up in a bus. The food can be plain, and you won't see milk or sugar for days at a time. All this, of course, comes on top of a hard day's ride along dusty roads in the hot sun. As Bicycle Africa's brochure says, this trip is for "good-natured realists."

Trips run during the "cool" season, from November through January.

RECOMMENDED READING

Conversations with Ogotemmeli by Marcel Griaule. A French anthropologist's classic account of his monthlong talk with a Dogon elder, during which details of the Dogon religion and myth were revealed to outsiders for the first time.

IN BRIEF

Bicycle Africa, 206-628-9314: 14 days, $1,190

Physical challenge, 3; Mental challenge, 3; Skills 2.

THE SAHARA
hanging out with
mauritanian nomads

Irma Turtle is not the first well-born woman of advanced civilization to be seduced by the Sahara Desert, to have her life permanently altered by sky and silence and shifting sand. Nearly a century ago—long before Turtle Tours, a one-woman adventure travel company trodding the unbeaten paths of North Africa—there was another female Sahara adventurer: Isabelle Eberhardt. Born of Russian parents in exile, Eberhardt fled her Geneva home at age twenty and for the remainder of her brief life wandered the Sahara in the garb of an Arab man, losing herself in the vast intrigue of the desert. "The Sahara has bewitched me for life," Eberhardt wrote in her diary. "As long as the Sahara is there with its magnificent expanse, I will always have a refuge where my tormented soul can go for relief from the trivialities of modern life."

Irma Turtle's escape from the trivialities of modern life took a little longer. She was a nice Jewish girl from Boston, daughter of a real estate investor, art major at Smith College. At about the same age that Eberhardt took off for the Sahara, Turtle read a book about the rock paintings of the Tassili n Ajjer in southern

Algeria. She was enthralled, and immediately began saving up for a pilgrimage there. But trivialities kept getting in the way, and before she knew it, Turtle was forty years old and an international vice-president for Ogilvy & Mather. Sent off to run the agency's Brazilian subsidiary in slum-ridden São Paulo, she came face-to-face with the staggering gap between rich and poor for the first time. "Living in Brazil blew the value system I'd been brought up with," recalls Turtle, now fifty-two. "It taught me how to be a human being."

Transferred back to New York, she immediately quit Ogilvy & Mather. The trivialities began to fall by the wayside, and six months later, there was Turtle, riding a Toyota Land Cruiser across the Sahara toward the rock paintings of the Tassili n Ajjer. The emptiness and tranquillity of the vast dunescape touched something in her soul from the first moment. "Waking up in the Sahara is like being in the arms of the Creator," she remembers.

What is it about the Sahara that so affects visitors? Many are drawn by the sheer nothingness of it, the solitary stillness of the senses that allows inner voices to be heard more clearly. Paul Bowles, the English language's master chronicler of North Africa, describes the "baptism of solitude" the visitor feels during his first Sahara night: "Immediately when you arrive . . . you notice the stillness. An incredible, absolute silence prevails. . . . You leave the gate of the fort or the town behind, pass the camels lying outside, go up into the dunes, or out onto the hard, stony plain and stand awhile, alone. Presently you will either shiver and hurry back, or you will go on standing there and let something very peculiar happen to you, something that everyone who lives there has undergone and which the French call *la baptême de la solitude.* It is a unique sensation, and it has nothing to do with loneliness, for loneliness presupposes memory. Here, in this wholly mineral landscape lighted by stars like flares, even memory disappears; nothing is left but your own breathing and the sound of your heart beating. A strange, and by no means pleasant, process of reintegration begins inside you, and you have the choice of fighting against it, and insisting on remaining the person you have always been, or letting it take its course. For no one who has stayed in the Sahara for a while is quite the same as when he came."

The eye of the visitor, as well as his ear, is stunned by the nothingness. Quentin Crewe, a modern-day motorized Sahara wanderer, writes, "At first the stranger to such vast spaces might see nothing. His eye, accustomed to an abundance of events, roves unchecked over wide vistas of sand or gravel or rock. It takes a few days to adjust to the extremes of scale—both to the seemingly unending space and to the minutiae. . . . When his eye steadies, the newcomer often finds that the austere majesty of desert scenery surpasses the more readily acceptable landscape of temperate climates."

And then there is the Saharan sky, compared to which, Bowles writes, "all other skies seem faint-hearted efforts. Solid and luminous, it is always the focal point of the landscape. . . ." In his novel *The Sheltering Sky,* Bowles's tormented antihero Porter Moresby notes darkly that "the sky here is very strange. I often have the sensation when I look up at it that it's a solid thing up there, protecting us from what's behind." When asked, "But what is behind?" Port answers, "Nothing, I suppose. Just darkness. Absolute night."

This feeling of protection from "what is behind" was apparently the Sahara's primary attraction for Isabelle Eberhardt, a tortured soul if there ever was one. Her identity was ambiguous literally from her birth in Switzerland in 1877, five years after her mother had fled Russia's tsarist regime without her husband, a general in Alexander II's army. Isabelle was told that she was the daughter of the general, by then deceased, and the polite fiction was maintained throughout her life. But her father was in fact the exiled family's live-in tutor, an eccentric anarchist named Alexander Trophimowsky. Isabelle called him Vava, or Uncle.

Isabelle's mother, sickly and reclusive, ceded virtually all family authority to Trophimowsky. There are hints that he sexually abused Isabelle as a child, and that she later had an incestuous relationship with her brother. In any case, the radically egalitarian tutor insisted that Isabelle dress as a boy from early childhood. Schooled at home, she rarely mixed with other children. Isabelle was apparently anorectic, and according to the editor of her diaries, a regular user of opium as a teenager. It is perhaps no surprise that, upon her arrival in Algiers after the deaths of her parents and the sale of the family villa, she wrote in her diary, "I feel I am coming back to life again."

For all her inner demons, Eberhardt knew herself well. "I am a dreamy eccentric, anxious to lead a free, nomadic life." But, she realized, "Everything in my childhood and adolescence prepared me for the fact that peace and good fortune would have no place in my life, that I would be doomed to a maddening struggle. . . . I know no other remedy than the silent contemplation of nature, far from people, face to face with the great Inconceivable, the unique refuge of souls in distress."

Once in North Africa, Isabelle shaved her head and adopted the traditional burnoose of the Arab man. With her remarkable facility for language—she had learned six of them, including Arabic, by the time she was sixteen—she absorbed local dialects quickly. Having dabbled in Islam back in Geneva, she now embraced it fully, taking the (male) name Si Mahmoud and eventually joining the Qadrya sect.

In her disguise—most Arabs saw through it immediately, but were too polite to mention the fact—Isabelle took up a nomadic life, wandering the Sahara from oasis to oasis, alone or with Arab companions, on trains and horseback, sometimes taking up residence for a few months, but always moving on eventually. She lived in poverty, often sleeping in the street and, well aware of the Arabs' extraordinary hospitality, showing up unannounced at acquaintances' houses at mealtimes. She took many Arab lovers, married one of them, confounded the French military authorities (who tried to expel her repeatedly), and, through her writings, became a sensation back in Paris—a sort of female T. E. Lawrence.

The apex of Isabelle's notoriety occurred in 1901 in the tiny Algerian village of Behima. Sitting in a mud house with a half-dozen fellow members of the Qadrya sect—all men, of course—Isabelle was attacked with a saber by a local villager. A clothesline that happened to be above her head deflected the sword and spared her life, although she suffered deep gashes in her head and arm. Her attacker—who claimed he had followed the voice of an angel of God to "kill Mademoiselle Eberhardt, who wore masculine dress" and "who was creating disorder in the Muslim religion"—was tried in a French colonial court. The magnanimous Isabelle, believing that her attacker had been hired by the leaders of a rival Muslim sect, argued for his acquittal on the grounds that he was merely "the blind instrument of a destiny whose meaning he doesn't understand." The court, however, sentenced the attacker to life at hard labor, and the higher-ups behind the plot, if any, were never arrested.

Her life spared by the miraculous luck of a clothesline, Isabelle's account with fate was squared three years later. Recovering from a bout of malaria (or perhaps syphilis), she lay in a small crumbling clay house in another, bleak, remote Algerian town, Ain Sefra. Suddenly, with no warning, a massive flash flood swept down the dry riverbed that ran through the town, inundating it in a few moments. According to the French soldiers who found Isabelle's body in the mud, pinned under a fallen beam, she was dressed as an "Arab cavalryman."

Irma Turtle's Sahara transformation was somewhat less

theatrical than Isabelle's. Upon her return from that first trip to Tassili n Ajjer, Turtle dropped everything, poured all her meager funds into starting up Turtle Tours, and a year later returned to Algeria with three paying clients. Over the next three years, the fledgling company racked up $50,000 in losses and debts. But, says Turtle, "I was doing what I wanted to do, which was to spend four to five months a year in the Sahara."

At the end of the company's fourth year, to Turtle's astonishment, there was $949 left over. The next year, 1991, the profit skyrocketed to $1,300. Turtle Tours is today a going concern, taking a hundred-odd clients a year to visit nomadic and tribal cultures all over the world. In the process, Turtle has accomplished her goal: to earn a living while at the same time immersing herself in the Sahara.

In 1992, however, Turtle Tours's Sahara business suffered a setback. Civil war erupted in Algeria, the focus of Turtle's desert passion. Militant Islamic rebels began shooting Westerners on sight. Turtle's local Algerian guides assured her that her clients would be perfectly safe once out in the desert, and figured they could probably hustle the clients in and out of Algiers before the AK-47-toting militants took notice. Turtle prudently settled on another alternative: the isolated, impoverished, and little-known desert nation of Mauritania, which borders Algeria to the west and encompasses the western end of the Sahara, where the sand dunes roll down to the Atlantic Ocean.

Mauritania has only one fifth the population density of Algeria, but more camels than any Saharan nation. The Mauritanian desert landscape is gentler, less threatening than Algeria's; nomads live out among the dunes, which are in some places inexplicably sprinkled with palm trees. Medieval villages pop up along the landscape at regular intervals. Though still a forbidding desert by any definition, the Mauritania Sahara has more vegetation than Algeria, more life, more people—which was just fine with Turtle, who had by now become more enchanted by the Sahara's nomadic inhabitants than even its solitary landscapes.

Mauritania is not without internal strife of its own, however; the ruling nomadic class of light-skinned Maures, or Moors, has for centuries enslaved and dominated the black African tribes who farm the southern edge of the country along the Senegal River. In a 1989 paroxysm of ethnic cleansing, hundreds of blacks were tortured and killed by the Moor-dominated military government, and thousands were expelled across the river to Senegal, their homes and land confiscated. A new civilian government, however, now disavows the events of 1989, and there is talk of a return of the deportees.

The lingering tension in the shabby capital city of Nouak-chott is today barely evident to the Western visitor, and it disappears entirely out under the sheltering sky of the desert, replaced by the traditional hospitality of the nomads, who greet strangers of whatever skin color with bowls of camel's milk. It is perhaps too much to ask of the modern traveler to emulate Isabelle Eberhardt, but with a little help from Irma Turtle, we can for a couple of weeks play modern nomads, following faint tracks across the sand and staying on the move, always on the move.

OUTFITTER

Turtle Tours's rugged 1,000-mile four-wheel-drive expedition is almost certainly the first—and at this writing, the only—trip in Mauritania by any American outfitter. The route begins in the nondescript capital of Nouakchott and follows one of Mauritania's two paved highways northwest to the former copper-mining town of Akiout. Here the road ends, and you'll follow faint tracks in the sand—or simply strike off across the dunes—for the next ten days.

The route winds through the Adrar massif, touching the religious mecca of Chinquetti, the trading town of Atar, and Azougi, the ancient Almoravidian capital of a thousand years ago. From the Adrar, you'll head south to the Tagant Plateau, a mountainous region of sand dunes and wadis (dry riverbeds) peppered with oases. Highlights include the dunes of El Khett, part of a continuous strip of sand that runs all the way to Algeria; the old Bedouin citadel of Rachid, from which local brigands would attack camel caravans; and the oasis town of Nbalka. Then you'll hit Mauritania's other paved road, "The Road of Hope," and complete the loop back to Nouakchott.

WHAT TO EXPECT

This is primarily an overland tour. Short day hikes and walks are easy and optional. The expedition will camp in the desert at night, whenever possible near nomad encampments. Though there are no guarantees, there is every likelihood that group members will spend some time hanging out with these nomads.

You'll stay in small two-person tents, with all meals provided. Temperatures are surprisingly moderate from November through February, with typical daytime highs in the 80s and nights in the 40s. The primary inconveniences are dust, rough roads, and a scarcity of water for washing. (Toilet facilities consist of the nearest sand dune.) Additional nuisances include wind, flies, and scorpions. Energetic outdoor types, accustomed to physical adventures like treks, should prepare mentally for being cooped up in vehicles for long stretches. And don't count on air-conditioning in the vehicles.

RECOMMENDED READING

The Sheltering Sky by Paul Bowles. The classic Saharan psychodrama of three lost souls trying vainly to figure out the meaning of life.

Sahara Unveiled by William Langewieche. A spare, unsentimental, but richly detailed account of the author's journey from Algiers to Dakar by bus, foot, camel, and riverboat.

IN BRIEF

Turtle Tours, 602-488-3688: 17 days, $3,650

Physical challenge, 1; Mental challenge, 3; Skills 1.

TANZANIA
climbing
mount kilimanjaro

For my first mountain, I chose Kilimanjaro. It seemed a good fit for a guy like me—goal-oriented, outdoorsy, in good aerobic shape but on the other hand middle-aged, unschooled in the use of ropes and crampons, and unwilling to risk death.

Kilimanjaro is a serious mountain, rising 19,340 feet above sea level, a mile higher than any peak in the lower forty-eight states. It has the romance of Hemingway and the cachet of being one of the so-called Seven Summits, the high points of each of the seven continents. And it looks great, an honest-to-God snowcapped peak rising dramatically out of the African savannah.

Yet Kilimanjaro is readily accessible to regular people like you and me. There is a jetport 40 miles from the main trailhead. The mountain requires no technical climbing; one essentially walks to the top along a hiking trail. The weather, by mountain standards at least, is benign. And, in a happy coincidence, there is just enough oxygen at 19,000 feet to sustain a well-conditioned and determined flatlander.

As a result, Kilimanjaro is too popular. Thousands of people trek there every year, and hundreds make the summit. The normal path up the mountain—the Marangu Route—at times resembles the queue for a Springsteen concert. The usual overnight stops along the Marangu Route, clusters of motel-like A-frame huts, teem each night with hundreds of climbers, porters, and guides.

In recent years, canny outfitters have begun offering alternate routes. I chose the Machame Route because it seemed like a good fit for a guy like me: a crowd-phobe in no particular hurry. The Machame is longer than the Marangu Route—five days up instead of four—and has tiny, wretched huts. It is therefore virtually untraveled. It offers the additional advantage of more time for climbers to adjust to the lack of oxygen at such altitudes.

Our trip leader, an easygoing Englishman named Clive Ward, started early with his litany about altitude sickness. We're not just talking huffing and puffing here, he warned. We're talking headaches of New Year's Eve–hangover caliber. We're talking nausea, disorientation, and worse. You can die from altitude sickness, he assured us, and ugly phrases like "cerebral edema" and "drowning in your own fluids" cropped up here and there. Adding to my sense of foreboding was the fact that altitude sickness is notoriously capricious; vegetarian marathoners are just as likely to be laid low as big fat chain-smoking slobs.

The keys to avoiding altitude sickness are to drink a lot of water and ascend gradually to allow the body time to acclimate. Tourists who jet in to Kilimanjaro Airport from sea level and zip up to 19,000 feet in seventy-two hours are often carried down on stretchers. In fact, it is said that more people suffer altitude sickness on Kilimanjaro than any other mountain in the world, simply because it can be climbed so quickly.

So it was with a certain trepidation that we set off in dense jungle from the village of Machame, at 6,000 feet on

Kilimanjaro's southwestern flank. Our group of seven climbers, supported by a dozen or so porters and guides, ranged in age from twenty-five to sixty-two, in temperament from ditzy to laconic, in fitness from decent to superb. Our professions included astronomer, social worker, agronomist, hardware store manager, and titan of industry.

As we ascended, the mossy, humid jungle gradually gave way to a forest of giant heather and pine trees. Our first overnight stopover, Machame Hut, was pleasantly devoid of human life when we arrived. But the hut itself was a crude claustrophobic shed of rotting corrugated steel, and so we pitched tents nearby amid dense, head-high bushes.

That first night, we were at 10,000 feet, about the elevation where many people start to feel altitude headaches. And so Clive began to preach the gospel of hydration. "Drink water until you slosh," he ordered us. "You should be pissing your brains out every couple of hours. And check the color. It must be clear. If it's even slightly yellow, you're not drinking enough."

Day two was a short one. We reached Shira Hut, another corrugated hellhole at 12,600 feet, by lunchtime and took the rest of the day off for altitude acclimatization. (So far, so good; I had no headache and was pissing clear as vodka.) We explored the surrounding plateau of rocks and bushes, and gazed up through broken clouds at the snowy summit a mile and a half above. It seemed inconceivable that we could ever actually make it up there.

On day three, we started a long traverse along the southern flank of the mountain, climbing only about 1,000 feet, to the edge of a monstrous abyss with the redundant name of Barranco Canyon. That night, the sky cleared, and I was awakened at three A.M. by a brilliant full moon. Crawling from my tent to relieve my swelling bladder, I was startled by the brilliantly glowing snow-clad summit, now looming larger than ever. Inconceivable.

Our gradual ascent was paying dividends; most of us were feeling no altitude symptoms. Ironically, it was Kathy—a twenty-five-year-old triathlete and probably the fittest member of the group—who had come down with a chest cold. She struggled gamely, wheezing and hacking, but the next morning Clive persuaded her to turn back. "No chest cold ever gets better at 16,000 feet," he told her. In an admirable display of gallantry, her friend Kent, still healthy and just as eager to reach the summit as the rest of us, agreed to accompany her and their porter/guide back down. (A wise move; shortly after returning to the States, she married him.)

The rest of us pushed on through fog and drizzle to our final jumping-off spot for the summit attempt: Barafu Hut, another grungy, graffiti-covered tin hut on a pile of rocks at 15,000 feet. For much of the day, the fog limited visibility to no more than a few hundred yards, and we had no sense of the summit towering over us. But we knew it was up there, waiting.

I had been dreading summit day for months. The itinerary called for a one A.M. departure, arrival at the top after "five to nine hours," and then a 6,000-foot descent along the Marangu Route to Hrombo Hut. "Hopefully, we will arrive by five to seven P.M." the itinerary had said, with what I thought was a startling lack of confidence. But I felt ready. I'd climbed easily so far, stayed healthy, and had suffered no altitude symptoms.

Clive warned us to eat hearty at our "last supper" at Barafu. I stuffed myself with soup, potatoes, rice, boiled chicken, and hot tea, and crawled into my sleeping bag about eight P.M., hoping to sleep a few hours before the wake-up call. No such luck. I was too pumped up to sleep. To make matters worse, whenever I did start to drift off, I would for some reason stop breathing, only to jerk wide awake a few seconds later, gasping for breath. (This is a common effect of altitude, I later learned.) Moreover, my stomach began feeling queasy. I lay in the dark, staring at the ceiling of my tent, willing the time to go by.

By the time the wake-up call came at midnight, my stomach malaise had worsened. We set off (five climbers, two Tanzanian guides, and Clive) under a brilliant full moon, the snows of Kilimanjaro glowing above, the lights of Africa twinkling below. The ascent was very steep, the footing poor in loose sand and scree. Single file, our headlamps turned off in the bright moonlight, we plodded rhythmically upward, switchbacking up the slope. Lift a foot, move it forward eight to ten inches. Put it down. Take a deep breath. Do it again. Step, breathe, step, breathe. *"Poli, poli,"* our Tanzanian guide, Joseph, kept saying. Slow. Slow.

My stomach got worse. Jay the astronomer had some stomach pills that helped a bit. Step. Breathe. Step. Breathe. But the nausea wouldn't go away, and finally I slumped down on the trail and faced the inevitable. But I never thought of quitting. Step. Breathe. Puke. Only five or six more hours of this. Concentrate. Step. Breathe. Puke.

So it went, stepping and breathing and puking in the moonlight. The lack of oxygen sucked the mental and physical energy right out of us. Nothing existed but the next footprint. Step, breathe, 6 inches at a time up the steep, rocky slope. The guides chanted a soft Swahili song in the darkness to encourage us and keep us in a rhythm. By 17,000 feet, I stopped taking the stomach pills because the task of unwrapping them and putting them in my mouth was simply too difficult. By 18,000 feet, I had stopped raising my head to look at the spectacular moonlit scenery around me; that, too, was no longer worth the effort. Although the nausea had receded, I began to feel dizzy and drunk.

Then—ten minutes later? an hour?—I heard a voice shout from above. "Nineteen thousand! We're almost there!" Suddenly, magically, all five of us were standing on top of the crater rim at Stella Point. We cheered. We hugged each other. Don, the agronomy professor, broke down and cried. Then the dawn began.

We rested for a while, watching mesmerized as the eastern sky turned pink, casting the glaciers behind us in an eerie glow. I asked Don, who was sitting next to me, "Am I crazy, or is this the greatest moment you've ever experienced in your life, too?" He pondered a moment before replying, "Well, I guess watching my son graduate from West Point might have been a little better."

Through thin, crunchy snow, we strolled giddily to the highest point on the mountain, a gentle bulge on the far side of the rim called Uhuru Peak. My nausea was gone, but I still felt weak and dizzy. We snapped the obligatory summit shots, but the lack of oxygen had numbed my brain; the mere task of retrieving the camera from my pocket and pressing the shutter button used up every single IQ point I possessed. As we stood there, the sun rose above the horizon, and we could see the mountain's shadow behind us, a crisp black triangle stretching to the horizon.

We went down the Marangu Route. With long, leaping glissades in the soft sand, we descended the summit cone to Kibo Hut at 15,000 feet in a couple of hours, then trudged a long, dusty trail across a high-altitude desert. We passed perhaps a hundred climbers coming up the lower slopes, the first people we'd seen in five days. "Did you make the top?" they asked eagerly. "How was it?"

"Not too bad," we answered.

OUTFITTERS

Dozens of companies can take you up Kilimanjaro, usually along the standard quick-and-dirty Marangu Route. To avoid the Marangu mob scene, however, we have listed only those companies that use longer, less crowded, and more scenic back routes, such as the Machame Route described above.

The mountaineering-oriented *Alpine Ascents International* offers its Kilimanjaro climb as a part of its Seven Summits program. Climbers use the Machame Route, with an extra day of acclimatization at Shira Hut, for a total ascent time of six days. Descent is via the Marangu Route. After the climb, guests go on brief safaris in Ngorongoro Crater and Masai Mara National Park.

Geographic Expedition's itinerary is unusual: The Kili climb, via the Umbwe Route, is preceded by a five-day trek on Mount Kenya, which serves as an excellent warm-up and acclimatization ascent. The Kenya climb uses the Chogoria Route, and trekkers will reach 16,335-foot Point Lenana. (The true summit of Mount Kenya, just over 17,000 feet, requires technical rock-climbing skills.) The Umbwe Route up Kilimanjaro, rarely used, approaches from the south and leads to Barranco Canyon, from which climbers proceed to Barafu and the summit. Descent is the quick-and-easy Marangu tourist route.

Mountain Travel-Sobek led the Kilimanjaro trek described in the preceding narrative. It has since abandoned that itinerary and now offers a choice of three "back-route" Kilimanjaro climbs, all combined with short wildlife safaris.

The first uses the hardly ever traveled Rongai Route through Kenya, which requires a special permit and is used by no other outfitter. The ascent/descent takes five days, including a rest day at Mawenzi, the craggy ancillary peak to the east of the main summit. Descent is along the Marangu tourist route. Before the actual climb, you'll warm up with a two-day walking safari, tracking elephants with Masai guides in Kenya's Amboseli National Park and visiting the camp of elephant researcher Cynthia Moss. After the climb, there's another two-day foot safari, in Tsavo National Park. The grand finale is a recuperation day in a deluxe beach hotel on Kenya's Indian Ocean coast.

MT-S also offers a six-day Kili climb along the Machame Route, preceded by a warm-up hike to the crater of Mount Meru in Arusha National Park and followed by a three-day safari in Ngorongoro Crater and Tanagire National Park.

A third option is a long eight-day climb along the Shira Plateau route, which approaches the summit through the Western Breach, a notch in the mountain's crater wall. The Shira Route is unusual because the last night is spent camped just below the summit at 18,300 feet. (On all the other routes, your final camp will be at about 15,000 feet.) The high final camp makes for a quick sprint to the summit the next morning—no getting up at midnight—but increases the chance for altitude sickness. On the other hand, the longer, more gradual ascent along the Shira Route helps climbers acclimatize to the altitude better.

Wilderness Travel also uses the Shira Plateau route, coming in from the west and proceeding up the Western Breach. Climbers will have time to explore Kilimanjaro's inner crater, a region very rarely visited. Because of the extra acclimation time, WT claims a summit success rate of nearly 100 percent. The descent is via the little-used Mweka Route. Following the climb, you'll do a weeklong safari through various parts of Tanzania, including Ngorongoro. Precise itinerary depends on the season.

WHAT TO EXPECT

People tend to underestimate Kilimanjaro; after all, it's only a walk-up. No climbing skills required, no ropes, no crampons, not even much scrambling. Just keep putting one foot in front of the other. But what a walk-up! The lower slopes, with daily ascents of 2,000 to 3,000 feet, are not difficult. But the final summit push, from about 15,000 feet to 19,340 feet, is extremely steep, and the footing at times soft and sandy. The altitude, of course, increases the difficulty by a factor of two or three. And the sheer length of summit day—typically eighteen hours or so of grueling effort, up and down—make this a physical challenge right up there with running a marathon.

Like a marathon, climbing Kili is as much a mental challenge as physical. The lower slopes are pleasant enough, with terrain and amenities comparable to Himalayan treks. But summit day is another matter. You must summon the determination to put aside exhaustion, cold, and possible altitude sickness and just keep putting one foot in front of the other. Not everybody can do it. I recall a well-known magazine writer who, a few years back, breathlessly wrote how he had discovered a whole new level of determination and inner strength while climbing Kilimanjaro—and then meekly turned back at the crater rim, not bothering to make the forty-five-minute walk around to Uhuru Peak, the actual summit. Reading that article, I was incredulous; once on the rim, I would have walked through gunfire to continue to the highest point in Africa.

Kilimanjaro can be climbed year-round, but January, February, and June through October are considered the prime months. Avoid April, the rainiest time of year. Try to pick a trip where summit day coincides with a full moon.

RECOMMENDED READING

The Snows of Kilimanjaro by Ernest Hemingway. Harry found his heaven in the great mountain, maybe you will, too.

IN BRIEF

Alpine Ascents International, 206-378-1927: 17 days, $3,495
Geographic Expeditions, 800-777-8183: 20 days, $2,795
Mountain Travel-Sobek, 800-227-2384: 14 days, $3,790
Wilderness Travel, 800-368-2794: 20 days, $4,485

Physical challenge, 4; Mental challenge, 4; Skills, 1.

UGANDA

trekking the
mountains of
the moon

White men were talking on the telephone and measuring the speed of light before they managed to locate the highest mountain range in Africa. The Ruwenzoris, rising 16,763 feet from the implacable dark heart of the continent, have for centuries been mountains of legend and illusion, shrouded in a historical fog, and in a quite literal one as well. Fittingly, the man who finally discovered them turned out to be a master of illusion himself, an inveterate liar whose public persona was more fantasy than reality.

Herodotus, the first great African traveler, pondered how the world's largest river could flow 2,000 miles out of a parched desert where rain never fell. He theorized that the source of the Nile must be melting snow "from parts beyond." On an exploratory journey up the river in 450 B.C., he was told by an Abyssinian sorcerer that the Nile flowed from a bottomless spring between two snowcapped peaks somewhere in central Africa. A hundred years later, Aristotle himself declared that the source of the Nile was "The Silver Mountain."

In A.D. 120, the Syrian geographer Marinus of Tyre wrote of

a Greek merchant seaman who had traveled inland from Zanzibar for twenty-five days and found a "silvery" mountain range that fed the Nile. Based on that account, Ptolemy, in A.D. 150, depicted the mountains on his celebrated map of the world. Apparently mistranslating "silvery" as "moon"—or perhaps simply displaying a flair for hype—Ptolemy called them Lunae Montes, or Mountains of the Moon. Thus grew the legend, spawned by a sorcerer's vision and nurtured by a catchy nickname.

For the next 1,700 or so years, every expedition that set out to locate the source of the Nile returned a failure, or not at all. In 1876, the journalist-explorer Henry Morton Stanley—the man who had five years earlier uttered the immortal "Dr. Livingstone, I presume"—while on the march through what was then known as Western Benga, "obtained a faint view of an enormous blue mass afar off." Offhandedly naming the distant range Mount Gordon-Bennett, after the degenerate drunkard editor of the *New York Herald*, who was the chief underwriter of his expedition, Stanley unaccountably kept going, entirely unaware that he had seen the legendary mountains. Ironically, Stanley subsequently claimed that his expedition had "in my opinion, proved the nonexistence of those Mountains of the Moon that had been drawn across Africa since Ptolemy's time."

Twelve years later, on an expedition to rescue Emin Pasha, the beleaguered governor of the British colonial province of Equatoria, Stanley nearly botched it a second time. Two of his staff officers, scouting ahead of the main expedition, looked up through a break in the interminable cloud cover and saw, to their astonishment, a huge snowcapped peak. When one of the officers, Arthur Jephson, informed Stanley of the brief sighting, he "laughed at me and pooh-poohed the idea," Jephson later recalled.

A month later, however, the clouds briefly thinned again,

and this time Stanley was in the right place at the right time. "I saw a peculiar shaped cloud of a most beautiful silver colour, which assumed the proportions and appearance of a vast mountain covered with snow. . . . I became conscious that what I gazed upon was not the image or semblance of a vast mountain, but the solid substance of a real one, with its summit covered in snow. . . . I have discovered the long lost snowy Mountains of the Moon, sources of the . . . Nile." His account conveniently failed to disclose that his staff officer Jephson had sighted the mountain a month previously and had called it to Stanley's attention.

Such self-aggrandizing deception came naturally to Stanley, an insecure and vainglorious blowhard. For most of his life he passed himself off as an American, but he was in fact born in north Wales, the unwanted offspring of a local trollop and—probably—a lecherous lawyer who paid off the town drunk to claim paternity. Stanley's birth record in the local church lists his real name as "John Rowlands, Bastard."

Quickly abandoned by his mother, Stanley/Rowlands, Bastard was initially raised by various relatives. At age six, his hired foster parents, dismayed at his increasing appetite, shunted him off to the local workhouse, a combination orphanage, asylum, and homeless shelter. Late in life, Stanley revealed his humble origins in his autobiography, describing the orphanage as a grim Dickensian house of torture, where "our poor heads were cuffed, and slapped, and pounded, until we lay speechless and streaming with blood." He recounts one incident in which a boy died mysteriously, after which Stanley and some pals snuck into the mortuary to peek at the body. They found it "livid, and showing scores of dark wheals," and concluded that the boy had been beaten to death by their despised schoolmaster.

According to Stanley biographer John Bierman, however, the incident is "total invention," and his descriptions of the orphanage a "dark fantasy." The orphanage was in fact a well-respected establishment, and Stanley was something of a teacher's pet. Indeed, after he found success in later life, he returned to the orphanage to sing its praises. Stanley's fabrications were apparently his way of bolstering an ego permanently wounded by his early shame and abandonment.

Stanley left the workhouse at fifteen. He claims he escaped, Nicholas Nickelby–like, over the garden wall after defiantly beating up the schoolmaster, who was about to inflict yet another cruel whipping. Orphanage records say he was routinely released to the custody of his uncle. Whatever the case, he subsequently ran away to sea, signing on as a cabin boy on an America-bound packet ship. Stanley found that life at sea was little better than the workhouse, centering primarily on "rum, sodomy and the lash," to use Winston Churchill's phrase. He jumped ship in New Orleans and adopted the name of a wealthy American who took a shine to him. He wandered from one menial job to another, and eventually joined the Dixie Greys, fought in the Battle of Shiloh, switched to the Union side after being taken prisoner, came down with dysentery, and finally ended up in the U.S. Navy. All the while, he filled his journals with preposterously tall tales of suffering and bravado.

At the age of twenty-five, Stanley discovered journalism, a trade for which his sense of inventive melodrama was perfectly suited. He covered the Indian Wars for the *Missouri Democrat* with energy and insight, then boldly sailed off for Ethiopia on his own initiative—and at his own expense—to cover the British campaign against the mad Emperor Theodore. Stanley had no firm assignment, only the vague promise of *New York Herald* editor James Gordon-Bennett to look over his dispatches and print them if they proved worthy. Once in Ethiopia, Stanley was dismissed by fellow reporters, mostly British, one of whom called him "a howling cad."

But Stanley got even; he bribed the local telegraph operator to send out his dispatch of the battle first, then watched in delight as a wire failure conveniently delayed his rival journalists' reports by several days. His worldwide scoop earned him a full-time job as a foreign correspondent for the *Herald* and, eventually, the assignment that would bring him world renown: to find David Livingstone, the beloved British missionary/explorer who had set off in search of the source of the Nile and not been heard from in four years. Not only did Stanley find Livingstone, but he eventually found the snowy peaks that had for so long eluded Livingstone and everyone else.

The Mountains of the Moon are now fully mapped and documented, of course. They have been confirmed as a source of the Nile, and a deep lake has been pinpointed between two of its snowcapped peaks, as the Abyssinian sorcerer had promised. But the precision of modern geography has little diminished the air of mystery that surrounds the Ruwenzoris. Partly this is due to the perpetual mists that shroud the mountains nine days out of ten, mists that concealed them from any number of unsuspecting explorers who passed nearby. A. F. R. Wollaston, a British naturalist who was among the first to study the area in 1906, wrote, "I was for many days a short distance from the mountains, and could not have even suspected their existence." When the Ruwenzoris do reveal themselves, it is usually in brief ethereal glimpses through gaps in the cloud, as Stanley experienced. "I rubbed my eyes and wondered whether the snow peak had been a reality or a dream," wrote Wollaston when he finally saw one of the massif's twenty summits after many weeks among them.

The other feature that lends the Ruwenzoris their air of mystery is the bizarre natural topiary that adorns their slopes. Wollaston, scarcely able to believe his eyes, called the plant life "unworldly." D. W. Freshfield, an early Ruwenzori wanderer, wrote, "That enchanted forest has a weird and grotesque effect that is all its own . . . in rain, a nightmare . . . in the rare sunshine, a Russian pantomime. . . ." The Duke of Abruzzi, the Italian climber who was the first to reach the main Ruwenzori summits in 1906, wrote of the lower slopes, "No forest can be grimmer or stranger than this."

An unusual combination of factors—steady moderate temperatures, copious rainfall, and intense ultraviolet radiation at this high elevation and low latitude—triggers in the Ruwenzori a botanical phenomenon called equatorial alpine gigantism. Grass grows 10 feet tall. Moss cushions are a foot thick. Heather plants grow 60 to 70 feet high, lichen dripping from their twisted limbs. Groundsel and lobelia, familiar at home a few inches high, grow to four times the height of a man here, and their phallic upper pods are the size and shape of a heat-seeking missile. Guy Yeoman, a modern authority on the Ruwenzori, likens the Ruwenzoris' giant lobelia to a sort of botanical big game. He notes that they "tend to occur in family groups, and in the mist there is a curious anthropomorphism about them—they suggest extraterrestrial beings that will move as soon as one's back is turned."

Even on the rocky summits, far above the level where plants can grow, the visual surrealism of the Ruwenzori doesn't quit. Because of the dense, almost constant cloud cover and barely subfreezing temperatures, ice accretes on the upper crags literally out of thin air, as supercooled water droplets freeze on contact. Depending on wind and cloud thickness, these rime accretions take on fantastic forms: mushrooms, gargoyles, great overhanging buttocks and breasts, wind-pruned cauliflowers, arthritic claws, hanging salamis, organ pipes, delicate crystalline flowers—a fantasy sculpture garden of ice.

The Ruwenzori trekker, his visual receptors unceasingly bombarded by the bizarre, may perhaps be excused a desire to fall into his tent at night and simply close his eyes, finally achieving respite from the supernatural. Fat chance. With the Ruwenzori night erupts the weird shriek of the rock hyrax, a creature that looks rather like a large guinea pig or rabbit but is zoologically a close relative to the elephant and rhinoceros. Patrick Synge, a young Cambridge naturalist who joined a 1934 British Museum expedition to the Ruwenzori, described the call of the hyrax as "gruesome shrieks and screeches which seemed to herald the approach of some dreadful monster, or the conversation of a party of prehistoric ghouls."

Ghouls, monsters, extraterrestrial beings—these are not words customarily employed for the description of mountains, particularly in the brochures of trekking companies. For those seeking reassurance in more conventional prose, we'll close with some brochurelike, but still heartfelt, words by the aforementioned Freshfield, a mountaineer of vast experience: "My impressions [of the Ruwenzori] are among the most vivid in a lifetime of travel . . . you may be familiar with the Alps and the Caucasus, the Himalaya, and the Rockies, but if you have not explored Ruwenzori, you still have something wonderful to see."

OUTFITTER

Sherpa Expeditions is a British company known for cutting-edge treks. Sherpa's Ruwenzori trek starts in Entebbe, from where you travel by van to Kampala for a city tour and overnight. Then it's a half-day drive to Kasese and, the following morning, to Ibanda, the start point for the trek. For the next eleven days, you'll hike up the Bujuku Valley to Elena Hut, then over the Freshfield Pass, then back down the Mubuku Valley and return to Ibanda. During that time, weather permitting, trekkers will make side hikes over the Stuhlman Pass and glacier ascents to three major summits: Vittoria Emmanuelle,

Edward, and Margherita, the highest point in the Ruwenzoris at 16,673 feet.

Upon completion of the trek, you'll spend three nights in a game lodge in Queen Elizabeth National Park, viewing chimpanzees and hippos, among other animals. From there it's back to Kampala and Entebbe.

WHAT TO EXPECT

Because the Ruwenzori is so little traveled and densely vegetated, the usual rigors of high-altitude trekking—long days, steep climbs, thin air—are compounded by poor footing on faint trails and occasional bushwhacking through dense growth. The word *slog* is often used to describe this arduous march. In addition, there are three days of moderate glacier-walking at altitudes above 15,000 feet.

The camping is more basic than one might be accustomed to in Nepal, but the trek staff handles the load-carrying and camp chores. Rain and clouds, however, make this a stiffer mental challenge than other high-altitude trekking trips. The pioneering botanist A. F. R. Wollaston put it nicely almost a century ago: "The atrocious climate and the chance of seeing nothing when you get there will keep away all but the most determined and enthusiastic mountaineers." Actually, it's not quite that bad; during the two trekking seasons (midwinter and midsummer) the clouds relent occasionally, and multiday stretches of fair weather are not unknown. But don't expect to come back with a tan.

Footing is wet and sloshy over much of the trekking route. In the notorious Bigo Bog, you'll either hop from tussock to tussock or wade through knee-deep slime. One Scottish trekker, a veteran of spongy bogs, reported that "the Ruwenzoris make Rannoch Moor look like concrete."

A modicum of alacrity is required for tussock-hopping. If you elect to make the summit climbs, very basic glacier-walking skills, including the use of rope and crampons, are required. These can be learned on the spot.

RECOMMENDED READING

Africa's Mountains of the Moon by Guy Yeoman. History, biology, and geology leavened with personal anecdotes by a British expat adventurer. And dig this opening line: "I was returning from a minor intelligence assignment in the Congo, the sort of gift that comes to you sometimes in war. . . ."

IN BRIEF

Sherpa Expeditions, 011-44-181-569-4101: 18 days, $2,825. This trip can also be booked in the United States through Himalayan Travel, 800-225-2380.

Physical challenge, 3; Mental challenge, 4; Skills, 2.

ZAMBIA

walking safari in
north luangwa
national park

In 1973, about seventeen thousand elephants wandered the forests and savannah of North Luangwa National Park, a remote, unpopulated, Delaware-size valley in eastern Zambia. By 1985, only about seven thousand elephants remained. The rest had been slaughtered by poachers who roamed the park at will under the averted eyes of inept and corrupt game wardens. The poachers' take was a thousand a year, a rate that would see the last elephant disappear from North Luangwa at about the time Bill Clinton took the oath of office for his first term.

Nineteen eighty-five was also the year that Mark and Delia Owens got kicked out of Botswana. The young American couple, both biologists, had camped for seven years in the vast Kalahari Desert, studying the habits of lions and brown hyenas. In the process, they'd discovered that government fences erected for wealthy cattle ranchers had disrupted the annual migration of wildebeests, killing a quarter of a million of them. The Botswana authorities, stung by the resulting outcry from wildlife advocates, ordered the Owenses out of the country on two hours' notice.

Traveling north, looking for a new site for their research, they asked a park official in Zambia about North Luangwa. The park had been closed for decades, he replied. No people. No roads. Impossibly remote and inaccessible. That sounded just fine to Mark and Delia. On a reconnaissance flight over North Luangwa in their Cessna 180 bush plane, they saw more wildlife than they'd seen anywhere else in Africa. On a follow-up overland exploration, they came upon a pod of hippos three hundred strong and watched lion cubs cavort around their Land Cruiser. One morning they awoke in their sleeping bags marooned in a sea of water buffalo.

But the only signs of elephants were the skeletons, dozens of them, bleached skulls with the tusks hacked off and bullet holes between the eyes. On the last night of their recon trip, camped by the Mwaleshi River, Mark and Delia finally caught their first glimpse of a North Luangwa elephant, a family of six walking toward the river 500 yards downstream. The elephants, terrified of humans, immediately caught their scent and fled without drinking. At that moment, Mark and Delia made each other a promise: No matter what it took, or how long, they would stay in North Luangwa until the elephants came to drink at the river in peace.

It took them more than a year to get the permits and approvals to operate in the park, and another year to build a base camp. To clear the airstrip, they arose at 4:30 each morning to attack the forest with axes, hoes, and shovels. With six Zambian helpers, they cut down three thousand trees by hand, and pulled out three thousand stumps. The sun beat down so fiercely that the chains they used to drag out the stumps burned their skin. They named their base camp Marula-Puku, after the huge spreading trees that sheltered their stone-and-grass bungalow, and the small gazelles that liked to graze nearby.

It was early in the morning, as Delia was mixing cornbread batter to bake over the campfire, that they first heard the poachers' guns. Mark recognized the distinct sound of AK-47 assault rifles, nine shots, just across the river. Unarmed and with no authority to arrest the poachers, they leaped into their Unimog off-road truck and drove the 18 miles of rutted dirt track to the park ranger station at Mano. They were met with quizzical looks. One Zambian game guard yawned, another walked away. "We have no ammunition," the chief ranger told them. "Only three of our rifles work. There is no food for a patrol."

When Mark offered to transport the game guards back to Marula-Puku in the Unimog, provide all their food, and pay a reward of 200 kwachas for each poacher captured, the game guards reluctantly agreed. One bullet was located.

Carrying food for a week, the ragtag group of game guards, some barefoot, set off from Marula-Puku in ostensible pursuit of the poachers. Three hours later, they returned and reported finding two dead elephants. They asked Mark and Delia to take snapshots of them with the carcasses. When Mark, struggling to stifle his outrage, explained that the idea was to catch the poachers, the rangers agreed to follow the poachers' tracks after lunch—but only if they could have more canned meat. Delia fixed them lunch, which they consumed hungrily, and gave them all but two of the cans of meat they had remaining. The rangers marched off again.

They did not return. Mark later learned that the "patrol" had gone directly back to Mano to share the food with their families.

All the next year, the Zambian game guards mounted not a single antipoaching patrol. The chief ranger told Mark he knew who the worst poachers were—five men from the nearby village of Mwamfushi. "But we cannot arrest these men," he said. They had juju, the special Zairian magic that makes men invisible. "They stand under a special tree, put on a special hat, pour magic potions over their heads, and turn in circles. Then they disappear. We can never capture them."

Mark began flying antipoaching patrols himself. To protect the Cessna from ground fire, he conjured up some juju of his own. Waiting until several game guards happened to be loitering nearby, he fired his pistol at the plane from close range. No bullet holes appeared in its skin, and word spread rapidly among the local people, including the poachers, that the Cessna was protected by magic. Apparently, the poachers didn't know about blanks.

Flying 1,000 feet above the Loukakwa River, Mark spotted a huge encampment of elephant hunters—dozens of campfires and wooden racks for drying meat. Vultures were already spiraling over the carcasses. Mark radioed the poachers' location to the game guards back at Mano and began to circle overhead. A man in a red shirt stepped out from behind a bush with an AK-47 and looked up at the Cessna. From the cockpit, Mark saw the puffs of smoke and the twitches of the man's shoulder. The bullets missed. He circled until his fuel gauges read empty, waiting for the game guards to arrive and arrest the poachers. Of course, they never did.

Impatient with merely observing the poachers, Mark began to harass them from the air. He spotted two men running across a sandbar with elephant tusks slung across their shoulders, and swooped down at 150 miles per hour, wheels at chest level. The men dropped the tusks and dived into tall grass. On the next pass, the Cessna's propeller chopped the grass to confetti above the poachers' heads. As the juju plane pulled up sharply, Mark switched the ignition rapidly on and off, triggering deafening backfires. The poachers fled, abandoning their kill.

One afternoon in 1990, an elephant, a medium-size male with a hole in one ear, appeared at the edge of Marula-Puku. It was the first one Mark and Delia had seen that close to camp. For twenty minutes the huge beast stood there, waving his trunk to catch a scent of these odd humans who didn't seem to be trying to kill him. Then he walked to within 10 yards of their hut and began to eat the marula fruits scattered on the ground. Mark and Delia named him Survivor, and he became a regular at the camp, even making an appearance for a visiting official from the Zambian tourist office. The official, who had never seen a wild elephant before, almost fell off his chair in excitement.

Mark's patrol flights and the 1990 international ivory ban seemed to be having an effect, for poaching began to decline in North Luangwa. Still, Mark and Delia's cautious optimism was shattered later that year, near the end of the dry season, when poachers brazenly attacked Survivor's herd almost within sight of Marula-Puku. When Mark found the carcasses, they were too mutilated to identify. Had Survivor been killed? They didn't know. Once again, the park's game guards declined to pursue the poachers. They had run out of salt, the guards said, and couldn't possibly go out on patrol without it.

Mark flew to Lusaka for a meeting with Zambian park and tourism officials. When Luke Daka, the visitor who'd been so excited to see Survivor, heard of the attack and the game guards' response, he exploded in anger and ordered a new commander and elite troops be sent to Mano ranger station. Mark and Delia had heard such promises before and nothing had happened. This time they kept their fingers crossed.

In the meantime, Mark stepped up his independent anti-poaching efforts. Using donations from wildlife enthusiasts, he bought a 300-million-candlepower aerial searchlight and a cherry-bomb launcher to harass the poachers at night. As word spread of the juju man who dropped thunder and lightning from the sky, the ivory hunters found it harder to hire the local people as scouts and carriers. The Owens's strategy was simple: Mark would chase the poachers and their helpers out of the valley with the Cessna; Delia would greet them at the edge of the park with a job, either on their road crew or with their village development and education projects.

For years, Mark and Delia had been warned that the village of Mwamfushi, home to five big commercial poachers, was too dangerous for them to enter. So, on their first visit there, in 1991, they took along a 9-mm pistol and a .38-caliber revolver. Thirty people awaited them warily in the barren schoolyard. Mark explained that they were not there to arrest anyone, and that they understood the villagers had little choice but to poach animals because they had no other food or work. "We are here to help you find alternatives," Mark said. "Any poacher who lays down his gun may come to work for us at a good salary." When this was translated, there were surprised murmurs from the crowd.

Delia continued, "We know that your whole village depends on poaching. Your own children work as carriers for the poachers. But you also know that soon the animals will be gone. Your fathers could find meat right around your village, but now you must walk 40 or 50 miles. Very soon the animals will all be gone, and you will have nothing. You must find ways to make money by other means. We are here to help you do that."

There was excited debate in the audience. Some of the village elders nodded enthusiastically, but the younger men argued among themselves. After forty-five minutes of shouted debate, several men applied for jobs with Mark and Delia clearing roads. Another said he was a skilled carpenter but his tools had been stolen. Mark offered to supply new tools and loan him the money to start a carpentry shop. Others asked about loans for sewing machines, presses to make cooking oil from sunflower seeds, and a grinding mill to grind their staple food, mealie-meal. The villagers seemed eager to make their own clothes, cooking oil, and mealie-meal instead of bartering poached meat and ivory for it, as they'd always done.

At a later meeting, a young man slipped through the doorway of the schoolhouse and handed Mark a scrap of paper. On it was written, "I want to joine yu. I give my weapon. Please to met me in shed behind the school before you going. Cum alone." It was signed "Chanda Seven." Mark knew he was one of the biggest poachers in Mwamfushi.

The Owenses hired him as a farm supervisor. A few months later, when an old poaching chum of Chanda Seven's approached him with a plan for an ivory-hunting expedition, Seven grabbed an ax and locked him in a room. The Mano game guards, now under new command and spiffily outfitted, arrived promptly and took the poacher into custody. But instead of going to jail, the second poacher happily accepted employment with Mark and Delia. His job: leading the game scouts on patrol against his former comrades.

In 1994, only six elephants were killed in North Luangwa National Park, and the population was growing. Survivor, true to his name, survived, and now drinks by the river in peace.

OUTFITTERS

In conjunction with Wild Zambia Safaris (see below), *Mountain Travel-Sobek* offers a walking safari that includes five days in mobile tented camps in North Luangwa, plus two days in South Luangwa, two days at a former British colonial estate north of the park, two days in the Bangweulu Swamp and two days in Kasanka National Park. It starts and finishes in Lusaka.

Remote African Safaris is owned by John Coppinger, one of the pioneers of walking safaris in North Luangwa. The trip starts in Mfuwe, where you'll be picked up and driven about two hours to Tafika, the company's base camp in South Luangwa Park. From there, it's a five-hour drive along a sand track into North Luangwa and Mwaleshi Camp, a seasonal thatched-hut base camp at the confluence of the Luangwa and Mwaleshi Rivers. Each day, you'll take morning and afternoon walks around the local area.

Trips are done on a custom basis, not scheduled. RAS prefers groups of four to six people, but says it will stretch to two or eight in a pinch. Trip length is optional, but the six-day package, with four nights at Mwaleshi and two at Tafika, is typical.

Instead of day walks from the base camp, *Wild Zambia Safaris* prefers the mobile approach. You'll hike along the length of the Mwaleshi River in North Laungwa, setting up camps along the way. The trip starts and finishes in Mfue, and the first and last nights are spent at Kapani, a luxurious lodge in South Luangwa run by old Africa hand Norman Carr, a renowned elephant-hunter-turned-conservationist/author. Trips may be extended to include walking safaris in South Luangwa and other Zambian parks as well.

WHAT TO EXPECT

The walking is generally easy over mostly flat terrain. Typically, you'll spend five or six hours a day on foot, in two or three separate outings timed to avoid the midday heat.

You'll stay either in seasonal bush camps made of wood and thatched grass, or stand-up safari-style tents with cots. The atmosphere in camp is nonetheless rather refined, with careful observation of the British colonial ritual of "sundowners," or evening drinks, and tea-and-biscuit breaks during the daily walks.

No amount of refinement, however, will change the fact that

the weather can be beastly hot and dusty, and occasionally buggy. And there's also the element—dare we say, the thrill—of danger in walking exposed among wild animals. There is a game guard with a gun on hand at all times, but if a herd of water buffaloes decides to trample you, his gun will be puny protection indeed. The element of danger is more theoretical than real, however; in twenty years of walking safaris in nearby South Luangwa Park, no tourist has ever been seriously injured by an animal.

Prime time for North Luangwa foot safaris is June through October.

RECOMMENDED READING

Eye of the Elephant by Delia and Mark Owens. A detailed first-person account of the Owens' antipoaching crusade in North Luangwa.

IN BRIEF

Mountain Travel-Sobek, 800-227-2384: 18 days, $4,290
Remote African Safaris, 011-260-1–291-764: 6 days, $1,320
Wild Zambia Safaris, 011-260-62-45015: 7 days, $1,955

Trips of African-based outfitters may be booked in the United States through such agencies as Africatours, 800-235-3692, Africa Adventure Company, 800-882-8453, and Bush Tracks, 415-326-8689.

Physical challenge, 2; Mental challenge, 2; Skills, 1.

ZIMBABWE

canoeing the

zambezi

The two most dangerous animals in Africa—the ones that kill the most people, year in and year out—are not those telegenic beasts so beloved by documentary filmmakers and safari-goers, the lion and the elephant. The leading perpetrators are in fact a decidedly uncharismatic and ignoble duo, the crocodile and the hippopotamus.

Both species, as it happens, are found in some abundance along the middle Zambezi River, where several outfitters run multiday canoe trips through one of Africa's wildest regions, an untouched Eden of broad savannah and dusty woodland. At this writing, no Zambezi canoe outfitter will admit to having lost any customers to crocs or hippos, but a journey down this remote and primitive river is nevertheless suffused with a sub-text unique in the adventure travel business: You could get eaten alive.

Of the two animals, crocodiles carry the more fearsome rep-utation, having aroused dread and loathing in humans for thousands of years. Crocodiles supposedly killed a thousand Roman soldiers trying to cross the Nile at Memphis. The seventeenth-century scientist E. Topsell wrote, "The crocodile is a devouring, insatiable beast, killing all that he lays his mouth on, without all mercy or exorable quality." More recently, the zoologist Bernhard Grzimek, editor of the authoritative standard reference *Grzimek's Encyclopedia of Animal Life,* noted in the sober tones of modern science, "People have always been deeply impressed with the crocodile's ability to kill human beings."

Unlike most African wildlife, crocodiles typically attack by surprise, without warning or threat display. The nineteenth-century English explorer David Livingstone, the first white man to travel the length of the Zambezi, said of crocodiles that "their nature leads them to show skulking habits." Floating silently just below the surface, eyes and nostrils protruding, crocodiles will dart out of the water to snatch people walking along the riverbanks. In one legendary case, a man was taken by a croc while urinating off the back of a good-sized boat.

On his epic 1858–64 journey along the Zambezi, Livingstone observed that local villagers had built anticrocodile barriers to protect themselves as they filled their water pots at the river. At two Portuguese missionary villages, however, he lamented that "although many women are annually carried off by crocodiles at Sunna and Tetta, so little are the lives of these poor drawers of water valued by their masters that they never think of erecting even a single fence for their protection." Livingstone offered one of the missionaries $20, a huge sum in those days, toward the construction of a crocodile fence to protect his flock of devoted converts. The missionary merely "smiled, shrugged, and did nothing."

The force of a crocodile's bite has been measured at about 3,000 pounds, the highest of any existing animal. (Paleontologists estimate that not even a Tyrannosaurus rex could out-chomp a big croc.) Once a victim is snared, there typically ensues a rather grisly procedure. Grzimek again: "Crocodiles tear mouthfuls of meat off a carcass by sinking their teeth in it and jerking around abruptly in the water. The tail usually breaks surface, exposing the pale underbelly. This twisting motion may be repeated up to 19 times in succession, often with such force that the crocodile turns completely on its own axis.

"The crocodile's digestive system is not very efficient or fast-working," Grzimek continues. He cites a case in which a 14-foot croc swallowed an eight-year-old African boy. Villagers were not able to spear the beast until the following day, and when they cut open the croc's belly, "the upper half of the child came to light in the stomach, quite recognizable and not in the least digested though it had been inside for twelve or fifteen hours."

It is not just Africans who get eaten by crocodiles. Some years ago, a group of six American Peace Corps volunteers, ignoring warnings from villagers, went for a swim in Ethiopia's Baro River. The group exuberantly swam 150 yards to the opposite shore, splashing and cavorting as they went. Five swam back together, but a twenty-five-year-old Cornell grad named Bill Olsen decided to linger for a while on the other side. Standing waist-deep in the water on a submerged rock, he leaned languidly into the current as a rippled vee of water swirled behind him. Olsen's arms were folded across his chest as he stood there, and "he was staring ahead as if lost in thought," according to the last person to see him alive, a hunting guide named Karl Luthy.

When Luthy glanced up a few moments later, there was no trace of Olsen. Fifteen minutes later a crocodile surfaced just downriver, carrying in its jaws a large, white, partially submerged object. Luthy's hunting client, perhaps getting more excitement than he'd bargained for, stalked and shot the animal. "The croc measured exactly 13 feet and one inch long, by no means a monster but still powerful enough to catch a human like a fish," Luthy later wrote. "There remained only the gruesome business of opening up the croc, and it was not long before Olsen's fate was established beyond all doubt."

Luthy went on to note, "The circumstances of Olsen's killing are of some interest in illuminating the way in which crocodiles set about taking their prey . . . no one saw any sign of the beast before the event, although it was flagrantly bold afterwards, illustrating the stealth and cunning with which a crocodile hunts."

There have been a number of more recently reported croc incidents along the Zambezi as well. A teenage canoeist had both legs bitten off when he snuck off from camp to swim in an unauthorized area. Two paraplegics were paddling through the Mana Pools area in 1995 when they startled a dozing 10-foot croc, which proceeded to leap out of the water and into their canoe. The paddlers prudently abandoned ship and swam ashore while the croc took over the helm, drifting downstream solo for some distance before eventually flopping overboard. Both paddlers and the canoe were eventually rescued unharmed.

For all its viciousness and cunning, however, the crocodile still rates as a mere runner-up in the pecking order of Zambezi manslaughterers. The hippopotamus is just as aggressive as the croc, just as ill-tempered, and has the additional dangerous traits of a wider range on land and superior size and speed. These attributes make the hippo the most dangerous animal in all of Africa.

This fact comes as a surprise to many people, for the hippopotamus has none of the crocodile's sinister appearance. The hippo's shape is benignly roly-poly, its proportions—the head large compared to its body—that of an infant, to which humans are genetically programmed to respond with warmth and affection. Even its name is vaguely comical. At first glance, one's instinct is to pat the endearingly clumsy and oafish beast on the nose.

Nor does the hippo have the crocodile's ancient tradition of dread. The animal was virtually unknown to the Western world until 1849, when an orphaned baby hippo arrived at the London Zoo, creating an instant sensation. Lewis Carroll and Charles Dickens wrote about it, and *Punch* magazine covered the extraction of one of its teeth. A song called the "Hippopotamus Polka" topped the charts that year, its sheet music depicting a smiling Victorian lady dancing with a slightly abashed-looking hippo who stood on its hind legs and wore a tuxedo.

Crocodiles aren't fooled by such trappings of cuddliness, of course; even the most vicious and aggressive 17-foot croc will meekly back down in a dispute with a hippo. Zimbabwean crocodile researcher C. P. Kofron, in a recent issue of the *African Journal of Ecology,* reports that during croc-hippo turf battles he has observed, the hippos would not hesitate to "snort at, charge, and shove aside" even large crocodile bulls—an observation of no little interest to canoeists, whose vessels unfortunately mimic very closely the shape and size of a large crocodile bull.

One can hardly blame the crocs for giving ground; the smallest adult hippo weighs as much as a Lexus, and the big ones go 7,000 pounds. The lower canine teeth are 20 inches long, a dimension sufficient to skewer two human torsos front-to-back, shish kebab–like. According to Grzimek, hippo teeth are as hard as glass, and were at one time in great demand for making human dentures.

Hippos subsist almost entirely on a diet of grass, emerging from the water at dusk to forage ashore all night. (For this reason, canoeists favor sandy beach areas for their campsites.) On land, a hippo has a very strong instinct to return to the water when threatened, and any impediment to its progress will be dealt with severely. When a hapless human comes between a hippo and his river, attempts to flee are usually futile; the hippo can gallop at speeds up to 18 miles per hour, the equivalent of a 3:20 mile—substantially faster than the current human world record of 3:44.

Once in the water, hippos are quite aggressive. But unlike crocodiles, which see humans as dinner, the vegetarian hippo is merely protecting his turf, or just being ornery. Grzimek reports that aggressive hippos twice attacked an amphibious car he was navigating along a Ugandan river. The intrepid naturalist brushed off the encounter, however, commenting, "I should only have been in trouble if the animals had decided to punch holes in the bodywork with their tusks."

Livingstone describes an encounter with a pod of hippos on his Zambezi expedition: "Our canoe men were afraid to venture down among them, because there is commonly an ill-natured one in the herd which takes a malignant pleasure in upsetting canoes. . . . we fired a few shots to drive them off; the balls often glanced off the skull, and no more harm was done than when a schoolboy gets a bloody nose."

Frederick Selous, another English explorer who traveled along the Zambezi in 1892, also had hippo troubles. "One of the paddlers . . . came running along the bank calling out 'The canoe is dead! The canoe is dead! A hippopotamus has killed the canoe!' We at once paddled back and soon met various articles floating down the stream, amongst them my cooking pot and the waterproof bag containing my blankets. . . . The canoe had been attacked and sunk in 12 feet of water, and now lay at the bottom of the river, with several tusks of ivory, all my provisions, cartridges, trading goods, and, in fact, everything I had with me. . . ."

Modern-day canoe voyagers along the Zambezi, of course, are at somewhat less risk than Livingstone and Selous. Yet dark possibilities remain. One veteran of a ten-day Zambezi run summed it up this way: "When you paddle by a pod of hippos over on the riverbank, and you watch some of them disappear under the water, and then you see the bubbles start coming up all around you, and you feel that bump and the canoe starts to lift, and you look down and see that shiny wet skin, and you remember all those pictures of those mouths opening up like huge suitcases, and you realize that this is not Disneyland or the zoo, and that your continued existence depends entirely on what that hippo decides to do in the next few seconds—well, I have to say that after an experience like that, you tend to look at the world a little differently."

OUTFITTERS

Goliath Safaris offers three self-supported "participatory" trips of four, five, and eight days, including two along the less-traveled section of the river between Mana Pools National Park and the Mozambique border. Canoeists typically camp out on islands, sleeping on the ground with a mosquito net but no tent. Prices include ground transfer from Kariba. Guides are typically not permitted to take paddlers farther than 50 meters from shore.

Nature Ways paddlers begin a five-day trip at the mouth of the Rukomechi River in Mana Pools National Park and proceeds 60 miles downstream to Chikwenya. (A four-day trip is also available in the same general area at $990.) Both are full-service Land Rover–supported trips with beds, a long-drop loo, and bucket shower. Price includes air transfers from Kariba. Nature Ways is owned by Garth Thompson, a certified professional guide and the largest land operator in Zimbabwe. All Nature Ways trips are led by professional-rated guides (an elite cadre, no more than thirty or so in all of Zimbabwe) who are permitted to lead foot safaris while ashore.

Ruwesi Canoe Safaris covers the four-day, 40-mile, border-to-border run along Mana Pools National Park. The trip is Land Rover–supported with full service, and prices include air transfers from Kariba. Like Nature Ways, Ruwesi uses only professional-rated guides who may lead foot safaris ashore. Ruwesi's director and head guide is Dave Christiansen, who has a superb reputation among canoeing clients. "He's not one of those bush geeks, he's got a real personality," says one former Ruwesi paddler.

Although *Safaris Par Excellence* is based in Zimbabwe, it is the only outfitter listed here that runs canoe trips along the northern shore of the river, under license from the Zambian government. In terms of amenities, SPE trips rank in the middle: They are vehicle-supported but don't always employ the professional-rated guides who are permitted to lead foot safaries on shore. Prices include transfers from Kariba.

Shearwater Adventures, the largest Zambezi canoe outfitter, offers the widest variety of itineraries, covering various parts of the entire 160-mile stretch of river between Kariba (just below the dam at Lake Kariba) and Kanyemba, at the Mozambique border. The shorter trips pass through Kariba Gorge, Mana Pools National Park, or Mupata Gorge. The full 160-mile trip traverses all three areas and takes ten days. Shearwater's trips are self-supported and therefore rather rustic, and they do not use professional-rated guides licensed to lead foot safaris when ashore. Transfers from Kariba are by ground or river.

Wilderness Travel combines a three-day canoe trip along the Mana Pools section with foot and vehicle safaris in Matusadona, Mana Pools, and Hwange national parks.

WHAT TO EXPECT

Canoeists typically cover 15 to 20 miles per day, paddling downstream in calm water for six to eight hours. This should be no problem for an experienced canoeist, but it may tax a beginner. Slackers may of course let their partners do all the work. The canoes on the self-supported trips (Shearwater and Goliath) are more heavily laden, and therefore require more muscle power to propel.

The Shearwater and Goliath trips are a bit spartan by traditional African safari standards; you'll sleep out in the open, with only a mosquito net, and be expected to help out with camp chores. All the ice will melt by the third or fourth day. And, in terms of safety, your guide will not be certified to carry a weapon for protection from animals, nor to take you farther than 50 meters from shore.

The Land Rover–supported trips are somewhat more luxurious, with large stand-up tents, cots with mattresses and pillows, shower and latrine tents. With the exception of Safaris Par Excellence, operators of the vehicle-supported trips use only armed, professional-rated guides who may take you on walking side trips away from the river. The vehicle-supported trips rate only a 2 in terms of mental challenge.

All Zambezi trips carry with them the potential of scary encounters with wildlife. The faint of heart should perhaps look elsewhere; you don't want to end up like the couple who bailed out of their trip on the second day after their canoe was rammed by a hippo and the guide's paddle got chomped in half by a croc. Another paddler reports being literally too frightened to sleep for several nights after an elephant took a midnight stroll through camp.

Basic canoe skills can be picked up quickly, and beginners do fine as long as they are paired with more experienced paddlers. (Two-novice couples should not plan on paddling together.) But don't underestimate the need for good paddling skills; quick, decisive action may be necessary to avoid aquatic onslaughts from our four-legged, sharp-toothed friends.

The high season for Zambezi canoe trips runs from May

through October. Game viewing is best in September and October, the end of the dry season, because the animals must come to the river to drink. But late September and October are so hot that it's called the suicide season. Trips during July and August sometimes face stiff headwinds. Goliath Safaris runs additional off-season trips from January through April.

RECOMMENDED READING

Eyelids of Morning: The Mingled Destinies of Crocodile and Man by Alistair Graham. A literary and philosophical narrative of the zoologist/author's yearlong study of the crocodile population of Kenya's Lake Rudolf, with sometimes startling photos by Peter Beard.

Narrative of an Expedition to the Zambesi and Its Tributaries by David and Charles Livingstone. The harrowing firsthand account of David Livingstone's (yes, he of "Dr. Livingstone, I presume") 1865 expedition up the Zambezi, the first ever by a white man.

IN BRIEF

Goliath Safaris, 011-263-4-390-263: 4–8 days, $450–$845
Nature Ways, 011-263-4-795-202: 5 days, $1,240
Ruwesi Canoe Safaris, 011-263-4-496-113: 4 days, $1,250
Safaris Par Excellence, 011-263-4-720-527: 3–5 days, $760–$1,090
Shearwater Adventures, 011-263-4-757-831: 3–10 days, $500–$1,200
Wilderness Travel, 800-368-2794: 19 days, $3,995

With the exception of Wilderness Travel, all of these outfitters can be booked through various American agents, at no additional cost and great savings in telephone costs and frustration. Try Africa Adventure Company, 800-882-8453; African Portfolio, 800-700-3677; Africatours, 800-235-3692; or Next Adventure, 800-562-7298.

Physical challenge, 2; Mental challenge, 2–3; Skills, 2.

A P P E N D I C E S

A P P E N D I X A

t r i p p l a n n i n g

c a l e n d a r

■ = Optimal Travel Months

	JAN	FEB	MAR	APR	MAY	JUN	JUL	AUG	SEP	OCT	NOV	DEC
NORTH AMERICA												
Alaska						■						
Arizona				■	■				■	■		
Canadian Rockies							■	■	■			
Florida	■	■		■							■	■
Mexico	■	■								■	■	■
North Pole			■	■								
Utah					■	■			■			
Wyoming	■	■										■
SOUTH AMERICA												
Antarctica	■	■									■	■
Argentina												
Belize	■	■		■	■							
Chile												
Dominica							■	■				
Patagonia	■	■									■	■
Peru										■		
Venezuela	■	■	■								■	■

	JAN	FEB	MAR	APR	MAY	JUN	JUL	AUG	SEP	OCT	NOV	DEC
EUROPE/ MIDDLE EAST												
England					▓	▓	▓	▓				
France					▓	▓			▓			
Greenland								▓	▓			
Italy					▓		▓	▓	▓			
Norway		▓	▓	▓								
Oman	▓	▓									▓	▓
Portugal						▓	▓	▓	▓			
Turkey				▓	▓				▓	▓		
ASIA/PACIFIC												
Borneo				▓	▓	▓	▓	▓				
Hawaii	▓	▓	▓	▓	▓	▓	▓	▓	▓	▓	▓	▓
Mongolia						▓	▓					
Nepal/Tibet				▓	▓				▓	▓		
New Zealand	▓	▓									▓	▓
Pakistan							▓	▓				
Sikkim			▓	▓	▓					▓	▓	
Vietnam	▓											
AFRICA												
Botswana			▓	▓	▓	▓	▓	▓	▓			
Ethiopia												
Mali	▓										▓	▓
Sahara												
Tanzania			▓			▓	▓	▓	▓	▓		
Uganda	▓	▓					▓					
Zambia												
Zimbabwe					▓							

APPENDIX B

how hard is

this trip?

P H Y S I C A L   C H A L L E N G E

	NORTH AMERICA	SOUTH AMERICA	EUROPE/ MIDDLE EAST	ASIA/PACIFIC	AFRICA
5				Tibet/Nepal	
4	Mexico The Arctic Wyoming	Patagonia	Norway	Vietnam	Tanzania
3	Canadian Rockies Wyoming Utah	Argentina Chile Dominica Peru	Norway France Portugal Greenland England	Hawaii Malaysia Pakistan Sikkim Vietnam	Mali Uganda
2	Alaska Florida	Belize	Italy England	Hawaii Mongolia Malaysia New Zealand	Zimbabwe Zambia
1	Arizona	Venezuela Antarctica	Oman Turkey		Sahara Botswana Ethiopia

* For physical-challenge rating description, see page 4.

M E N T A L   C H A L L E N G E

	NORTH AMERICA	SOUTH AMERICA	EUROPE/ MIDDLE EAST	ASIA/PACIFIC	AFRICA
5	Arctic	Patagonia		Nepal/Tibet	
4	Mexico Wyoming	Peru Chile	Greenland	Pakistan	Ethiopia Uganda Tanzania
3	Canadian Rockies Alaska Wyoming Utah Florida	Argentina Venezuela Belize	Oman	Hawaii Mongolia Sikkim Vietnam	Sahara Zimbabwe Mali
2	Arizona Canadian Rockies	Antarctica	Italy Norway Turkey	Malaysia New Zealand	Botswana Zambia Zimbabwe
1		Dominica	France Portugal England	New Zealand Hawaii	

* For mental-challenge rating description, see pages 7–8.